Fabien Patrick Viertel

Heuristic and Knowledge-Based Security Checks of Source Code Artifacts Using Community Knowledge

Logos Verlag Berlin

 λογος

Bibliografische Information der Deutschen Nationalbibliothek

Die Deutsche Nationalbibliothek verzeichnet diese Publikation in der
Deutschen Nationalbibliografie; detaillierte bibliografische Daten sind
im Internet über http://dnb.d-nb.de abrufbar.

ISBN 978-3-8325-5349-4

Logos Verlag Berlin GmbH
Georg-Knorr-Str. 4, Geb. 10,
D-12681 Berlin
Germany

Tel.:   +49 (0)30 / 42 85 10 90
Fax: +49 (0)30 / 42 85 10 92
http://www.logos-verlag.de

Heuristic and Knowledge-Based Security Checks of Source Code Artifacts Using Community Knowledge

Von der Fakultät für Elektrotechnik und Informatik der
Gottfried Wilhelm Leibniz Universität Hannover
zur Erlangung des akademischen Grades

Doktor-Ingenieur

(abgekürzt: Dr.-Ing)

genehmigte Dissertation von Herrn

M. Sc. Fabien Patrick Viertel

geboren am 07.04.1990 in Salzgitter, Deutschland

2021

1. Referent: Prof. Dr. Kurt Schneider

2. Referent: Prof. Dr. Jan Jürjens

Prüfungsausschussvorsitzender: Prof. Dr. Daniel Lohmann

Tag der Promotion: 28 Mai 2021

Abstract

Currently, software applications operate using highly sensitive data that only a limited number of people can access. In some cases, human lives might depend on the continuous and correct deployment of these applications. Due to the rise of cybercrime and reported vulnerabilities, organizations now consider security a top concern. Therefore, it is problematic that software developers generally have no security experience, which could be a reason for occurring vulnerabilities. A further problem that underlines the criticality of missing know-how is that the presence of a security expert within projects is not always guaranteed. A frequent practice to address knowledge gaps is to ask the developer community for help in solving concrete implementation concerns.

In addition to websites of the Stack Exchange network, such as Stack Overflow, developers can use the National Vulnerability Database (NVD) to discover vulnerabilities in concrete software artifacts or products. Using vulnerability databases to find security flaws within written source code is complex. Much information has to be considered, which can overwhelm developers. Moreover, the NVD does not directly provide code fragments showing the expression of vulnerabilities in source code. Sometimes NVD provides links to other websites containing proofs of concept or a security-patch code.

The goal of this dissertation is to support developers in applying security checks using community knowledge. Artificial intelligence approaches combined with natural language processing techniques are employed to identify security-related information from community websites such as Stack Overflow or GitHub. All security-related information is stored in a security knowledge base. This knowledge base provides code fragments that represent the community's knowledge about vulnerabilities, security-patches, and exploits. Furthermore, meta information regarding vulnerability types and identifiers of concrete security flaws are provided. Comprehensive knowledge is required to carry out security checks on software artifacts, such as data covering known vulnerabilities and their manifestation in the source code as well as possible attack strategies. Approaches that check software libraries and source code fragments are provided for the automated use of the data.

Insecure software libraries can be detected using the NVD combined with metadata and library file hash approaches introduced in this dissertation. Vulnerable source code fragments can be identified using community knowledge represented by code fragments extracted from the largest coding community websites: Stack Overflow and GitHub. A state-of-the-art clone detection approach is modified and enriched by several heuristics to enable vulnerability detection and leverage community knowledge while maintaining good performance. Using various case studies, the approaches implemented in Eclipse plugins and a JIRA plugin are adapted to the users' needs and evaluated.

Keywords: Community knowledge, Security, Vulnerability detection, Machine learning, Natural language processing, Artificial intelligence, Code clone detection, Software libraries, Source code

Zusammenfassung

Derzeit arbeiten Softwareanwendungen mit hochsensiblen Daten, auf die nur eine begrenzte Anzahl von Personen zugreifen können. In einigen Fällen können von der kontinuierlichen und korrekten Bereitstellung dieser Anwendungen Menschenleben abhängen. Aufgrund des Anstiegs der Cyberkriminalität und der in diesem Zusammenhang gemeldeten Schwachstellen ist Sicherheit für Unternehmen mittlerweile ein wichtiges Thema. Vor diesem Hintergrund ist es als problematisch zu bewerten, dass Softwareentwickler in der Regel keine Sicherheitserfahrung haben (was seinerseits ein Grund für die oben genannten auftretenden Schwachstellen sein könnte). Da in vielen Projekten nicht immer die Anwesenheit eines Sicherheitsexperten gewährleistet ist, wird damit die Kritikalität des fehlenden Know-hows unterstrichen. Stattdessen besteht die Praxis, um Wissenslücken zu schließen, häufig darin, die Entwicklergemeinde punktuell um Hilfe bei der Lösung konkreter Implementierungsprobleme zu bitten.

Um Schwachstellen in konkreten Software-Artefakten oder Produkten zu entdecken, können Entwickler neben Webseiten des Stack-Exchange-Netzwerks, wie z. B. Stack Overflow auch die National Vulnerability Database (NVD) nutzen. Die Verwendung solcher Schwachstellendatenbanken zum Auffinden von Sicherheitslücken in geschriebenem Quellcode ist jedoch komplex. Denn es müssen viele Informationen berücksichtigt werden, was Entwickler überfordern kann. Außerdem stellt die NVD nicht direkt Codefragmente zur Verfügung, die die Ausprägung von Schwachstellen im Quellcode zeigen. Manchmal stellt die NVD nur Links zu anderen Websites bereit, die Proofs of Concept oder Sicherheits-Patch-Codes enthalten.

Das Ziel dieser Dissertation ist es, Entwickler bei der Anwendung von Sicherheitsprüfungen mit Hilfe von Community-Wissen zu unterstützen. Dabei werden Ansätze der künstlichen Intelligenz mit Techniken der natürlichen Sprachverarbeitung kombiniert und dazu eingesetzt, um sicherheitsrelevante Informationen von Community-Websites wie Stack Overflow oder GitHub zu identifizieren. Die so gesammelten sicherheitsrelevanten Informationen werden in einer Sicherheits-Wissensbasis gespeichert. Diese Wissensbasis enthält Codefragmente, die das Wissen der Community über Schwachstellen, Sicherheits-Patches und Exploits repräsentieren. Darüber hinaus werden in der Wissensbasis Metainformationen zu Schwachstellentypen und Bezeichnern konkreter Sicherheitslücken bereitgestellt. Um Sicherheitsüberprüfungen von Software-Artefakten durchführen zu können, ist umfangreiches Wissen erforderlich, wie z. B. Wissen über Daten zu bekannten Schwachstellen und deren Manifestation im Quellcode sowie über mögliche Angriffsstrategien. Für die automatisierte Nutzung der Daten werden Ansätze bereitgestellt, anhand derer Softwarebibliotheken und Quellcodefragmente überprüft werden können.

Unsichere Softwarebibliotheken können mit Hilfe der NVD in Kombination mit den in dieser Dissertation vorgestellten Ansätzen für Metadaten und Bibliotheksdateihashs erkannt werden. Anfällige Quellcodefragmente können mit Hilfe von Community-Wissen identifiziert werden, das durch Codefragmente repräsentiert wird, die von den größten Websites der Coding-Community extrahiert wurden: Stack Overflow und GitHub. Ein hochmoderner Ansatz zur Erkennung von Klonen wird modifiziert und mit mehreren Heuristiken angereichert, um die Erkennung von Schwachstellen zu ermöglichen und das Wissen der Community zu nutzen, während gleichzeitig eine gute Performance beibehalten wird. Anhand verschiedener Fallstudien werden die in Eclipse-Plugins und einem JIRA-Plugin implementierten Ansätze an die Bedürfnisse der Anwender angepasst und evaluiert.

Acknowledgments

During the time I have been writing this dissertation, I have had many informative conversations and discussions about scientific issues with researchers and practitioners. All these exchanges have contributed meaningfully to this dissertation.

First of all, I would like to thank my supervisor, Prof. Dr. Kurt Schneider, for giving me the freedom to conduct my research with my own interest and for always being there to give me advice. I would also like to thank Prof. Dr. Jan Jürjens, who acted as the second examiner for this dissertation and supported me in the sense of professional exchange during the preparation of the dissertation.

In addition, I would like to thank my former colleagues from the Software Engineering Group at Leibniz Universität Hannover and the members of the SecVolution@Runtime project for the many comments on the research applied for my dissertation. Especially Dr. Jens Bürger, Martin Obaidi, Dr. Javad Ghofrani and Dr. Tobias Baum . Furthermore, I would like to thank all collaborators and co-authors of scientific publications that were produced during the course of my doctoral studies: Dr. Oliver Karras, Wasja Brunotte, Yannik Evers, Leif Eric Wagner, Dr. Daniel Strüber, Huu Kim Nguyen, Joshua Garlisch and Alexander Threptau. Besides, several students contributed to my research by their final bachelor and master theses; thanks to all of them.

Thanks to my long-time friend and colleague Fabian Kortum in particular, with whom I was always able to discuss essential topics of the dissertation and who frequently supported me with advice.

I would like to thank my beloved family and friends, who always showed understanding towards my demanding work during the years of my doctorate. Many thanks to my parents who have always supported me in my endeavors. In particular, I thank my beloved mother Silke Maria Viertel, who always motivated and supported me during my education. Without her, this dissertation would not exist.

Contents

ix

List of Abbreviations

A Accuracy

AR Action Research

Ch Challenge

CPE Common Platform Enumeration

CSRF Cross-site Request Forgery

CVE Common Vulnerability Exposures

CVSS Common Vulnerability Scoring System

CWE Common Weakness Enumeration

F1 F1-Measure

GN Google News

ID Identifier

IDE Integrated Development Environment

IDF Inverse Document Frequency

JAR Java Archive

JS JavaScript

LOC Lines of Code

MITM Man in the Middle Attack

M Metric

NN Neural Network

NPM Node Package Module

NVD National Vulnerability Database

OWASP DC Open Web Application Security Project Dependency Checker

P Precision

R Recall

RQ Research Question

S Specificity

SCCD Security Code Clone Detector

SCKB Security Code Knowledge Base

SKB Security Knowledge Base

SMO Sequential Minimal Optimization SVM

SO Stack Overflow

SVM Support Vector Machine

UML Unified Modeling Language

XML Extensible Markup Language

XSS Cross-site Scripting

Chapter 1

Introduction

Headlines frequently report security incidents. Due to the rise of cybercrime and incidents of reported vulnerabilities [124], security is a top concern for organizations organizations [45, 153, 20]. Security is also an essential quality aspect in recent software projects. In the past, there were several examples of insecure software that lead to leaks of sensitive data. The consequences of security breaches for software companies can be severe due to reputational damage to corporate identity and fines [82, 159]. Furthermore, the impacts of security incidents could harm private users and enterprises. Undetected vulnerabilities during implementation can lead to increasing maintenance costs and financial penalties that can exceed the development budget [38]. Moreover, human lives can depend on software that ensures the continuous and faultless provision of service, for example, the software that manages the cooling of radioactive centrifuges within a nuclear reactor [36].

Software project security relies on the expertise of project members. One reason for security issues could be the absence of security expertise in developers [60]. For instance, a study by Acar et al. [2] reviewing 307 professionals and students revealed that developers usually have no security expertise. They discovered that there is no difference between students and professionals considering their security know-how. Furthermore, the availability of security experts within a project is not always guaranteed. Moreover, if an expert is available, it is usually not for the entire development phase.

Ideally, security experts should review the complete source code of a project for vulnerabilities. Considerable knowledge is required to search for vulnerabilities in self-written source code [73]. This knowledge includes information about attack strategies and patterns of previously occurred vulnerabilities. Additionally, knowledge of the top libraries and insecure hash algorithms used to exploit vulnerabilities can help prevent their usage, which leads to a more secure source code. Furthermore, guidelines or examples of code for the secure implementation of concrete concerns could help as well.

This dissertation investigates how developers can be supported within the knowledge-based task of security checks on source code artifacts. For this purpose, freely accessible historical community knowledge of vulnerabilities should be used. Section 1.1 describes community knowledge and potential knowledge sources. The problems and concrete challenges (Ch's) considered in this thesis are summarized in Section 1.2. The underlying research methods and questions are presented in Sec. 1.3, and the contributions of this dissertation is placed in Section 1.4. Section 1.5 shows the structure of this thesis.

1.1 Security Community Knowledge

Developers can research security flaws within publicly available vulnerability databases such as the National Vulnerability Database (NVD) [129] to obtain information about almost all already identified vulnerabilities. In practice, additional effort is required to ascertain that the necessary information is non-trivial. Unfortunately, the associated manual process to find vulnerabilities in projects is time-consuming and error-prone: Developers need to use a search engine to find relevant entries based on the names of the libraries used. Then, developers must manually scan the source code to uncover problematic uses of the affected libraries. Even worse, the support with available examples of vulnerabilities, patches, and exploit codes in the databases is scarce. Vulnerability entries sometimes just contain a link to a report or to a repository that provides additional information on proofs of concept, patches, and exploits.

Furthermore, security knowledge is also included in user contributions to coding community websites such as Stack Exchange [69] and GitHub [112]. Part of the Stack Exchange network is the well-known website Stack Overflow [9], which developers use to find implementations that solve specific problems. Stack Overflow contrasts with NVD, which is a similar workflow for coding communities to find security flaws in source code. NVD makes a distinction regarding the availability of source code contributed within user posts. The NVD partially provides links to other websites that provide source code related to listed vulnerabilities. On Stack Overflow, predefined areas can be used to post source code fragments.

Within a search, developers can be overwhelmed by the vast number of results on these websites. The resulting information can be both natural language texts and code fragments, and the information contained in posts is not restricted to security issues. If security-related content is found, it exhibits granularity, which makes it challenging to obtain the necessary security information for developers without security experience. For example, content could be about a concrete software library, a native Java method, or a program that has security issues. Furthermore, if security-related content is found, it is not easy to distinguish whether the information is about code that is securely patched, vulnerable, or describes the exploit [169]. Without any security knowledge, developers can only trust into contributions of the community. If developers are looking for security information about a concrete concern, they have to interpret the statements of numerous posts.

Developers can use several sources of security community knowledge that affect the implementation of secure software. Figure 1-1 shows some of these knowledge sources with various information affecting selected software development phases. The center of the visualization contains the specific kind of information that influences the software development phases. All knowledge sources are visualized in a surrounding cloud containing examples of concrete sources providing this specific information. Thereby, security patterns and bug reports are expressed by security experts' user contributions or experienced developers using the remaining knowledge sources.

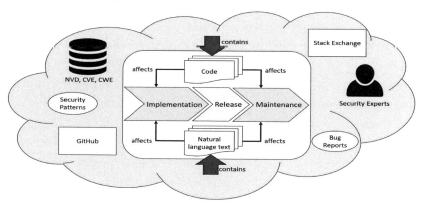

Figure 1-1: Effects of Security Knowledge on Software Implementation.

These knowledge sources partially contain natural language texts and code fragments consisting of security-relevant data. In a way, the users' contributions to community websites reflect their security knowledge. Some of the posted code fragments will be identified as vulnerable or secure by the community. The decisions about the security relevance of code express the state of security know-how. In summary, this dissertation considers the following aspects:

1) Extraction of Security knowledge from various sources for identifying vulnerabilities in source code artifacts.

2) Automation of security checks during software development.

1.2 Challenges

In practice, security knowledge is insufficiently integrated into the software development process [76, 84], which leads to vulnerabilities in software projects. Preventing vulnerabilities during implementation is cheaper than removing them during later maintenance phases [97]. US-Cert has announced that a system is only as secure as its weakest component, which implies that a single weakness within a written code fragment or a used library can make a whole system insecure [164, 73]. Also, the Open Web Application Security Project (OWASP) [32], identified the use of third-party software libraries with known vulnerabilities as one of the ten most significant risks for web projects [133]. This means that if a developer implements a code fragment with a vulnerable method in it or uses an insecure third-party software library, the entire project becomes susceptible to hackers. A single line of source code can invoke a vulnerability. Therefore, the apparent granularity for detecting vulnerabilities is on the file-level while considering the containing source code. Knowledge of security-related topics on the web pages of the coding community is expressed in two types of information: source code and natural language texts.

For interleaving security knowledge expressed by distinct types of information, it is necessary to store data in a reusable manner. Information provided by different knowledge sources makes it essential to structure it within a unique scheme. This security knowledge can be used to identify vulnerabilities during the implementation of software. As Figure 1-1 shows, the security community knowledge from various sources should be used to make developers aware of potential security risks in source code artifacts. Thus, this dissertation

4

aims to develop an approach for extracting community knowledge to store provided data in a unique structure and enrich it with further information. Furthermore, a semi-automated procedure is offered to systematically support security checks within the software implementation phase.

For the identification of vulnerabilities, the knowledge of already-occurred security flaws can be beneficial. With this knowledge, it is possible to avoid making the same mistakes so that known vulnerabilities will be mitigated. The effort to obtain, enrich, and apply this security knowledge has to be minimized so that the time consumption is not excessive. Simply providing community security knowledge to developers will result in them being overwhelmed by the vast amount of information. Therefore, support for using this information during software development is required.

Existing challenges are listed and divided into the two previously named aspects:

Using Security Knowledge

- **Challenge 1.1 - Identify sources of reusable security knowledge:** There exist distinct sources to obtain security knowledge. In this thesis they will be sighted and evaluated for their suitability to deliver reusable security knowledge.

- **Challenge 1.2 - Identify security knowledge:** Not all of the coding community websites like the NVD contain only security-related content. Usually, they contain information about coding from which only a small portion considers security. This makes the identification of security-related content in the context of this dissertation necessary because the plan is to use security community knowledge to identify vulnerabilities.

- **Challenge 1.3 - Distinguish security information into three classes - vulnerabilities, patches, or exploits:** For security experts, it is probably easier to determine whether security-related content belongs to any of these classes. Developers with no security experience more tend to confuse the classes. They get overwhelmed by multiple statements referred to source code fragments, which makes it difficult to interpret whether code contributes to a vulnerability, patch or exploit.

- **Challenge 1.4 - Store security knowledge in a reusable manner:** Security community knowledge is distributed over multiple websites and accessible in different formats. Some data representing security knowledge are natural language texts and some are source code fragments. These data are yet not stored in a consistent and reusable way; thus it is difficult to leverage it for semi-automated security checks. Therefore, the data preparation and transformation in a uniquely shared scheme is a part of that challenge.

Automatization of security checks

- **Challenge 2.1 - Reuse security knowledge on reported vulnerabilities:** Based on the available security information, developers should be supported during the implementation of source code with security checks. Software developers should not be prevented from carrying out their work. Thus, a goal is to provide security checks with less user interaction as possible. Suitable procedures have to be found for integrating them into the software development process.

- **Challenge 2.2 - Security checks for different source code artifacts :** Source code could be placed within raw source files and also be part of software components like libraries. Not for all programming languages, libraries and source files can be treated equally. There are languages which not always obtain raw source code of libraries. Therefore, security checks for software libraries and source files have to be processed differently.

To support developers in solving these challenges, approaches have been developed to fulfill the two derived tasks: extraction and the use of security knowledge. These approaches have been implemented in tools for enabling their use.

1.3 Research Questions and Methodology

Exploratory research is a well-known research design [88, 31]. The center is the construction of an artifact, such as a product or system. Typically, this artifact is a prototype to solve a domain-specific problem, such as the tools created for this dissertation. The approaches, or formed tools, are evaluated with suitable metrics to measure their performance.

To emphasize the research perspective of this thesis, the identification and use of community knowledge in different forms is focused upon to support security checks on source code artifacts. At first, related work was considered to identify a domain-specific problem, which is reflected in the challenges. Concerning the challenges of this thesis, the following research questions (RQ's) arise:

- **Research Question 1: Can security knowledge be semi-automatically extracted from coding communities?**

- **Research Question 1.1: Can security information be semi-automatically differentiated into vulnerabilities, patches, and exploits?**

- **Research Question 2: How can the extracted community knowledge be used for heuristic security checks on source code artifacts to identify vulnerabilities?**

- **Research Question 2.1: How valuable is the use of community knowledge about security in detecting vulnerabilities?**

- **Research Question 2.2: How useful are the developed approaches for detecting vulnerabilities?**

The origin of each research question resulted from one to multiple challenges. Table 1.1 shows the constraints of the research questions to the challenges.

Table 1.1: Research Questions and Challenges Relationship.

Challenges \ RQs	C1.1	C1.2	C1.3	C1.4	C2.1	C2.2
RQ1	✔	✔		✔		
RQ1.1			✔			
RQ2				✔	✔	✔
RQ2.1				✔	✔	✔
RQ2.2				✔	✔	✔

The validity of the community knowledge of IT-security was determined via a sample of Stack Overflow contributions. For identifying the performance of developed approaches, different case studies used common metrics for the information retrieval. To measure the success of developed tools for real software projects, a qualitative analysis was applied within case studies during the development of two software projects in a cooperating software house. To obtain insights across the use of created tools, an experiment was applied in which the manual task of detecting vulnerabilities through the use of the NVD and handed source code verification is compared to the software. Furthermore, the resulting security knowledge base containing security-related code fragments is validated within a further case study. Figure 1-2 visualizes the described constructive research process.

Figure 1-2: Constructive Research Process.

1.4   Contributions

To address mentioned challenges and solve the research questions identified to be relevant for this dissertation, the following contributions resulted from this.

- An automated approach is employed to detect vulnerabilities within source code artifacts based on community knowledge about security. Therefore, eclipse plugins and a JIRA plugin were created.

- A tool-based approach to obtain, enrich, and maintain security information and knowledge from coding communities such as Stack Overflow and GitHub. The results are stored in a repository containing security-related code examples for previously reported vulnerabilities, security-patches, and their exploits.

1.5   Structure

The dissertation is organized into three parts: the introduction, main part, and the evaluation. The introduction contains the research motivation and describes some background information to understand the thesis.

The main part contains its own related work section for each chapter in addition to the prototypical implementation. This is due to the broad scope of approaches. The main section describes the concepts of every sub-step necessary to realize security checks using community knowledge. The solutions of RQ1 and RQ1.1 are shown within the concepts described in Chapter 4.2. Chapter 5 and 6 show the solution for RQ2. The technical validation (Ch. 8 shows the performance of approaches using community knowledge and responds thereby to RQ2.1.

The thesis is finalized with the evaluation, technical validation, case studies, and conclusions that address the research questions and fine-grained contributions to challenges. RQ2.1 and RQ2.2 are thereby answered during the case studies. Figure 1-3 provides an overview of the complete thesis.

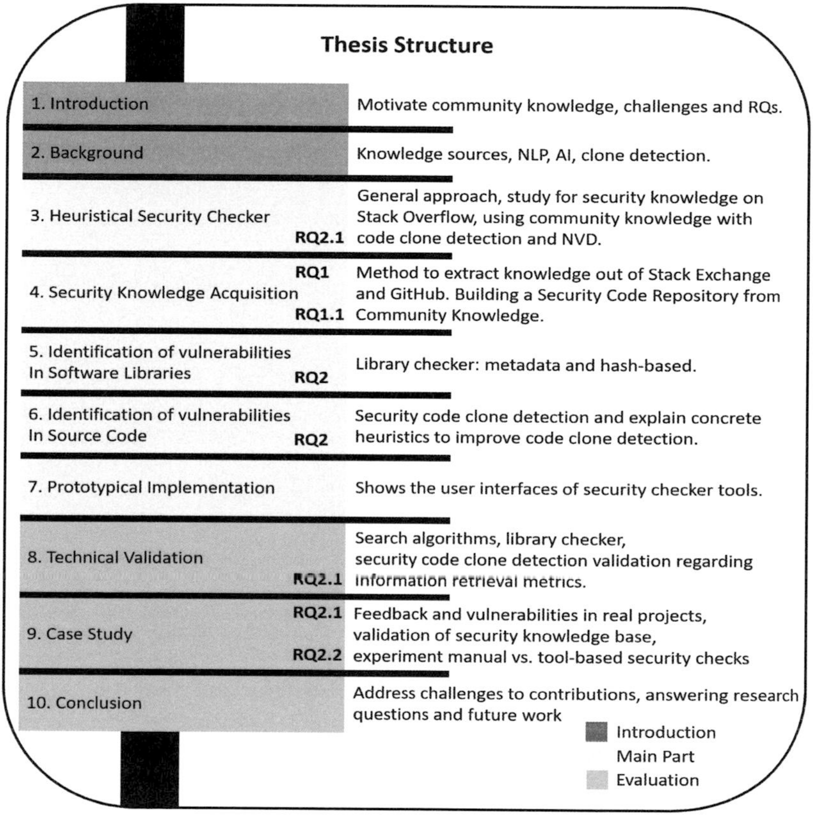

Figure 1-3: Thesis Structure.

Chapter 2

Background

The background of the topic is sketched in this chapter to inform the thesis. In particular, vulnerabilities, patches, and exploits are described based on the vulnerability lifecycle. The terms "data," "information," and "knowledge" are defined, as there has been disagreement about their meaning. Furthermore, knowledge sources containing security-related data are introduced. General techniques to access or identify this knowledge, such as artificial intelligence, natural language processing, and code clone detection, are outlined. Furthermore, metrics from the information retrieval to measure the performance of the classification techniques are introduced. The final section shows types of threats to validity from the software engineering research.

2.1 Vulnerabilities, Patches, and Exploits

Software products will likely encounter security issues during their life span. A general software security life cycle (SSLC) can be described as follows [74]: A new attack strategy is developed, or a previously unknown vulnerability is discovered. An attacker maliciously exploits the functionality of a software system using the new information and techniques. The security incident is detected and it probably punishes in some manner the customers using the attacked software product. Vendors of the developed software publish security patches to close these vulnerabilities. The SSLC is visualized in Fig. 2-1.

Within the vulnerability lifecycle mentioned above, there are three types of source code that are generated. These types are vulnerabilities, patches, and exploits, defined as follows.

- **Vulnerability.** Within the common vulnerabilities and exposures (CVE) database, a "vulnerability" is defined as a "weakness in the computational logic (e.g., code) found in

11

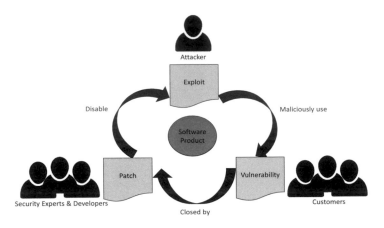

Figure 2-1: Generalized Software Security Life Cycle.

software and some hardware components (e.g., firmware) that, when exploited, results in a negative impact to confidentiality, integrity, OR availability..." [125].

- **Patch.** Removes a potential vulnerability so that it no longer can be exploited.

- **Exploit.** Maliciously uses a vulnerability to invoke a negative impact on the confidentiality, integrity, or availability of a software system.

2.2 Data, Information, and Knowledge

In the literature, there are multiple definitions of the terms "data," "information," "knowledge," and "relationships" [154]. Therefore, there is disagreement in understanding the terms. Some authors, such as Nonaka and Takeuchi, only distinguish between *information* and *knowledge* [121]. They do not define data as a separate term.

These inconsistencies underscore the importance of defining the terms. In the context of this dissertation, the author agrees with the definitions of Spek and Spijkervet [165]:

- **Data.** Not yet interpreted symbols.

- **Information.** Data assigned with a meaning.

- **Knowledge.** The ability to assign meaning.

12

Each posts' content is data, expressed as the symbols of natural language texts or source code fragments. These code fragments can be interpreted by community members' contributions with natural language texts to form information that expresses community knowledge. Within this dissertation, "security community knowledge" is defined as the ability to categorize concrete content as a vulnerability, patch, or exploit. The community's knowledge is, therefore, statements in natural language texts that identify the security of code fragments.

2.3 Sources of Security Knowledge

Some sources are limited to providing security-related content and others contain additional information. For the latter, approaches to identifying security-related content are required. This section describes the different knowledge sources in the context of security.

2.3.1 Vulnerability Databases

Several vulnerability databases are freely accessible to the public, of which NVD is a widely used resource [129]. The NVD contains data synchronized with the Common Vulnerability and Exposures (CVE) database [30]. In comparison with CVE, the NVD contains additional search functions to discover vulnerabilities. Both databases display all entries with a CVE identifier (CVE-ID), which uniquely identifies a security flaw found in a concrete product. A CVE-ID can be used when referencing a specific vulnerability. Therefore, it is appropriate to use this identifier when discussing a concrete vulnerability. In January 2021, CVE and NVD databases have tracked 155514 reported vulnerabilities [128]. Entries usually do not contain the source code revealing further detail about the occurrence, security patch, or exploit. However, some entries contain links to other websites that display the relevant data.

Vulnerabilities are further grouped by type using the common weakness enumeration (CWE) [29]. The CWE compresses various types of weaknesses, all identified through a unique CWE-ID and categorized into different vulnerability manifestations. The catalog now compromises about 600 types and sub-classes of vulnerabilities. One example of these types is CWE-306: Missing Authentication for Critical Function. All CVE entries referencing CWE-306 listings are weaknesses due to the absence of authentication for critical functions.

An issue for the NVD is that 38% of the NVD stored entries are missing assigned CWE-IDs [170].

Common Platform Enumeration

The common platform enumeration (CPE) is a standard designed to reference IT products so that they are interpretable and processable by machines [116, 126]. The platform provides a dictionary containing detailed information for comparison of products and platforms based on their CPEs. Detailed versions and configurations of products can therefore be reflected. The syntax of the CPE follows the generic syntax of uniform resource identifiers (URI). The NVD supports CPE version 2.3, which forms product strings as follows:

- cpe:2.3:part:vendor:product:version:update:edition:lang:sw_edition:target_sw: target_hw:other

The contained attributes are explained in Table 2.1.

Table 2.1: Description of Attributes for CPE2.3 [25].

Attribute	Description
CPE:2.3	Shows the used CPE version 2.3.
part	Indicates whether CPE belongs to a application ('a'), operation system ('o') or a hardware device ('h').
vendor	The person or organization, who created the product.
product	Identifies the most common product name.
version	Shows the vendor-specific release version of product.
update	Shows the update version of the product as alpha or beta.
edition	Deprecated for version 2.3 for backward compatibility to CPE version 2.2 'Any' is assigned.
lang	Language tag for the user interface language as English.
sw_edition	Identifies manifestations of product-tailoring (e. g. professional and standard products)
target_sw	Product-operating software computing environment.
target_hw	Product-operating instruction set architecture (e.g. x86 or x64).
other	Any other vendor- or product-specific descriptive information.

Common Vulnerability Scoring System

The risk and severity of vulnerabilities can be expressed by the common vulnerability scoring system (CVSS). The CVSS has the purpose of defining and communicating the characteristics of vulnerabilities. In January 2021, the NVD supports CVSS2.0 and CVSS3.1 [127]. Older entries in the NVD database only provide CVSS2.0. In addition, a newer version provides the scores of both CVSS2.0 and CVSS3.1. Therefore, this dissertation considers the use of CVSS2.0 for scoring vulnerabilities. The score can take numeric values from 0 to

Table 2.2: CVSS2.0 Severity Scoring Ranges [127].

Severity	Score Range
Low	0.0-3.9
Medium	4.0-6.9
High	7.0-10.0

10. Therefore, the scoring is divided into low, medium, and high severity scores. The scores are summarized by the NVD as shown in Table 2.2:

The scoring is calculated using different aspects separated into base, temporal, and environmental metric groups. The base metric group represents time-constant intrinsic and fundamental characteristics such as access vector, access complexity, and impacts on confidentiality, integrity, and availability. The temporal group defines time-variable factors including exploitability, remediation level, and report confidence. Environmental characteristics are relevant to a particular user's environment. For example, the collateral damage potential is considered, as well as the target distribution and requirements of confidentiality, integrity, and availability [111].

2.3.2   Question and Answer Websites

Several online communities exist for developers, including for topics about source code, which is frequently discussed. Some websites are members of the Stack Exchange [69] question-and-answer network, on which this thesis focuses. The network consists of about 130 web pages, for example, Stack Overflow [9], Super User[10], Information Security[7] and Server Fault[8]. In 2020, Stack Overflow represents the largest related website, with 13.2 million registered users. In total for 2019, Stack Exchange recorded about 3.3 million questions offered with 3.6 million answers and 13.7 million comments [43]. Software developers have identified these websites as useful for discussing program-specific content [46, 26, 162, 135].

Each main post is a description of a problem, question, or a statement for discussion. Posts can be answered by several contributors who can be rated by community members. Ratings are expressed by a positive or negative number and are increased or decreased by one every time a user assesses them. The questioner can accept an answer when it helps in solving a concern. Stack Overflow introduced a reputation system to improve the quality of the information on the website. Users can earn reputation points if others' questions are answered or their own written question is answered. With only a slightly increased reputation, users can unlock different features and permissions, such as rating the capabilities of user contributions.

For every question, single to multiple tags can be assigned, for example, to identify whether a post treats issues for concrete programming languages or possibly security-related content. The tags for programming languages are useful, but the security tag is often not set in comparison. This fact makes it necessary to find other ways to identify security-related posts on the platform. Furthermore, in this thesis, it was identified that CVE-IDs are rarely mentioned when security issues are discussed. More often, attack strategies such as Cross-Site Scripting (XSS) are used to identify vulnerabilities.

2.3.3 GitHub

GitHub [112] is a versioning system for software development. Many open source projects appear on the platform, which means that no institution can ensure that the developers have a minimum amount of security experience. GitHub also lists vulnerable source code and related security patches that can be part of projects' code commits. On the platform, there are mechanisms to support developers to find vulnerabilities inside of their git repository. The GitHub advisory database stores all the vulnerabilities they are aware of in packages. A dependency graph then knows which repositories use which packages. For example, suppose a repository is using a package with a known vulnerability. In that case, GitHub creates a security alert to notify the repository owner and attempts to fix the vulnerability if users have enabled automated security updates. For detecting vulnerabilities, GitHub takes advantage of the semantic code analysis engine CodeQL [55], which uses static code analysis with patterns added by security experts. Also, GitHub relies on community knowledge about security. GitHub provides security advisories [113] which enables GitHub users to discuss potential security issues. Users can comment about concrete advisories that were previously created by repository administrators.

2.4 Artificial Intelligence for Text Classification

Over 80% of the world's existing information is in the form of natural language text, making up a large part of the Stack Exchange network web pages [86]. Therefore, texts are the most valuable source of knowledge. Text classification exists in different forms such as supervised,

16

unsupervised, and semi-supervised learning [151]. These forms contain machine-learning techniques such as neural networks, and can be enriched by natural language processing (NLP) methods to discover patterns and automatically classify text into different types. This procedure is knowledge-intensive and reflects the use of knowledge within the textual information. Concrete approaches are described in Sec. 4.2.3.

2.5 Code Clone Detection

Code clone detection aims to locate exact or similar code fragments, called clones, in or between the source code of software [150]. For code clone detection, different approaches exist with distinct recognition capabilities. These approaches have different levels of granularity, such as code lines, tokens, nodes of abstract syntax trees or nodes of a program dependency graph. In the following section, the logic security examination of these granularity levels is described. Sheneamer et al. created a survey of code clone detection techniques, summarizing the approaches as follows [150].

Textual: Text-based methods compare the similarity of code fragments by using the contained textual terms such as represented by comments as well as within class, method or variable names. These techniques can only find Type 1 code clones without preprocessing. Furthermore, they are language independent and easy to implement.

Lexical: These methods are also called token-based clone detection techniques. All source code lines are divided into a sequence of tokens. The tokens are converted into token sequence lines. Then, the approach looks for a match. Several state-of-the-art techniques belong to this class of code clone detection approaches. The lexical approaches are among the best of such methods and can detect various code clone types with higher recall and precision than text-based techniques.

Syntactic: These methods are split into two types of techniques: tree- and metric-based. For tree-based techniques, the source code is parsed into abstract syntax trees and its subtrees are compared to find cloned code parts using tree-matching algorithms. In comparison, metric-based approaches calculate and compare a number of metrics rather than checking the similarity of source code fragments directly. The comparisons are based on metric vectors created for each code snippet. Examples of metrics used are the number of declaration, loop, executable, conditional, and return statements, as well as function calls and parameters. Metric-based techniques can detect Type 1 and Type 2 clones with high time complexity. The technique reduces the complexity of text-based approaches.

Semantic: This method detects two code fragments that perform the same computation but have differently structured code previously categorized as a Type 4 clone. Semantic methods are separated into graph-based and hybrid techniques. Graph-based approaches use a graph to represent a program's data and control flow, for example, a program dependency graph. Hybrid techniques are a combination of two or more techniques that can overcome problems encountered by single tools and approaches.

In Sheneamer et al.'s [150] survey of code clone detection approaches, the authors also compared code clone detectors. According to their analysis, only two clone detectors, SourcererCC and CCFinderX, are applicable for huge data sets containing 100 million lines of code (LOC). This dissertation's goal is to use information systems with big data content of vulnerable source code snippets. Therefore, this capability is essential. The source code of SourcererCC is publicly accessible, whereas the code of the CCFinderX is not. Furthermore, for distinct programming languages, SourcererCC achieves the best recall. Therefore, based on its benefits, SourcererCC is used as a base for the approach described in this dissertation.

2.5.1 Code Clone Types

The common taxonomy of code clones and its implications for security were instrumental in defining code clone types. Within the common taxonomy of code clones [87] four existing clone types are distinguished based on the degree of similarity:

Viertel et al. [170] defined these clone types as follows: "*Type 1* clones are code fragments that are accurate copies of each other, excluding whitespaces, blank lines, and comments. *Type 2* clones are structurally identical code fragments that may differ in the names of variables, literals, and functions. *Type 3* or *near-miss* clones are syntactically similar code fragments that, as opposed to Type 1 and Type 2 clones, may include changes such as added or removed statements. *Type 4* clones are code fragments with a different syntax but similar semantics.".

The example in Fig. 2-2 shows a code fragment CF_0 together with clones of each type, one to four.

Security considerations Clone types have different implications for security vulnerabilities. If a vulnerability exists in a source code fragment, then type 1 clones of that fragment

18

Initial Code Fragement CF$_0$	CF$_1$ – Type-1 Clone	CF$_4$ – Type-4 Clone
```for(i = 0; i < 10; i++)` `{` ` // foo 2` ` if (i % 2 == 0)` ` a = b + i;` ` else` ` // foo 1` ` a = b - i;` `}```	```for(i = 0; i < 10; i++)` `{` ` if (i % 2 == 0)` ` a = b + i; //cmt 1` ` else` ` b = b - i; //cmt 2` `}```	```while(i < 10)` `{` ` // a comment` ` a = (i % 2 == 0) ?` ` b + i : b - i;` ` i++;` `}```

CF$_2$ – Type-2 Clone	CF$_3$ – Type-3 Clone	
```for(j = 0; j < 10; j++)` `{` ` if (j % 2 == 0)` ` y = x + j; //cmt 1` ` else` ` y = x - j; //cmt 2` `}```	```for(i = 0; i < 10; i++)` `{` ` // new statement` ` a = 10 * b;` ` if (i % 2 == 0)` ` a = b + i; //cmt 1` ` else` ` a = b - i; //cmt 2` `}```	

Figure 2-2: Clone-Types: Type 1 to Type 4 [170].

are usually also vulnerable. In most programming languages, code containing whitespace, blank lines, and comments does not change its execution behaviour. Therefore, the assumption is that the vulnerability in a code fragment would also occur in all of its Type 1 code clones.

The situation is different when changing variable names in Type 2. However, the change of literal and method names can impact a vulnerability when a specific method is called or when specific literals are used. This means that Type 2 code clones might no longer be insecure but are quite similar to referenced vulnerable code clones.

A particular challenge for the vulnerability detection described in this thesis is the support of type 3 clones. A single line can invoke a vulnerability and vice-versa. The notorious buffer overflow vulnerability, for example, represents that a buffer is not checked before it is read or written. A simple range check before accessing the buffer would close this vulnerability, but the resulting code fragment counts still as a Type 3 clone. For security code clone detection, this means that a secure code snippet will be detected, as seen in a code clone of a weak fragment. Otherwise, if an arbitrary statement is added into a vulnerable code snippet, it is still insecure. Therefore, to obtain a higher recall, it is necessary to consider Type 3 clones as well.

The crux of Type 4 clones is code snippet semantics. That is, two code fragments with entirely different syntax are still detected as code clones if they share the same semantics.

19

Since many vulnerabilities are product-specific as listed in the NVD and caused by syntactical uses of particular software artifacts, Type 4 clones are not considered for the vulnerability detection described in this thesis. Code vulnerabilities address the insecure implementation of a particular code snippet or structure. Thus, the assumption is that if code differs in the context of structure and statements used, then the decision about the security of an insecure code clone is impossible. Hence, this dissertation focuses only on the approaches toward code clone types one to three.

2.6   Performance Metrics

To investigate the performance of classification approaches, metrics introduced within the information retrieval are employed [106]. The metrics comprise precision, recall, F1-measure and accuracy. These metrics are based on the confusion matrix, which shows how many items are properly assigned to the correct class and the number of incorrectly classified items for each binary classifier. To be more precise, the matrix distinguishes between true positives (TP), false positives (FP), true negatives (TN) and false negatives (FN). A "true positive" is an item that is correctly assigned to a concrete class, while a "true negative" indicates that something was correctly recognized to do not corresponding to this class. False values, as false positives or negatives, identify the error of classification. While "false positives" are falsely assigned to a certain class, "false negatives" are the elements that are falsely recognised as not belonging to this class. An example of the confusion matrix structure is shown in Table 2.3.

An example classifier could use textual descriptions in a concrete Stack Exchange post to determine whether the post contains security-related content. True positives are posts that are correctly recognized as handling security-related topics. A false positive would be a post that does not consider security at all but is identified as such. True negatives are the ones that are correctly recognized not to handle security of any kind. In the end, false negatives are security-related posts that are not properly classified as such.

Table 2.3: General Confusion Matrix [106].

	Relevant	Non-relevant
Retrieved	True Positives (TP)	False Positives (FP)
Not retrieved	False Negatives (FN)	True Negatives (TN)

20

Precision: The *Precision* measures the fraction of retrieved to relevant items. Within the context of the posts' security classification, this is the ratio of posts correctly classified as security-relevant to all recognized posts. Thus, the denominator includes the false and the true positive predictions. The equation is shown in the following:

$$Precision = \frac{TP}{TP + FP} \tag{2.1}$$

Recall: The *Recall* is defined as the measure of the fraction of relevant items retrieved. As in the precision classifier, recall compares the number of correctly identified posts to those that must be recognized as such. Therefore, the denominator also considers posts that are falsely classified as irrelevant. That is, the recall classifier considers the number of relevant posts that could correctly be identified as such. The equation is shown as follows:

$$Recall = \frac{TP}{TP + FN} \tag{2.2}$$

To achieve perfect precision and recall of 100% is usually impossible. Often, a drawback exists in keeping both metrics high. Therefore, for vulnerability detection, this dissertation prioritizes recognizing as many vulnerabilities as possible, which means that recall is more important than precision. However, precision is also important. For instance, if the precision is too low, developers get false warnings about secure source code fragments, which can lower the trust in the tools [178].

F-Measure: A combination of precision and recall is called the "F-Measure." This measure represents the weighted harmonic mean of precision and recall. However, it is unnecessary to weight precision and recall differently. An example of equal weighting is the F1-measure shown in the following equation:

$$F1 - Measure = 2 \times \frac{Precision \times Recall}{Precision + Recall} \tag{2.3}$$

Accuracy: A further alternative to express the performance of classification algorithms is accuracy, which is defined as the fraction of correctly classified items. This is the ratio of all correctly identified posts (whether security-related or unrelated) to all existent classifications within the security example.

$$Accuracy = \frac{TP + TN}{TP + FP + TN + FN} \tag{2.4}$$

The introduced metrics that share the result always have a value between zero and one. They can also be expressed as percentage values by multiplying the result by 100.

2.7 Threats to Validity

Wohlin et al. [175] defined types of threats to validity for empirical software engineering research. The authors distinguished between conclusion, internal, construct, external, credibility, dependability, and confirmability. The threat types are summarized and described within Table 2.4.

Table 2.4: Types of Threats to Validity [44].

Validity type	Explanation
Conclusion	Statistically significant effects of the treatment on the result.
Internal	Effect cause by the treatment.
Construct	The relationship between the outcome and the observed effect.
External	Generalized or situational effects.
Credibility	Confidence that findings are true.
Dependability	Consistent findings that can be repeated.
Confirmability	Findings are attributed to the participants and not by the researcher.

These threats are partially considered during each step of technical validation and in the case studies.

Chapter 3

Heuristic Security Checker

During software development, security checks on code artifacts have already been applied in the past to produce more secure software. The full source code and imported software libraries must be sifted for vulnerabilities to find insecurities in a software project. These vulnerability checks are a very time-consuming and challenging task. Much knowledge is required to achieve satisfactory results for applied security checks [68]. Within the software development process, many software artifacts are created. Section 3.1 partially describes emerging software artifacts and the scope of relevant representations for this dissertation. One goal of this dissertation is to actively support developers in the task of implementing secure software. In Section 3.2, the points of contact for the phases of the software development process are highlighted. For the investigation carried out in this thesis, reference is made to specific programming languages. The selection of these languages is described in Sec. 3.3. Within coding communities, discussions occur about vulnerabilities and their manifestations in source code. To take advantage of community knowledge about security content, a semi-automated process for extracting and using community knowledge within security checks is described in Sec. 3.4. Furthermore, the relevance of using community knowledge is discussed. A study was applied to underpin the idea of considering community knowledge from Stack Overflow to apply security checks on source code artifacts [15]. This study is described in Sec. 3.4.1. To apply these security checks, a heuristic-based approach was developed. Sec. 3.5 provides a general description of a heuristic as it is serves as the basis for enhancing existing algorithms to improve their validity in security prediction. Code clone detection, described in section 3.6, allows the use of community knowledge about security, expressed in the form of code fragments, to perform vulnerability checks. At the end of the chapter, Sec. 3.7 lists related work aiming to extract knowledge from developer community websites and directly use it to support software development.

3.1 Software Code Artifacts

To identify suitable development artifacts to focus on during security look-ups, NVD content was investigated [170]. Different reasons for vulnerabilities to occur in software products include hardware issues, configuration mistakes, or vulnerabilities induced by insecure software code artifacts such as source code and software libraries. The open web application security project (OWASP) named the use of reusable components, for example, software code libraries, as one of the top 10 most significant security issues for web development [133].

In the context of this investigation, the ratio of vulnerabilities that induce source code problems to those that do not are reviewed. The more that source-code based weaknesses are stored, the better the concentration of source code artifacts, which aids in detecting them. A larger number of code-based vulnerabilities also substantiates the capability of using the publicly accessible NVD to recognize security flaws invoked through source code. For classifying the NVD content, a CWE identifier is assigned to them. The CWE compresses different types that categorize almost all kinds of vulnerabilities. They enable it to receive all vulnerabilities assigned to a specific CWE-ID, such as CWE-306: Missing Authentication for Critical Function. All entries associated with this type are security flaws because of the absence of authentication for critical functions. Unfortunately, a CWE-ID has not been established for every vulnerability. The NVD comprises about 103,745 entries as of August 2018 and a CWE is known only for approximately 62 % of them.

Furthermore, no identifier exists for a type that identifies all security issues belonging to source code. Therefore, the NVD content was analyzed, including the assigned CWE-IDs. For every set CWE type, it was systematically proven whether it was possible to retrieve their origin by using its description, induced by source code or a configuration.

Vulnerabilities without any assigned CWE-IDs were investigated using their description. Randomized manual checks of 20 entries showed that it was possible to find security issues induced to source code vulnerabilities via checking reports of them for the occurrence of substrings. Therefore, terms are separated into five groups: (1) file endings, (2) attack strategies, (3) configurations, (4) rejects, and (5) unclassified. The partition of the NVD regarding the mentioned groups is summarized in a pie chart in Fig. 3-1.

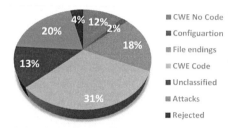

Figure 3-1: Classification of National Vulnerability Database Content [170].

Based on attacks, file extensions and CWE IDs that can be assigned to the source code, the results show that 69% of NVD entries are due to source code problems. Furthermore, considering the part attribute 15,094 of stored CPEs belong to hardware, 26,166 to operation systems and 189,987 to software applications. Therefore, it is a well-suited idea to focus on source code artifacts for identifying known and reported weaknesses in software projects. Unfortunately, the focus on source code artifacts is not the only opportunity to detect these vulnerabilities. There are also traces back up to the requirements. However, source code artifacts are identified as the scope for the vulnerability detection mechanisms described in this dissertation.

3.2 Integration of Approach into Software Development

Security holes in software applications are common and a growing problem [110]. For supporting developers to apply security checks during the software development process, different phases can be considered. This section compares various phases within the software development life cycle (SDLC) and limits the scope to specific phases attributed to created artifacts [50]. Each stage delivers various software development artifacts.

As an example of a general software development process, the Waterfall model is visualized in Figure 3-2. Examples of created software artifacts are assigned to each phase. Currently, approaches already exist for considering project security in each development phase. Right from the beginning, it is possible to identify security-related demands in the requirements elicitation. Natural language processing and ontologies consisting of terms that identify security-related content can be used and manually enriched with domain-specific terms [51, 49]. Within the design phase, there are guidelines, best practices, and approaches to building software on an architecture while considering security [85, 58]. Several tools already exist that allow for security checks during implementation [24]. Furthermore, these tools partially enable the generation of security tests for the verification phase [77]. Also, there are approaches using model checking for the verification of the security requirements of software products [4].

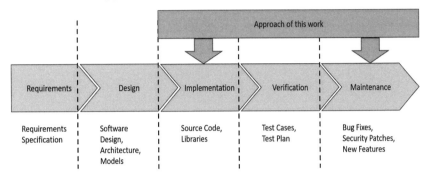

Figure 3-2: Integration of Approach into a General Waterfall Process.

The implementation and maintenance phase are appropriate process steps within the SDLC. New source code artifacts are created or imported into the project to construct a specific software product during the first phase. The second phase is placed after the project release so that new functionality can be added or bugs removed. Usually, some regression testing is applied to ensure that previously required software still meets its requirements after the changes are executed in this phase. In this context, security checks should be done because the evolving information about known vulnerabilities, technologies, and new uprising attack strategies can change a system's security so that it could become insecure. During these phases, notable software artifacts relevant to this dissertation's approach are libraries and source code files written for or imported into a project. A single vulnerable file can cause an entire project to be insecure. Therefore, it would be desirable to support security checking in all phases generating files.

3.3 Programming Language Selection as Research Base

For investigating this thesis's approach feasibility, the Java programming language has been selected. Java is widely used across numerous communities, taught at the authors' university, and frequently used by both beginners and professional developers. Furthermore, Java is the third most popular programming language on GitHub, which indicates the necessity for considering security for that language [56]. This popularity is measured by the number of total pushes within all repositories. Furthermore, Java was voted as the most popular programming language by communities [160]. For the first investigation described in this dissertation, Java source files *.java* and libraries expressed as file type *.jar* are considered.

Furthermore, as another widely used language, JavaScript is selected to investigate the effects of the described approach on other programming languages. JavaScript is the most popular programming language on GitHub in 2020, which also indicates the necessity for considering security for that language [56]. For Javascript, there are no particular library files. In contrast to Java, all content is simply stored in *.js* files. Additionally, JavaScript differs from Java in terms of syntax rules and other restrictions, which are explained with more detail in later sections. Within software projects at the author's university, JavaScript also plays an increasingly significant role.

3.4 General Approach

Security checks can be done manually and with tools, as already mentioned within the security development life cycle (SDLC) by Microsoft [98, 66]. Such tools can find vulnerabilities in software artifacts that damage the security of a system. Many of these tools rely on pre-defined static patterns that have been previously identified and defined by the community and security experts [55, 152].

These patterns represent a kind of knowledge about security. They must be manually defined in a machine-readable format such that security checkers can recognize particular vulnerabilities. Within coding communities, there are discussions about these vulnerabilities and their manifestation in the source code. To take advantage of community knowledge about security content, a semi-automated process for extracting and using community knowledge within security checks will be described in this section.

Accessing community knowledge about security is cumbersome. The search engines of community knowledge sources have to be scanned via delivered search functions for each software code artifact inside of a software project. Developers could be overwhelmed by this mass of security information. Therefore, it is not always easy to select relevant content. In this dissertation, the simplification and automation of using community knowledge about security are investigated. This approach is divided into the two steps previously used to separate the challenges and research questions: (1) identifying and (2) using security knowledge through semi-automated tool support.

First, it is vital to identify sources of knowledge regarding security. These sources could be the CWE, CVE, NVD, or the Stack Exchange question-and-answer networks such as Stack Overflow or GitHub. The CWE categorizes information regarding vulnerabilities, which are reported to the NVD and CVE. Therefore, these sources contain only security-relevant information. As already mentioned, Stack Exchange also includes Security Exchange, which only considers security-related content, but the number of contributions is lower than that of Stack Overflow. As the largest website of the network, the Stack Overflow community discusses a variety of topics according to software development, including security. The community thereby forwards affected source code artifacts. In comparison, many projects on GitHub are stored by version and made publicly available to the community. Developers' knowledge is expressed by the contained source code and related commit messages that also handle security-related issues. The knowledge sources are described in detail in Sec. 2.3. All the named sources consist at least partially or completely of security-related data. For knowledge sources that only partly contain security data, it is necessary to identify the security content. For this thesis, a security knowledge base is created to receive a repository that contains only security-related information. The data is then stored in a machine-readable manner.

Regarding the security knowledge base, the database is enriched as information about security evolves and the associated community contributions increase. To counteract potential incorrect results delivered from the approach developed in this dissertation, manual auditing and correction were provided. This knowledge was then stored in a machine-readable manner to enable the use of other tools such as code clone detectors, with the goal of automatic vulnerability detection.

The available security-related knowledge gathered and stored in the knowledge base from

28

the sources mentioned above is designed to support developers in security checks on software code artifacts. If a vulnerability mentioned in the identified knowledge sources is detected, the potential exposure and location are shown to the developers. Therefore, the heuristic approach developed for this work is used. To provide the most precise feedback possible, the different granularity for software artifacts' security assessments from the block or method up to the file level is considered. The results of vulnerabilities have to be manually validated and patched by developers. An example of code concerning an occurrence, its exploit, and the patch of the detected security flaw is reported to users to aid in addressing the vulnerability. This process is visualized in Fig. 3-3.

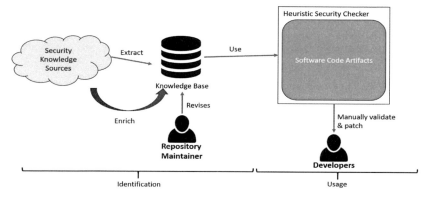

Figure 3-3: General Approach.

3.4.1 Study: Community Knowledge about Security

A central concept of this work is to use community knowledge about security. However, several studies have conclusively demonstrated that using code fragments from community websites such as Stack Overflow can make a project insecure [46, 26]. Unfortunately, the trend of developers is using posted code from scratch without checking its security. Stack Overflow contains insecure code fragments, which underscores this platform's relevance to get insights into examples of vulnerabilities.

Chen et al. [26] conducted a study to identify the reliability of crowdsourced community knowledge about security implementations. Results indicated that 45% of inspected answer posts were insecure. The authors attempted to measure the reliability of community knowledge about security using only code clone detection. Code clones, however, are not considered text contributions of users, which are likely to identify vulnerabilities in code fragments. Thus, the validity of their results and the research method employed is limited. Chen et al. could not draw any valid conclusions about crowdsourced community security knowledge.

Another study showed that 15% of 1,305,820 Android applications contained vulnerable code fragments that handled cryptographic issues and were likely copied from Stack Overflow [46]. The authors used a program dependency graph clone detection to identify vulnerable code snippets in applications. Their procedure, however, did not consider whether the community was able to detect that the posted insecure code fragments were secure. To derive the impact from the community's knowledge of security, it is therefore necessary to consider not only the code fragments but also the user contributions that are written in natural language.

To close this gap, the real security knowledge of Stack Overflow regarding the user contributions in natural language was manually investigated regarding their security know-how [15]. In both studies previously mentioned [46, 26], security experts manually labeled a set of code fragments extracted from Stack Overflow, regarding their security. Chen et al. [26] did not provide links to the original posts within their manually classified data and did not store the posts' texts. To retrieve the texts, a search using the code fragments was applied on Stack Overflow. Both works manually labeled 1,429 unique posts for which the original post text could be retrieved. For the posts, 785 contained code fragments labeled as secure and 644 were identified as vulnerable. For labeling, the authors considered only the source code. In the same way, contributed text or answers for these code fragments were not considered. At first glance, it appears as if it is ill-advised to use community knowledge about security to help developers implement secure software. In contrast, their study does not consider the real security knowledge of the community.

Therefore, all the insecure and 100 secure posts were manually reviewed for user posts that identified or provided hints that a code fragment might be insecure. For the subset of secure posts, whether the community saw insecurities where none exist was investigated. This was not the case for any secure posts. Therefore, only the examples classified as insecure were proven. Furthermore, Fischer et al. [47] introduced a new set of 10,558 manually labeled data samples enriched by a more precise categorization of security issues. For each category,

100 results were investigated manually. This way, the time until members of the community detected a vulnerability was considered. Furthermore, the types of security issues assigned in the previous work were utilized to determine whether the community knowledge varied with different security concerns; for instance, initialization of cipher, hash, transport layer security protocol, setting hostname verifier, override hostname verification, server certificate verification, generation of symmetric key, and initialization vector [47].

This thesis shows that security knowledge is not as poor as it seems in previous studies [46, 26]. In total, for 73,21% of investigated Stack Overflow posts, the community expresses positive security expertise. Posts considering secure implementations are combined with posts providing vulnerable code fragments that can be recognized as insecure by the community. For 40,68% of the insecure code fragments contributed within posts, the community correctly identified them as vulnerable. Considering the different security concerns, 20% to 50% of each insecure post was identified as such. The worst results for insecure recognition appeared in the community for hashes and trust-manager affected topics. In the median, the community detected all categories of vulnerabilities as insecure within 2.18 hours after their contribution.

The use of posts on Stack Overflow is therefore a good option to obtain security-related information about security. In this thesis, code examples and natural language texts can therefore be retrieved to form a security knowledge base.

3.5   Security Heuristics

Many decisions are made under uncertainty, where the probability of several options could be weighed against each other [163]. Todd [161] defines a heuristic as follows:

- *"Heuristics are approximate strategies or "rules of thumb" for decision making and problem solving that do not guarantee a correct solution but that typically yield a reasonable solution or bring one closer to hand. More specifically, heuristics are usually thought of as shortcuts that allow decisions or solutions to be reached more rapidly and in conditions of incomplete or uncertain information—often because they do not process all the available information."*

A possible question could be: What is the chance that object A belongs to class B? To respond to equivalent questions, the answer could rely on representative heuristics that consider probabilities of the degree that object A is a representative of class B. That means if A is most similar to B, the likelihood that A belongs to that class is higher than to all other classes. To the contrary, class B's low similarity indicates that object A probably cannot be assigned to class B. These rules can lead to severe and systematic errors, but they also enable decisions on unclear issues.

In computer science, different areas contain heuristics for a wide variety of purposes. For example, there is a heuristic to calculate the complexity of methods called McCabe metric. Heuristics can also likely be used to decide about the security of source code fragments or to transform data in natural language into information. A more general problem could be whether a code fragment contains a vulnerability or is secure in the security context. To define the problem more formally within a question, it can be asked: Does a code fragment A belongs to the class of vulnerability B? To simplify this task, another class could be the opposite, which means that A does not belong to a vulnerability B. Formally, this can be expressed by the following equation.

$$P(B) + P(\overline{B}) = 100 \tag{3.1}$$

This formula means the sample heuristic delivers only the probability of a code fragment being vulnerable. To solve the research questions of this dissertation, heuristics of different purposes are leveraged.

3.6 Code Clone Detection

Many vulnerability detection approaches check the occurrence of previously defined patterns. These checks have to be manually created by security experts. One sample pattern could prove to be the correct parameterization of a cryptographic algorithm to hash a password. For example, MD5 and SHA-1 are susceptible to length-extension and collisions [13]. The correct use of these encryption algorithms can be checked within such a sample pattern. However, defining these patterns automatically from community knowledge stored within the posts in Stack Exchange or GitHub is difficult and not possible from the author's experience.

An approach to automatically using the information stored on these platforms is code clone detection, which uses pre-identified code fragments tagged as vulnerable. This mechanism prevents the need of manual definition of patterns for applying security checks based on the knowledge from coding communities, which is one goal of this work.

3.7 Related Work

Integrating the community knowledge from question-and-answer websites such as Stack Overflow for software development is an approach known in the research of knowledge engineering and application. This section describes related work that extracts community knowledge from Stack Overflow to automatically support developers' software generation.

Ponzanelli et al. [135] introduced an eclipse plugin named SEAHAWK for permitting the context change from web browsers to the integrated development environment. The authors presented an approach to automatically querying Stack Overflow knowledge by extracting keywords of previously selected code fragments directly in eclipse. This approach enables drag-and-drop code fragments to be pasted within a developer's own project source code through interactive and ranked lists. The traces back to the original Stack Overflow posts of the copied source code fragments are stored. Ponzanelli et al.'s approach attempts to solve missing documentation issues, for example, in open-source projects. Within their work, they did not consider security in any manner.

A further approach that automatically uses knowledge stored in Stack Overflow was developed by Huang et al. [67]. The authors used graph-based clustering and latent factorization combined with a software-specific knowledge base to recommend software experts as a service. Huang et al. trained word embedding on user contributions to the platform to fulfill their service. Moreover, Huang et al. derived domains by clustering word representations. The approach enabled the location of experts in certain domains for the users of Stack Overflow. The method only considered text in natural language contributed to Stack Overflow. The authors disregarded the security of discrete posted code fragments.

Treude et al. [162] augmented API documentation via the use of machine learning. The authors mentioned that API documentation captures functional and structure information but does not provide other types of information, such as concepts or purpose. Therefore, the purpose of their work was to close this gap inside of the documentation to leverage insight from sentences on Stack Overflow to enhance API documentation. Treude et al. did not consider security.

Ragkhitwetsagul et al. [139] attempted to find code clones on Stack Overflow and GitHub software projects using a code clone detection approach. Indeed, they noted that copying and pasting code from Stack Overflow can lead to license problems and vulnerabilities. The authors analyzed 2,289 code clones, of which 214 could violate original software licenses, which occurred 7,112 times in 2,427 GitHub projects. Furthermore, the authors identified 100 code snippets as outdated, of which 10 were buggy and harmful for reuse. They did not consider a security checker to support developers using code clone detection nor a vulnerable code repository created out of community websites such as those introduced in this thesis.

Regarding the unsystematic literature review done for this dissertation, no known approach automatically extracts and reuses the security knowledge on programming community websites to apply security checks within software applications.

Chapter 4

Security Knowledge Acquisition from Coding Communities

The previous chapters provide the motivation and identify the scope of research, introducing the overall conceptional idea of this dissertation in an abstract way. This chapter addresses the first part of the approach which tackles the following research questions:

- **RQ1:** Can security knowledge be semi-automatically extracted from coding communities?

- **RQ1.1:** Can security information be semi-automatically differentiated into vulnerabilities, patches, and exploits?

At first, the conceptional solution of creating a security knowledge base out of community knowledge is presented abstractly. This semi-automated approach to building such a repository is introduced within Section 4.1. Therefore, the most significant coding and security knowledge sources are interleaved to form a central repository containing security-related code and information among software vulnerabilities. Afterwards, the process is enriched with more detailed information. Section 4.2 introduces machine learning and natural language processing mechanisms combined to identify security-related content on Stack Exchange. Furthermore, a simplified approach for GitHub is presented in the same way. To distinguish between vulnerable, security-patch, and exploit information, the same artificial techniques are applied to achieve that goal, described in Section 4.3. Finally, the post-processing of the resulting classifications is required, as presented in Section 4.4. At the end of this chapter, Sec. 4.5 describes the related work of creating such a repository.

4.1 General Approach

To create a suitable security knowledge base out of different sources, a uniform structure would be essential. To support the use of security-relevant information with heuristic security checking approaches, it is necessary to store data in an automatically accessible way. Due to the rapid evolution of security knowledge, it has to be possible to build and sustain the knowledge base iteratively. The data is separated into the three identified types of security-related information introduced through the vulnerability life-cycle described in Sec. 2.1. This eases access to the different types of security-related information, which is required to apply code clone detection to identify vulnerabilities. As data in the knowledge base consists of previously known vulnerabilities, a CVE-ID is assigned, if available. Furthermore, for every vulnerability, a CWE-ID is allocated so that the context of issues could be more understandable. Through the missing code examples stored in the NVD, this knowledge base should contain source code examples of vulnerabilities, security-patches, and exploits to understand insecure source code better and provide a reference knowledge base for the security code clone detection.

The process for creating a suitable security code repository relies on programming community websites on which such code snippets can be found. To this end, Stack Exchange [69], a well-known question and answer platform for developers and GitHub [112], a versioning system for software projects of almost every programming language is used [169, 170]. Both are freely accessible to the public. In the context of this dissertation, the security knowledge base consists of community knowledge represented by security-related source code fragments. These fragments are example code of vulnerabilities, their exploits or patches. As the center of this data collection, count vulnerabilities, for which additionally available meta-information as CVE-ID and CWE-ID are stored. The process for creating this repository is shown in Fig. 4-1, and contains the steps *Identification*, *Classification*, *Storage*, and *Verification*.

During the identification step, the content on these platforms is searched and classified as security-related by textual descriptions of user contributions. Therefore, simplified string search and comparison are used as well as artificial approaches. Meanwhile, the classification of the resulting security-specific content is assigned by almost the same algorithms for up to three different types of security information: vulnerability, patch, or exploit. This

36

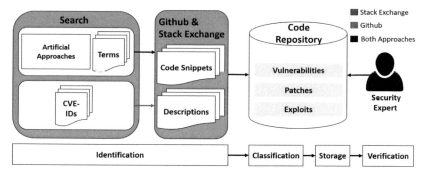

Figure 4-1: Abstract Knowledge Base Creation Approach [169].

information is stored within its categories and enhanced with metadata such as CWE-IDs and CVE-IDs. A repository maintainer now has to recheck previous miss-classifications, and in the same way, extracted code fragments for their relevance. The maintainer has to assign CWE IDs to the extracted code fragments manually for vulnerabilities where they are not set or could not be retrieved.

4.2 Identification of Security-Related Information

Both platforms consist of much programming-specific information and source code examples. However, they are not restricted to security content, which makes the identification of information on vulnerabilities difficult. Due to the lack of setting the security tag for Stack Overflow posts and the absence of any possibility to filter security-related code from GitHub, other approaches are required for the search. In addition to source code, a massive amount of text describes the content, some findings, and statements about the code fragments' security. This abundance of information makes it necessary to consider natural language texts to identify security-related information and code fragments. Right now, there are a lot of algorithms that ease the processing of text, as introduced in this section. The repertoire of approaches encompass strategies of simple string comparison up to natural language processing and artificial intelligence mechanisms. Regarding the absence of CVE-IDs on Stack Exchange, it is more difficult to identify security content on the question-and-answer network than on GitHub [170], where developers frequently use CVE-IDs in commit messages.

An example is a post where a user asks whether a code snippet using an MD5 hash is secure or not for password encryption. The question could be, "Does the following code perform a secure password-encryption?". The created question text contains some evidence that the post handles a security-related topic. This thesis assumes that posted code fragments on Stack Exchange have relationships to the text published in the same context. This assumption obviously holds, but it was also manually validated by investigating a subset of randomly picked security-related posts from Stack Overflow.

Random sampling also showed that security classifications are misleading when questions are considered individually to answer posts. Most interrogators have no professional knowledge of the content in the created post, which is usually the reason for a question posted on Stack Overflow. Rigby and Robilliard came to similar conclusions about the search for code fragments on Stack Overflow [142].

Nevertheless, dependencies are identified, that do indicate the conclusions about security among the main post, also named question, with its answers. This is because answers usually appear on the original post. An example is that the interrogator sometimes posts vulnerable code and asks the community about its security. Often interrogators do not have security in mind and are pointed to a containing vulnerability inside posted source code by answers of the community. This relationship is bidirectional, which means that the answers usually help to decide about the security of the question content and vice versa.

Therefore, to discriminate about posts' security relevance, they are grouped with each of their answers into pairs for their security types classification. Tuples are build, whose formal definition is as follows: $< Question, Answer_n >, n \in \mathbb{N}$

The n is an index representing a concrete answer responding to a question, where n can be a number from one to the total amount of answers to that question. The problem is that Stack Exchange tuples partially cannot be assigned to just a single type because they contain multiple types of data. For example, this can happen if a interrogator adds insecure code to a question answered by a post identifying the code fragment as vulnerable and referencing a securely patched code. In this case, the tuple would be classified as having vulnerable and patched information, for example, source code. For these situations, usually manual rework is required to remain within files only containing the content of specific security types.

4.2.1 Keyword-Based Search

A keyword-based search is an investigated procedure to find security-related content. To locate security-related content, a simple approach utilizing terms likely to be associated with the security content are used. Therefore, search engines of knowledge sources are leveraged. To determine adequate terms for the identification of security-related content, different knowledge sources are needed.

One possible step to identify a concrete vulnerability might be its unique CVE identifier (ID), which places a definite product-specific vulnerability stored in the NVD. Therefore, these CVE-IDs were extracted for a check-up of their existence on Stack Exchange and GitHub. Using CVE-IDs in the search for security-related content on GitHub delivers numerous results. On the other contrary, using the same IDs within a search on Stack Exchange is insufficient, simply because of their absence. Unfortunately, the community seldom mentions concrete CVE-IDs in their contributions. More often, they name types of vulnerabilities. The Common Weakness and Exposure (CWE) summarizes types of vulnerabilities in a list. To obtain reasonable terms for the search on Stack Exchange, the CWE-types are manually inspected.

The Open Web Application Security Project (OWASP) lists the 10 most infamous weaknesses within internet applications, which are used to obtain more valid search terms. Terms indicating security content were included in the initial set of terms used for the search.

Furthermore, the systematic manual searches on Stack Overflow for security-related posts identified terms to find posts with security affiliation. Therefore, general terms identifying security as *security*, *vulnerability*, *patch* and *exploit* were used. From found posts manually identified as security-relevant, additional keywords were extracted that could potentially discover new security-relevant posts. If an unknown keyword was identified this way, it was checked whether it revealed recent posts that were not returned with previous keywords. For keywords that do find revelant posts, they would be added as a term for keyword-based searches. The process was canceled when no new entries were found within the top ten returned posts. Moreover, in a group of three security experts, brainstorming was made to find further security-related terms. To this end, it is necessary to emphasize that the identified terms form a non-enclosed set of keywords.

An experiment with ten subjects [161] was conducted to retrieve community knowledge

Table 4.1: Search Terms of Security Experts [169].

TN	Terms
1	security issues, open cve(s)+, security (vulnerabilities)+
2	vulnerabilities, exploit
3	lib bug, (lib)+ security leak, login hack, (libs)+ cve, cve (login)+ bypass, cve (exploit)+, data exploit, vulnerability.jar, vulnerability example, bugs in lib, bugs in jdk, (security(bypass|vulnerabilities|bug|gaps)+
4	security vulnerabilities, secuirty bugs,
5	fix (security flaw)+, exploit(s)+, security (issues)+, exploit, vulnerabilities
6	security issue, security vulnerability, insecure library, sql injection
7	(vulnerability)+ fix, exploit, vulnerable code, fix vulnerability, exploit
8	exploit (jackrabbit|(apache+(commons|structs)|invoke(cve)+|fix apache| fix security)+, vulnerability (cve|rce|structs|injection|struts rce| sql jdbc+|fix)+, rce fix
9	vulnerability, bufferoverflow, cve (code)+, "sql injection", injection FindBugs (plugin|code|cve|vulnerability)
10	cve (vulnerability)+, vulnerability security exploit fix, cwe (answers)+, security flaw malicious

of security experts (Appendix A.8) [169]. The subjects attempted to find security-related Java content on Stack Overflow using the provided search engine. Based on the longest time an automatic keyword-based approach required, the time to fulfill the task was restricted to 17 minutes. The search-terms were enriched by all suitable words the experts used. Table 4.1 summarizes all terms used within the search of the security experts. The terms are listed within an abstracted regex syntax. The "+" symbol means that the terms occur once or can be omitted. A "|" indicates an "or" relationship.

Among others, it has turned out that the search for attack strategies such as cross-site scripting (XSS) and others were expedient. Furthermore, the security experts used many general terms such as vulnerability, security, patch, fix or exploit. All the automated search terms utilized are listed as follows:

- Terms: attack, security weakness, "prone to", vulnerable, security bug, weak security, XSS, insecure hash, sql injection, session fixation, shell injection, exposing sessionid, command injection, "remote code execution", injection attack, weak password hash, cross site scripting, "deserialization attack", request forgery, man in the middle attack, insecure encryption, reflection attack, veracode, CWE.

The pre-extracted terms (Stack Exchange) and CVE-IDs (GitHub) are used to search security-related posts on these platforms. With these terms, a hypothesis can be formed:

- **Hypothesis H(x):** All posts x on Stack Overflow are considered to have security-relevant content if they contain at least one of the keywords.

4.2.2 Data about Security

To apply supervised artificial intelligence algorithms as neural networks, prior training of these algorithms is required. Therefore, the labeled training data described in this section is used. Identifying security-related content or distinguishing between information about a vulnerability, security-patch, or exploit means data containing examples of this kind of information are partially available. For using these supervised learning algorithms within this thesis's approach, data from Stack Overflow is used that is identified as security-related in other work [26, 46, 47, 169, 92]. For training the classifiers, data formatted as question-answer pairs including their comments is used, as described above.

The data sets of Chen et al. [26] and Fischer et al. [47] are described in Sec. 3.4.1 with more details.

Chen et al. [26] delivered a data set only consisting of code fragments from Stack Overflow and assigned to a security state (secure or insecure). To obtain the textual descriptions of posts contributed along with source code, the code fragments were used to retrieve the text. These texts sometimes contained information about the security relevance of code fragments distributed in the same course.

Fischer et al. [46, 47] provided 4,067 data samples of answers, which could be used to create question-answer pairs for the training of classifiers. Again they also give information about the security of code contributed within the answers.

Viertel et al. [169] provided data samples of 159 security-related posts about vulnerabilities, patches, and exploits. These posts were generated by analyzing 200 randomly picked posts identified as security-related by the keyword-based search described in Sec. 4.2.1.

In addition to examples with a security affiliation, posts that do not have a direct security relationship are also required. This is necessary to enable the supervised methods to be able to process security-unrelated information. Therefore, a blacklist containing the terms used for the keyword-based search to identify security-related content on Stack Overflow was utilized. This means that posts not containing any of these security indicating keywords are considered as posts that are not security-related. To relate this to the hypothesis made for the keyword-based search, the hypothesis can be negated.

Table 4.2: Stack Overflow Posts of Datasets for the Training of Textclassifiers [46, 47, 26, 92].

Sources	Vulnerable	Secure/ Patch	Exploit	Non- related	Total
Fischer et al. [47, 46]	2437	1627	-	-	4064
Chen et al. [26]	35	216	-	-	251
Viertel et al. [169]	124	29	7	-	160
Kupczyk [92]	-	-	-	4475	4475
Total	2596	1872	7	4475	8950

- **Negated hypothesis** $\bar{H}(x)$: All posts x on Stack Overflow are considered as non security-related if they do not contain any of the keywords.

Bosu et al. [22] introduced terms extracted via text mining from open source software projects that identifying security-related code reviews. These terms are assigned to CWE-IDs, which they should represent. To enhance the capability to find posts with no security-relevance, these terms were also considered for the blacklist. General terms such as "string" and "integer", and duplicate terms identified by Viertel et al. [169] were disregarded. Conclusively, the enhancing terms are listed as follows:

- **Terms:** hole, buffer, overflow, format, CSS, improper, unauthenticated, access, denial service, DOS, race, CSRF, XSRF.

This approach identifies no security-related content with a precision of 97,91% which was evaluated by drawing 96 random data samples from the results [92].

Table 4.2 summarizes the balanced data sets used for the training of classifiers. The data contains question-answer post pairs that contribute code fragments retrieved of different works in which the code is manually identified as secure or vulnerable [46, 47, 26], as well as automatically identified pairs that provide code that does not consider any security purpose [92]. Furthermore, one work made a more precise manual classification into vulnerable, security-patched, and exploit code fragments [169].

For training the classifiers, the data were picked in a balanced way. Question-and-answer tuples, including their comments from Stack Overflow, were used. The approaches were trained with cross validation variations to test the trained models regarding the prediction of unseen data. In this way, problems such as overfitting can be avoided.

Pre-Processing of Training-data

For the training of text classifiers, different works considered pre-processing, such as tokenization, stopword-removal, stemming lemmatization, and cleaning. The evidence of these approaches is highly related to their suitability. In the following, the named methods are introduced.

- **Tokenization:** Splits a sentence into words and parts. Therefore, the single tokens can be processed independently [83]. The implementation is based on the linguistic system of language families; for example, the tokenization for languages with a similar syntax to English can be done using the spaces seen as dividers. Other languages, such as Mandarin, do not share this behavior.

- **Cleaning:** Removes noise inside the text of user contributions of Stack Overflow. For example, this could be HTML patterns included in the running text of posts, numeric values, or other non-alphabetic signs.

- **Stemming:** This approach transforms words into their root form [136]. An example is shown in the following Figure 4-2. This example also includes non-real words, such as "thu" that are built through the stemming process.

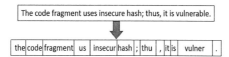

Figure 4-2: Example of Stemming.

- **Lemmatization:** Aims to obtain the canonical, that is, grammatically correct forms of words. These forms are also known as lemmas. For example, the words hacks, hacking, and hacked are forms of the word "hack;" thus, "hack" is the lemma. This approach is disregarded for this thesis because of its minimal and partially negative impact on performance [140, 37].

- **Stopword-removal:** Removes words with no particular meaning and high term frequency, called stopwords [140]. They are commonly used in every language. The idea is to give machine learning algorithms the possibility to focus on meaningful words and disregard others. The implementation of this approach only checks the occurrence of words inside of a list consisting of stopwords. If a word is inside this list, it is disregarded for further training. These words can be prepositions (e.g., in, over, under, before), coordinating conjunctions (e.g., but, yet, for, an), determiners (e.g., a, an, the), and more.

Almost all these pre-processing strategies except lemmatization are used before the classification and training of the classifiers.

4.2.3 Combining Artificial Intelligence and Natural Language Processing

In this dissertation, different text-classification approaches to identify Stack Overflow posts as security-relevant are used. Therefore, posts were classified into two classes: security-related and not security-related. The classifications are defined as follows.

- **Security-related:** A post contains information and code that has security relations. This includes security-patch, vulnerability, or exploit information.

- **Not security-related:** A post that does not contain information and code that has any affiliation to security. These posts are about general programming discussions or solving concrete coding belongings.

For training the supervised learning and natural language processing techniques, the textual descriptions of Stack Overflow posts were utilized, which express the security relevance of in the same manner as contributed code fragments. Therefore, Sec. 4.2.2 describes the used training data. This section describes the manifestations of the machine learning and natural language processing approaches to investigate their classification ability. In the following, the algorithms and their configurations are described in more detail. Before their training, a pre-processing of the training and classifiable data is necessary to improve their quality (Sec. 4.2.2).

Naive Bayes with Bag of Words. A linear naive Bayes classifier is known as a supervised learning approach that is simple but effective [140]. The algorithm is frequently used for text classification. The probabilistic model of the Bayes classifier relies on the Bayes' theorem:

$$P(A \mid B) = \frac{P(B \mid A)\,P(A)}{P(B)} \tag{4.1}$$

Using this classification, the elements of the formula expresses the following probabilities:

$P(A \mid B)$ Object B belongs to class A.

$P(B \mid A)$ Object of class A has the property B.

$P(A)$ Object belongs to class A.

$P(B)$ Object has the property B.

The Bayes' theorem's naive assumption is that every element's probability is independent of other elements' occurrence due to classifiable items. For the mentioned example, this means that the likelihood of occurrence of a word A is always independent of the presence of a word B. Obviously, this assumption tends to be not always correct. If the word security is part of an arbitrary text, then the word weakness is more likely to occur. However, the classifier ordinarily produces suitable results despite of this naive assumption and its simplicity.

There are different strategies to represent natural language text. Natural language processing (NLP) procedures introduce a widely known model to transform text into suitable properties called *Bag of Words*. The basic idea is to transform each text before the classification into an unordered set, which includes each word assigned with its number of occurrences. For example, the sentence *Each question and each answer belongs to a security type* results in a set S = each: 2, question:1, and:1, answer:1, belongs:1, to:1, a:1, security:1, type:1. Therefore, case sensitivity is ignored, and only words that are part of the text can also be part of the set. None of the words is counted to 0. Usually, such a set contains each word inside the training data. For the classification of texts, existing words are counted and the value increases for each occurrence. The result is taken as input for the classifier. A major disadvantage of this procedure is that the words' order is not considered, which impacts a sentence's semantics. For instance, the question "Will you do it?" contains the same words as "Do you will it?" but has a different meaning, which highlights the limitations of this method.

Naive Bayes with N-grams. To remove Bag of Words' weakness, the missing recognition of word order, the naive Bayes classifier could be enriched by *N-grams*. Words can now be grouped as sequences of words to a size of N. The higher N is chosen, the more context information is considered. Therefore, the problem is that the word combinations with increasing N occur less frequently, making them less informative. For example, the number of N-grams is investigated that performs well for the described approach by using the search on Stack Overflow with general security-related terms such as "security" and "vulnerability." For the resulting posts, the N-grams up to a size of five N are created. However, larger N-grams are seen not to contain additional discriminatory information about the security of texts. Thus, two and three are identified as valid values for N.

Support Vector Machine. Introduced by Vapnik [166], support vector machines are a further supervised machine learning approach. Often, support vector machines are applied to text classification issues [144]. They were designed with a focus on minimizing the absolute error obtained for the classification of unseen data. Before the classification, every object is transformed as a vector in an n-dimensional space. To achieve satisfactory results, it is necessary to choose classes suitable for the complexity of the training data [166]. For each class, an SVM is trained for assigning a text to a given class, which resolves in a binary classification. Figure 4-3 shows an example of a linear division of vectors within a two-dimensional vector space. In the described approach, a vector is represented as the pre-named Bag of Words model combined with N-grams. Rarely occurring words are removed so that vectors reduce their size to a fixed number of elements. Five hundred attributes were thereby identified as a valid threshold by examining applied classifications with different sizes using cross validation. For N-grams, this defines the number of word groups.

Another algorithm to enhance SVM's is the sequential minimal opimization (SMO)[134]. SVM's scale based on the training set size between linear and cubic. SMO's scales linearly and quadratically, which reduces training time of SVM's. Thereby, the SMO utilizes set of heuristics to partition the training of classifiers in smaller analytical chunks. Within this thesis both approaches are considered.

Neural Network with Word2Vec. Neural networks deliver accurate results for speech-recognition. Recurrent neural networks (RNN) is an architecture that considers the word order in sentences [157]. RNN's maintains a kind of memory of previously processed data. This enables the model to predict current input concerning unseen data. In this way, an RNN can learn from the dependencies within the data. The deficit of the model is that it can only learn about recent information. Long short-term memory (LSTM) NNs can solve

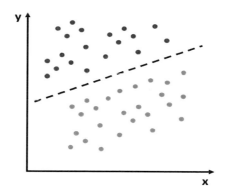

Figure 4-3: Example of a Hyperplane in a Two-Dimensional Vector Space [151].

this problem. These networks are a special implementation of RNNs. LSTMs can better understand contextual information. Within the identification and exposure of long-range dependencies in data, LSTMs surpass RNNs, which is useful for processing textual sentence structures.

The LSTMs adopted in this dissertation provide one input, a hidden, and an output layer. The output layer contains two neurons for each: the textual input belongs (or not) to a given class. For each class, a new network is trained.

In this case, the input is single words, which are added to classify a whole text up to its last word. After each word of a text has been processed, the final output is used for its classification.

Mikolov et al. [114, 115] of Google introduced an approach called Word2Vec to transform the textual representation into a vector consisting of descriptive attributes. For each word, a vector in an n-dimensional space is generated. In this representation, terms with a semantically equivalent meaning have a smaller distance to each other, which shows their relationship. An example of an optimal model is the following calculation: $Father - Man + Woman \approx Mother$

If the vector for "man" is subtracted from the vector for "father" and the one for "woman" is added, it approximately results in the vector for "mother."

For text classification, Word2Vec determines the number of neurons for the NN input layer by its generated vector size. Within a security use case, only a few examples of the training of a neural network exist, which leads to a concentration of specific attributes so that only the words of the training data can be classified. Thus, the network only recognizes the terms of the training data. This is a widespread problem within neural networks, also named *overfitting*. The network can classify these data well, but it prohibits the security type of the unseen text inadequately. This is due to the absence of learning relationships between terms. One way to solve this phenomenon is to deactivate single neurons to learn more characteristics of the words. For the training of the networks, the available training data is used three times. Thereby, in each training step, 40% of the neurons were randomly disabled to prevent an overfitting.

For the proper training of a model such as Word2Vec, much domain-specific text for the classification is required. The algorithm considers each word as well as its surrounding words and its ordering. Word2Vec uses a further NN internally, which is described in detail within the previously-referenced work. A pre-trained, generally valid NN for Word2Vec could be used, with the one disadvantage that domain-specific vocabulary is usually not included and could not be considered for the classification. Alternatively, the training could be applied to specific texts that suitably represent a specific domain. Within such a network, a domain-specific vocabulary could also be considered with later classifications.

Two types of NNs that differ regarding the Word2Vec were investigated. One was a pre-trained network on Google News contributions delivered by Google. The second was a self-trained network based on security-related posts found on Stack Overflow. For the pre-trained Google News version, 300 dimensions were chosen as a valid value for the vector size, which was also adopted for Stack Overflow. An example of the visualization of an LSTM is shown in Figure 4-4.

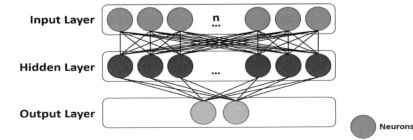

Figure 4-4: Example of a Neural Network [157].

ULMFiT. Howard and Ruder introduced a novel training procedure for a NN called universal language model fine-tuning for text classification (ULMFiT) [65]. To fulfill the training, they used LSTMs, as previously described.

The authors aimed to distinguish movie reviews of the Internet Movie Database (IMDb) within the classes of positive or negative reviews [118]. Again, an additional language model was trained as for Word2Vec on Wikipedia texts. Their approach considers a further step to enrich the trained general language model with domain-specific information, which can be sparsely available. After this adoption, the NN still remembers the pre-learned general language knowledge but is enhanced by the information of a few available domain-specific texts. The authors emphasize that the required training data for obtaining satisfactory results within the text classification can be highly reduced. Indeed, Howard and Ruder only used 100 training samples and showed that they receive as good a performance as traditional approaches with one hundred times the data. Their approach reduced errors by 18-24%. For this thesis, the process is adopted concerning the domain-specific language model. The IMDb domain-specific language model was exchanged with a model trained on Stack Overflow posts containing security-related content. An abstract view of this approach is visualized in Figure 4-5.

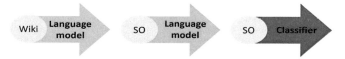

Figure 4-5: Example of the ULMFIT Adaption [65].

4.2.4 Filter for Programming Language

Within this dissertation, the focus is on a repository containing Java and Javascript code fragments. To filter source code fragments for concrete programming languages, multiple methods were used. One method was lexical analysis, as it is also used for processing compilers. This procedure is also called tokenization, which applies program language-specific grammars to source code for further processing. If the resulting source code does not match a specific program language or contains syntactic errors, the tokenization cannot be successfully completed. If this is the case, the findings are excluded for further processing so they are not considered for the security code repository. Furthermore, for Stack Overflow, the Java and Javascript tags and file-endings (.java and .js) on GitHub are considered. To limit the number of results, the focus in this dissertation's approach is on the Java and Javascript programming languages.

4.3 Classification of Security-Related Information

If security-related information in the form of source code and its textual descriptions is identified on Stack Overflow, the result is security-related content. At this point, all identified information is treated the same, and no distinction is made between the security-related information. As already mentioned in the vulnerability life cycle, there are different kinds of security-related code artifacts. For processing, the information obtained regarding the various types of security-related information post-processing is required, particularly for the security code clone detection to identify vulnerable code in projects. As described in Sec. 2.5, it is necessary to distinguish between vulnerabilities, patches, and exploits within clone detector's reference code repository. Otherwise, the vulnerability detection would flag securely-patched code fragments as vulnerable when using a code repository with security-related content that is not distinguished. For this dissertation, these three security content types are described in Section 2.1. To distinguish these security types, the approach relies on the dependence of the main elements on their responses, as mentioned earlier. Therefore, tuples of question and answers including their comments are again considered. (Sec. 4.2). Furthermore, the same artificial algorithms combined with natural language processing were used.

A new training and test set is necessary regarding the different goals, which represents Stack Overflow posts of vulnerabilities, security-patches, and exploits altogether. Creating a training and test set for the classifiers is a labor-intensive task. Regarding the enormous effort to creating such a training set, a subset of 200 examples were randomly drawn from the results of the keyword-based search. These examples of Stack Overflow posts are assigned by hand, if possible, in the three mentioned types vulnerabilities, security-patches and exploits. The data proportion is shown in Section 4.2.2. Within this sample set, only 5% of the data is expressed by exploits. For every of these three security types, a classifier is trained. If a Stack Overflow post is classified, the categorization is done by all three classifiers. If one classifier reaches a probability higher than 50% the post is assigned to the specific security type.

In addition to the machine learning classifiers, again, a keyword-based classifier is created. The classifier utilizes a list of keywords assigned to each security type: vulnerability, patch, or exploit. If at least one of these keywords is contained within the posts' natural language text, they are classified into the related classes. Thereby, question-answer pairs including their comments are considered. Each pair can be assigned to multiple classes. The keywords are retrieved from the manual analysis of randomly picked security-related Stack Overflow posts, found by the keyword-based search described in Section 4.2.1. This process is aborted when no new keywords are found anymore by newly drawn posts. The used keywords are differentiated in terms representing vulnerable, patch or, exploit information. These keywords are summarized in Table 4.3. All terms are listed in a syntax similar to regular expressions. Therefore, the "|" indicates an or operation. Placing terms within quotes means that they must occur in the same order.

Table 4.3: Terms of the Keyword-Based Classifier [169].

Class	Terms
Vulnerability	vulnerable, issue, you shouldn't, you should not, side note, dangerous, do not use, risk, wrong way, not advised, cause of vulnerability, not safe, is unsafe, vulnerabilit(y | ies), you should (read|inform), is sensitive to, awful, you are not, less vulnerable
Patch	add this, safer, better, suggest, "insted use", instead of, fix, you should (not | read | inform), you can use, you also should, less vulnerable, resolve, prevent, right way, patching, better is to, you may (not), (n't | not) use
Exploit	exploit, (someone | somebody | attacker | user) (could | can), (illustration of | that is | that's) why, demonstrate

Furthermore, in a pair review of two security experienced developers, it was identified that vulnerabilities and security-patches are often mentioned in the same posts. For 33 Stack Overflow posts that contained vulnerable and secure patch content, it was checked whether the secure patch closes the vulnerability itself. These posts were retrieved by randomly picking data from the training data received from the manual classification of 200 posts considering only the posts containing both vulnerable and security-patch information. This heuristic holds for 29 of 33 of the investigated posts, which remains in a sufficiency of 87,88 %. The heuristic will be applied after the classification of user posts in the search for security-related content on Stack Overflow.

4.4 Postprocessing of Data: CWE Assignment, Relationship between Posts and Verification

The classified findings are stored in a knowledge base expressed as a code repository with an SQLite database inside of its root. Through this repository, security code clone detectors should identify vulnerabilities or at least security-relevant fragments in the source code of software projects. The related meta-information provided by Stack Exchange posts and GitHub commits is saved for all found security-related content. This information consists of the post URLs, textual descriptions, mentioned security-related terms and—if found—a correlating CVE-ID and CWE-ID. The included terms are a subset of previously listed ones used for the search on Stack Exchange. The last part of the repository creation is the manual verification by security experts. This step is inevitable because of the error spectrum that automated assignment methods could have.

Post-processing mainly validates falsely identified data as security-related and removes an incorrect classification into vulnerability, patch, or exploit information. Furthermore, for code fragments classified as vulnerable, not each part contributes to a vulnerability. This means that code snippets not having any security-affiliation are also exported and might not be important for better understanding the context. Removing these parts increases the validity of data. Therefore, unrelated parts must be detached so that only critical code remains. The integrity of data for this purpose is essential. For each extracted code fragment stored in the security knowledge base, it should be proven whether the code is really security-related, contains the relevant code, and is correctly assigned to one of the security types: vulnerability, patch, or exploit. It would be advisable that security experts perform these verification's.

Otherwise, developers and approaches using the repository may have difficulties recognizing a vulnerability in code fragments. For example, if secure parts remain in code that has been identified as critical in the security knowledge base, code clone detectors could identify secure code as vulnerable.

Before using the retrieved data within the clone detection, it is recommended to check the suitability of the representation of security flaws within the code fragments.

For example, ineligible vulnerabilities can only be patched by importing a newer library version or dynamically loading using string literals. Vulnerabilities distributed over several methods were also partially ignored. This is due to the fact that in most cases the code changes were too small for code clones to be meaningfully detected by clone detection. All inadequate elements must be removed. Additionally, for posts that mention no specific CWE-IDs, they have to be addressed manually. The information provided with the warning messages from the clone detectors is thus enriched. The described approach of verifying the repository content and enriching by missing information takes a median time of 36 seconds per element.

4.5 Related Work

Software security is the science of implementing software to always provide service even under malicious attacks. The subject covers the security knowledge of common threats and continuous use of this knowledge over the software development life-cycle [110]. Previous research has already considered the systematic organization and management of software security knowledge. For instance, Barnum and McGraw [18] introduced a model representing seven concepts and their relationships to software security knowledge. They identified attack pattern, vulnerability, guideline, historical risk, rule, principals, and exploits as knowledge elements for their model. This dissertation focuses on vulnerabilities, patches, and exploits, which are considered in these models. The security knowledge regarded for this thesis is expressed as code fragments and texts from past code commits on GitHub and user contributions on Stack Exchange. Hazeyama [62] considered this model and enriched it by adding three nodes: process, concepts, and security patterns and their interactions with each other.

Much of the literature focuses on Stack Overflow for extracting source code and related data. Wong et al. [176] introduced a procedure to enhance source code fragments with comments by the text of Stack Overflow posts. They used code clone detection to find clones between the source code of a project and posted on this platform. Whenever a code clone is found, they extract and add a comment out of the post's related text. Security was not considered for their approach.

Rigby and Robillard [143] noted that to access knowledge within developer communications, it is useful to determine the code fragments contained. The authors' consider documents include posts on Stack Overflow, email discussions, and formal documentation such as tutorials and Javadoc for their approach. The idea was to find good usage patterns, bug workarounds, or alternatives for specific software (API) elements. Furthermore, Rigby and Robillard [143] developed a tool called an automatic code element extractor (ACE), which also leverages code on Stack Overflow to classify posts into Java-specific artifacts as packages, classes, and methods. For these artifacts, the authors distinguished between them that are the center of the posts and those rarely mentioned. Furthermore, they check whether the artifacts are only part of source code blocks and do not occur within posts' texts. Therefore, they are able to search for code examples or workarounds of a bug for a concrete method.

Approaches exist for analyzing texts and classifying them into various types. For example, Cicero and Maira [39] used deep convolutional neural networks for sentiment analysis of short texts such as single sentences and Twitter messages. As a result of their approach, texts are classified according to positive or negative content. They estimate this task as difficult due to the limited contextual information the texts usually contain. For training their network, the Stanford Twitter Sentiment Corpus was used, consisting of Twitter messages and the Stanford Sentiment Tree-bank, which contains sentences of movie reviews.

Compared to the approach described in this dissertation, the related work mentioned do not consider security whatsoever. Furthermore, from the literature review done and authors' related knowledge, no work recognizes the distinction of security-related content into vulnerable, patch, or exploit information.

Yang et al. [177] analyzed security questions on Stack Overflow to highlight the popularity and difficulty of different topics. The authors used tags that could be set on the question-and-answer platform to identify security-related questions. Latent Dirichlet Allocation tuned with Generic Algorithm to cluster metadata was used for their analysis. Thus, they recognized that the questions cover a wide range of security topics. The identified topics mainly belong to five categories: web security, mobile security, cryptography, software security, and system security. In contrast to this dissertation, Yang et al. did not differentiate between the three mentioned types of security content. Furthermore, they did not consider answers of Stack Overflow posts.

Chapter 5

Identification of Vulnerabilities in Software Libraries

The motivation for using community knowledge for security checks is discussed in previous chapters. Security knowledge sources such as the NVD also have been introduced. Chapter 4.2 shows how to build a Security Code Knowledge Base containing security-related code fragments contributed to Stack Overflow and GitHub. For detecting vulnerabilities in software libraries, code fragments are not required.

The solution to the research question RQ2 is distributed over multiple chapters: "How can the extracted community knowledge be used for heuristic security checks on source code artifacts to identify vulnerabilities?". The answer is distinguished between source code and software libraries. This chapter delivers the solution for RQ2 regarding software libraries. At first, the manual approach without using any tools is introduced in Section 5.1. The first challenge is to identify software libraries used within projects. Different sources can be used, which are described with the associated challenges in Section 5.2.

Due to these sources, two approaches to check the security of libraries are introduced. Strategies attempt to solve problems that arise in connection with the security analysis. The investigation of the feasibility of the identified approaches relies on the Java and JavaScript programming languages because of the reasons mentioned in Section 3.3. To support developers with these problems, two approaches for identifying libraries as vulnerable are investigated: a metric and metadata-based library check using the NVD search engine (Ch. 5.3) and a hash-based library checker interleaved with the same database (Ch. 5.4) [172, 119]. The concepts of both approaches are described in this chapter. The end of this chapter summarizes related work attributed to vulnerability detection in software libraries (Ch. 5.5).

5.1 Manual Approach to Identify Insecure Software Libraries

Acar et al. [1] have shown that developers prefer functional software artifacts over secure ones, even for security-related tasks. Therefore, developers may look for third-party libraries in the same way and probably select them only for their functional needs. Usually, developers import external software libraries into a software project to enhance its functionality. At that point, the software might become insecure. Security knowledge evolves over time and soon becomes obsolete. New attack vectors and innovative technologies can make a previously secure system vulnerable. The security community submits newly discovered vulnerabilities to the NVD to fill it with proper content.

Due to the continuously evolving number of reported vulnerabilities, recurring and iterative security checks are required to reveal security flaws inside of software projects. Security information systems such as the NVD can be checked to receive new data about weaknesses. This can be done by entering an input string containing, for example, information that identifies a library into the search engine to receive a list of potential vulnerabilities. This list matches the search input, but not every entry found this way is relevant. Therefore, the developer has to filter the results for all vulnerabilities that belong to the exact product version, which probably can be an overwhelming task. Furthermore, developers can partially check company internal vulnerability databases, if provided. Capable management is required to process the continually growing knowledge of security. If a security flaw for a concrete software library name and version is found, the developer has to decide whether to use the library or to search instead for another one with similar functionality. The previously described procedure of manually using the vulnerability databases is visualized in Figure 5-1.

Steps for a general approach to applying vulnerability checks on software libraries can be determined. These steps include the identification of concrete software libraries, searching for known vulnerabilities using databases, filtering and interpreting reported results to deduce whether a library is secure. These steps are also represented within the developed approaches introduced in this chapter.

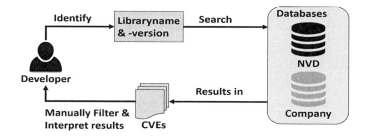

Figure 5-1: Manual Search for Insecure Libraries Using Vulnerability Databases.

5.2 Sources and Challenges for Identifying Software Libraries

Depending on each programming language, the availability of metadata about software libraries is different. Various recommendations outline which metadata should be set for identifying software libraries. Even for the same language, really accessible metadata for libraries is different. Despite name conventions and regulations, not every third-party library provides the metadata for software libraries. Therefore, metadata vary concerning their format and storage location. However, one thing is the same for many programming language specifications - the provision of metadata for software libraries is optional. For some programming languages, such as Java, the provision of metadata is a voluntary guideline that does not have to be implemented. Metadata of software libraries could be part of the library filename or stored inside of separate files located in- or outside of the library. In the following, the sources of potential meta information of Java and JavaScript software libraries will be analyzed concerning the purpose of unique library identification.

5.2.1 Filenames

One source for identifying the Java and JavaScript library names is the library filename as well as the version number, which is used to highlight a concrete revision. The 20 most-used Java libraries of the Maven repository were analyzed, and they confirm this statement. A general format of the library filenames is *Libraryname-Version.jar*, whereby the library name can consist of multiple words, and dashes separate them. An example of a real library filename is *slf4j-api-1.7.25.jar*. Within this record, the library name is *slf4j-api* concatenated by a dash and its version *1.7.25*, ending with the Java archive datatype *.jar*. Dots separate the library version number. Preston-Werner described the version number's division into major-, minor-, and patch-versions [137, 138]. This version segmentation is regular for most filenames of software libraries. However, the filename is insufficient to obtain results for identification. Sometimes library filenames are confusing and do not identify the library itself. Filenames can be abbreviated to short forms, which contain only the first letters of words. A further problem can be renamed libraries by software developers. This can be due to malicious purposes, such as hiding insecure library versions. Only using library filenames can produce ambiguous results, which makes the identification of libraries imprecise. In addition to library filenames, there are other sources to improve the unique identification of libraries.

5.2.2 JAR-Manifest

For Java, there is the *JAR-Manifest* file containing libraries' metadata stored inside the software library zip-file named *Java archive (.jar)*. The JAR-Manifest file contains meta-information about the Java library itself. The manifest file structure is described in the official JAR file specification [132]. Its main section declares attributes that are relevant to the entire jar file. The specification recommends creating extra sections to consider custom file entries, separated by empty lines. In Figure 5-2, the sample content of a manifest file of the *Jetty* library is visualized. The main part is covered within lines 1–11 of the figure. The manifest contains three custom sections comprising line numbers 13–15, 17–18, and 20–21.

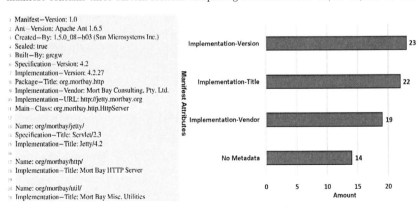

Figure 5-2: Manifest Example and Distribution of Attributes [172].

The main part of the manifest file is identified as relevant to the approach of this thesis. The main part includes the *version number*, *ant version*, the development *company* or *group*, *sealed state*, *specification version*, *implementation version*, *package title*, *implementation vendor*, and *URL*, as well as the name of the *main class*.

Although these values are optional, *vendor*, *product* and *version* are recognized as useful attributes for the precise identification of software libraries. These values could be part of the filename and the manifest file but are not mandatory information, which means that they are not set in every filename or manifest file. In some cases, only one or two entries are set in arbitrary combinations. An additional attribute named *update version* is required to identify pre-release library versions, such as alpha or beta.

The occurrence of attributes stated as relevant is investigated within the manifest file for a set of 38 software libraries (Appendix A.3) [172]. These libraries have known vulnerabilities derived from the NVD and the top-20 used Maven software libraries for Java.

The most significant problem in identifying libraries is that 14 libraries do not have any metadata inside the manifest file. Only the filenames remain for them to retrieve metadata. The other 24 libraries contain at least one of the attributes. The most frequent occurred attribute is the *implementation-version*, which occurs 23 times, followed by the *implementation-title* with an amount of 22, and the *implementation-vendor* attribute was found 19 times. It can be noted that these results also implicate the necessity of further steps to take care of specific cases. Only using the manifest file is probably not enough to draw conclusions about the actual library that partly does and does not have any metadata stored.

Another problem is the inconsistency of manifest files in libraries. For example, within the three libraries *Struts*, *Commons HttpClient* and *Axis* of the Apache company, the attribute implementation-vendor should be the same, but indeed, it has different naming for the same vendor. The following enumeration summarizes the three library names assigned with their vendor naming inside of the manifest file [173]. Each line starts with the addressed vendor and ends with the library name from which it was derived in brackets.

- **The Apache Software Foundation** (Struts)

- **Apache Sofware Foundation** (Commons HttpClient)

- **Apache Web Services** (Axis)

The listed examples are long forms of the vendor name. Another possibility to represent the vendor is chosen by the Common Platform Enumeration (CPE) standard for the documentation of vulnerabilities that are used in the CVE and NVD database [25]. The CPE uses short and concise names for the CPE-Vendor-Attribute instead. For example, to identify the three mentioned libraries, a unified short form Apache is used. Due to their various occurrences, a pure string comparison would not deliver meaningful results for searching vulnerabilities in software libraries.

A similar problem occurs by comparing the product names obtained in a filename, manifest file, and the CPE product. For instance, the filename of the *axis2* library, resulting tokens are *axis2* and *kernel*. Both can probably be used as the potential product name. In contrast, the CPE's product name is *axis2*, which only fits the first token. A related problem arises for the *Struts Framework* library when comparing the exact representation in the metainformation with its opposite CPE product names "struts". In this case, the only difference is using a single capital letter in the token "Struts" of the library's meta-information. An ambivalent representation is used for the Commons FileUpload library. The library's product name in the manifest and the CPE product name differ in an additional underscore and capital letters. By comparing further metadata with their CPEs and filenames, another problem arises between the *xalan-2.7.0* library as expressed in its file name and their CPE product name *xalan-java*.

Thus, the naming of attributes that should express the same charcteristics can be different between filenames, metadata in manifest files and its relating CPEs. For the same attributes, their representation distinguishes due to the substitution of single whitespace with an underscore and the case sensitivity of letters. Furthermore, additional tokens that are not part of the library name can be placed inside the CPE product name, such as *java*. The compared libraries' metadata is aggregated to their CPE product names in Table 5.1.

Metadata-Type	Value	CPE-Product
Filename	axis2-kernel-1.4.1	axis2
Implementation-Title	Struts Framework	struts
Implementation-Title	Commons FileUpload	commons_fileupload
Filename	xalan-2.7.0	xalan-java

Table 5.1: Example: Comparison of Manifest Metadata and CPEs [172].

5.2.3 Build Systems

In addition to the sources already mentioned, there are also build systems such as Gradle, which handle library dependencies for a variety of programming languages such as Java and JavaScript [42]. In this way, Gradle supports the Maven build system and Ivy compatible repositories and file systems. With Gradle, the library version handling can be eased. For both build systems, the library dependencies are stored in an external file. The maven build system library dependencies can be stored inside of a *Project Object Model (.pom)* file [108], which contains the dependency attributes *groupId*, *artifactId*, and *version*. A groupId is unique among organizations or a project. Apache's multiple products, for example, share the same groupId prefix and partially end with a more specific project name, such as *org.apache.commons*. In this case, org.apache is the prefix, and commons is the name of the project. The words inside the groupId are divided by dots . or dashes /. The artifactId is generally the publicly known name of the product, which can differ from the ending of the groupId. An example library name for that groupId is the *commons-collection*. The version attribute defines the library version number, such as *3.2.1*, which must be used. The version follows the same notation previously explained within the Java library filenames section [137]. An abstract example of a POM file with the described information is shown in Listing 5.1.

```
1   <dependency>
2       <groupId>org.apache.commons</groupId>
3       <artifactId>commons-collection</artifactId>
4       <version>3.2.1</version>
5       <type>jar</type>
6   </dependency>
```

Listing 5.1: NPM Dependency Example [105].

Libraries added using the POM file to a project are usually not stored within the project's root. JAR library files' storage depends on the Maven base repository location on the local machine, which contributes to a relative path such as */m2/org/apache/commons*.

Gradle provides almost the same information inside its dependency section of the *gradle.build* file. The difference is that Gradle combines the whole information inside of a single string added after the keyword implementation *'org.apache.commons:commons-math3:3.5.1'*. The versioning systems automatically download the required libraries considering the added library version during the building of the software. These libraries are mentioned in the dependencies within the external files.

5.2.4 File-Hashes

A common procedure for many applications is using digital fingerprints expressed by hashes. For example, hashes are the basis of blockchain technology, cyber forensics, secure password storage, and more [41, 168, 3]. On the one hand, hashes can encrypt passwords that theoretically cannot be deciphered. This facility is important for secure password storage. On the other hand, one approach to identify a file without using its metadata is the file verification through file-hashes, which is also used within file systems [93]. They are utilized to check the integrity of a file and to detect corrupted files. A file can become corrupt for several reasons: errors in transmission, errors during copying or moving a file, or manipulation through man-in-the-middle attacks. The idea is to create a hash from a file with a cryptographic algorithm such as MD5, AES, AES2, SHA1, SHA2, or BLAKE2. The hash is compared to the original file hash to ensure its equality. Identifying software libraries requires a massive amount of data on all file hashes and their existent versions.

The Java library repository provides versioning of Java libraries containing SHA1 hashes to uniquely identify them. However, some library repositories for other languages do not provide any usable hashes, such as the node package manager (NPM) for the JavaScript programming language [104]. This circumstance makes it difficult to identify the libraries based on hashes. Furthermore, a Java library is usually a single .jar file, which does not hold for JavaScript. In JavaScript, a library could be stored in a single *.js* file, but it also can be split over multiple. This fact makes the building of file hashes more difficult.

5.2.5 JavaScript File

JavaScript does not contain any separate file extension that identifies software libraries. This makes it more challenging than it is in Java to distinguish between source code files and third-party library files. For JavaScript, both are files with the extension *.js* and can contain the same raw source code. Therefore, JavaScript libraries have to be identified as such. Problematically, if the NPM is not used, there is usually no external file containing metainformation about a software library, which means that metadata is not directly available. The most-starred GitHub JavaScript libraries with more than 40,000 stars from

July 2019 were investigated to find an alternative to identifying JavaScript software libraries uniquely and differentiate them between source code files. Sixteen repositories were analyzed regarding metadata content. This shows that it appears to be common in the JavaScript software development that meta-information for software libraries is added to the main library's first block comment of the main library *.js* file. For 14 of 16 libraries, its version number is added within the first comment at the beginning of the file. Furthermore, the library filename identifies the library name itself for 15 libraries, which are almost all the investigated libraries. Only two of the considered libraries also use their version number directly within the filenames. The version number also follows the previous named semantic versioning principle [137]. The investigated libraries are listed in Table 5.2.

Table 5.2: Metadata for the Most Starred JavaScript Libraries on GitHub [53, 5].

Name	Lib Name in File Name	Version in File Name	Version in Comments	File Name
vue	✔		✔	vue.js
bootstrap	✔		✔	bootstrap.min.js
react	✔		✔	react.development.js
d3	✔	✔	✔	d3.v5.min.js
react-native	✔		✔	react.development.js
axios	✔		✔	axios.min.js
Font-Awesome			✔	all.js
angular.js	✔		✔	angular.min.js
three.js	✔			three.min.js
jquery	✔	✔	✔	jquery-3.4.1.min.js
material-ui	✔		✔	material-ui.production.min.js
reveal.js	✔			reveal.js
socket.io	✔		✔	socket.io.js
Semantic-UI	✔		✔	semantic.js
Chart.js	✔		✔	Chart.min.js
moment	✔			moment.js

Therefore, to identify JavaScript libraries, it is a promising approach to check if any version number occurs inside the first comment. Those files do not contain any version information, are assumed to be no libraries. The version number is important information for detecting vulnerabilities in concrete software libraries. Without considering this information, it would probably result in many false positives because then it is not possible to detect discrete vulnerable libraries considering their versions. In that case, all libraries that had a previous vulnerability would always be vulnerable, which is illogical.

5.2.6 Node Package Manager

A further opportunity to identify JavaScript libraries emerges through the use of the Node Package Manager (NPM) in projects [104]. The manager allows for the management of Node.js libraries and automatically resolves dependencies. NPM hosts over a million JavaScript packages [158]. Furthermore, NPM is dissimilar to Maven, which is a repository for standalone libraries. Package providers generally offer the possibility to obtain a standalone library version, but this is not mandatory.

NPM is the major source of JavaScript third-party libraries, which are also called packages. Therefore, NPM has become one of the central components within JavaScript development. To provide a short impact on the relevance of NPM, the top trending JavaScript repositories are checked for their use. Therefore, 14 out of 20 repositories are using NPM. The results are summarized in Table 5.3 [5].

A file including the dependencies of an NPM project is called *package.json* and *package-lock.json*. Inside of these files, there is information such as the NPM project name, version, a description, keywords for discovering the project, a homepage set by the package author, license, contact data in case of bugs, and all required dependencies to external libraries. Relevant information to identify third party libraries uniquely is stored inside of the dependency section, which contains the unique product name followed by the used version. Thereby, the versions can be set by ranges of accepted library versions, but they can also be set to concrete values. An excerpt of the dependency for the most used package *lodash* is shown in Listing 5.2.

```
1    "lodash": {
2        "version": "4.17.20",
3        "resolved": "https://registry.npmjs.org/lodash/
4        -/lodash-4.17.20.tgz",
5        "integrity": "sha512-3e585d15c8a594e20d7de57b...ac698"
6    }
```

Listing 5.2: lodash NPM Dependency Example [105].

64

Table 5.3: Use of NPM in the 20 Trending JavaScript Repositories on GitHub [54, 5].

Repository Name on GitHub	Uses NPM
gothinkster / realworld	✔
algorithm-visualizer / algorithm-visualizer	✔
pixijs / pixi.js	✔
jaywcjlove / awesome-mac	✔
vuejs / vue	✔
bannedbook / fanqiang	
strapi / strapi	✔
azl397985856 / leetcode	
elastic / kibana	✔
mui-org / material-ui	✔
haotian-wang / google-access-helper	
facebook / react-native	✔
hasura / graphql-engine	
yangshun / tech-interview-handbook	
gatsbyjs / gatsby	✔
GoogleChrome / puppeteer	✔
carbon-design-system / carbon	✔
trazyn / ieaseMusic	✔
syhyz1990 / baiduyun	
axios / axios	✔

The package name in this example *lodash* and its version *4.17.20* is the required information to identify a library. The libraries do not need to be derived from filenames, as in the previous example, to identify libraries that are not part of an NPM project. The first approach is probably more error-prone. For NPM, all package names are unique identifiers; therefore, it is possible to uniquely identify packages by only using their names aggregated with the concrete version number.

5.2.7 Relevance of Sources

All sources provide similar information to uniquely identify a library: vendor information, a product name, and a version number. For JavaScript libraries, a vendor is not present in the meta-information. Generally, metadata for software libraries are sporadically provided. On the one hand, build systems need them to automatically download the correct dependencies during the building process. However, the group ids only partly contain vendor-specific information.

On the other hand, build systems are not always utilized with software projects. Their use during the software implementation induces an overhead of 12% in the development effort [90]. Therefore, just one example of build systems is considered, which are the pom files used by Maven. Two approaches are supposed to identify libraries:

- **Metadata approach:** The available meta-information of libraries is utilized to identify them and detect vulnerabilities using the CPEs stored in the NVD.

- **Hash approach:** A hash database is created, and file signatures of library files are generated for a lookup in the database. If projects use a build system, the library storage location is derived from the information provided by the build system files.

5.3   Metadata Library Checker

A general workload to identify vulnerabilities among software libraries has been introduced above. The previous section highlighted characteristics of various information sources to uniquely identify software libraries. This section describes the overall idea and the resulting approach to identify and security-check libraries based on metadata. Section 5.3.1 introduces the general steps. The search for vulnerabilities using the NVD and applied techniques to improve the results are introduced in Section 5.3.2. At the end of the section, the scope and limitations of the introduced approach are highlighted.

5.3.1   General Metadata Library Checker Approach

It is possible that the metadata of Java libraries can be found in the file name as well as in the manifest file. Both provide the same information that can also be leveraged to find product-specific vulnerabilities through the NVD search engine. Therefore, these two information sources are considered to identify Java software libraries used in a software project and to detect contained vulnerabilities.

Although a unique file extension exists for Java libraries, this is not the case for JavaScript libraries. JavaScript source code files and libraries have the same file extension. Therefore, another strategy is necessary to differentiate source code files from libraries. Two options for projects using libraries for JavaScript are possible: from within an NPM project or from scratch without any package manager. Both provide their distinct meta-information about the software library, whereby the first usually contains the second's metadata.

Compared to Java, JavaScript libraries also provide metadata in filenames to identify libraries in projects, which are contained in the first block comment within some JavaScript files and the *package.json* for NPM projects.

If a software library is determined, the vulnerability detection is based on previously occurring vulnerabilities reported by the NVD community. The vulnerability detection uses the extracted metadata for a lookup in the CPE information of the NVD.

To be more precise, the described approach considers five distinct major steps: identification of libraries, search for vulnerabilities, report results, enrichment, and the use of security knowledge.

An example use case is that a developer selects a software library concerning functional needs. This library partially provides metadata of any kind. The library is imported into a project, which may now becomes vulnerable. The use of this library inside source code files is therefore unnecessary. Its presence inside of a project could be enough to harm the project's security. On the one hand, the library can now be identified through the approach of using its library filename and its metadata stored in the manifest file for Java files. On the other hand, for JavaScript files, the filenames as well as the first block comment in some JavaScript files and the *package.json* for NPM projects, can be used to uniquely identify a library. This information is utilized by a search on the NVD and other databases, such as company-based ones. For the searches, an additional string similarity approach is considered, which is described in Section 5.3.2. If vulnerabilities are detected, they are reported regarding to the correct library version to the developer to avoid overwhelming them with a flood of information. Furthermore, the description of the vulnerability and its CVSS criticality value added to the NVD are presented. The described procedure can be seen in Figure 5-3.

5.3.2 Search on the NVD

A simple method exists to discover vulnerabilities in software libraries, which is the trivial string comparison between libraries' metadata and data entries of the NVD, expressed by

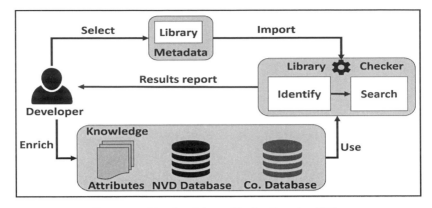

Figure 5-3: Metadata Library Checker Overview [172].

CPE-products.

Indeed, it is not easy to find a match between this information. For instance, only a few of the above-mentioned libraries would be detected as vulnerable in a simple string comparison. This situation requires an alternative approach. The present thesis introduces an enrichment of the procedure with similarity metrics.

One such metric is the *Levenshtein-Distance*, which comes from the field of information retrieval [106]. This metric measures the minimum number of insert, substitution, and delete operations related to single characters such as letters or symbols required to transform a given string A into another string B. This measurement is also called the *edit distance*. An edit distance of zero means that two strings are the same, so they are equals regarding all their containing characters. Various weights can be added to make some operations more valuable to others. Furthermore, the difference in substitutions of single letters can be detected. This means for the two cases of substituting two letters (1) a with z and (2) a with b, the distance from the original and the replaced letter within the alphabet can be seen as a possible weight. The heuristic can thereby distinguishes the same operation on two different single letters. However, for this approach, an equal weighting regarding operation and letters is made. The time complexity of the edit distance between two strings can be calculated by $\mathcal{O}(|s_1| \times |s_2|)$, where $|s_i|$ denotes the length of a string s_i. The similarity computation between two strings can be represented in a two-dimensional matrix. Figure 5-4 shows the equations for the Levenshtein distance and an example of calculating the distance between the two strings *Back* and *Book*.

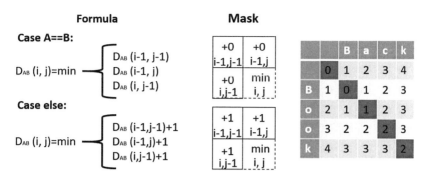

Figure 5-4: Levenshtein Formula and Example [172].

In the first row and column, the case's values for which each character must be deleted for the transformation is shown. This scenario expresses the case whether two words distinguish each position regarding the letters as for the strings *case* and *book*. Every cell contains the value of operations necessary to transform a character of string A into a character of string B. For equal characters on the same definite position inside the strings, the number of operations required to transform into equal ones is zero. Therefore, the value of operations would not be increased regarding previously needed transformations. Suppose two characters are different, so that an action is necessary. In that case, the weight of that operation will be allocated to the cell with respect to the minimum of the previously essential transformations. Within this dissertation, each additional required operation increases this value by one. The diagonal of the matrix displays the value of operations, which are needed to transform two strings. Therefore, the result for the edit distance is the lowest value in the lower right corner, which shows the required operations to transform word A into word B. In the example, the edit distance for changing the word Back into Book, the result is two, which means two operations must be applied for building this word. The first letter for that transformation is *a* of string B, which has to be replaced by an *o*. Secondly, the letter *c* has to be replaced by an additional *o* to form string A out of string B. After this transformation, both strings are equal "Book".

Merely using the Levenshtein distance is not a sufficient strategy to get a good match between metadata and CPE-Products. For example, the distance's computation of the metadata library name *Framework struts* and the CPE library name *Struts* results in 11, which is an unsuitable threshold for this distance metric. Such a high threshold, would lead to many erroneous results for the vulnerable library search.

To remedy the above-described problem, the single words of a string have to be viewed more individually. Therefore, the tokenization of strings is considered. Concerning the two tokens *struts* and *Struts*, the Levenshtein distance results in 1 merely by replacing the lowercase character *s* with an uppercase *S*, which ends in an acceptable threshold of 1.

For creating tokens, the advantage of regular expressions (regex) is taken. By using regex's, it is possible to distinguish between *version numbers* and terms that can be the *vendor* attribute or the *title of the library* itself. The regex *.*/d+.** can recognize version numbers within the structure of the beforehand explained version hierarchy. Library names and its vendor can be identified by the regex **/pL.**. The *implementation title* of libraries can also include numbers; therefore, it is not valid to find the library version just by checking for their occurrence in a string. For example, there is the library *axis2*.

Some libraries still cannot be uniquely identified if there is a too significant of a distinction regarding libraries' metadata and its CPE-Product. Furthermore, there is the case that a library contains no metadata, and the library file name was changed so that it does not provide any of the approaches' considered attributes. In these situations, user interaction is required to add missing and modify wrongly derived attributes. Developers are able to manually set the three attributes title, vendor, and version number, which enriches the knowledge of the library checker to improve future vulnerable library detection.

Redundant tokens in product, version, and vendor are cleared automatically by transforming these data into a set. This powerset $\mathcal{P}(X) := \{U \mid U \subseteq X\}$ excluded the empty set, where X is a list of the tokens vendor, title and version number, is created directly after the tokens are identified. An example of tokens are {apache, commons, fileupload} which results into a power set of {{apache}, {commons}, {fileupload}, {apache, commons}, {apache, fileupload}, {commons, fileupload}, {apache, commons, fileupload}}. The described procedure of identifying library content, its tokenization, power set generation, Levenshtein calculation, detect vulnerabilities and the knowledge enrichment is displayed in Figure 5-5.

Overall, the combination of the Levenshtein distance, power set generation, and tokenization increases the capability to identify libraries uniquely and finally to find matches with vulnerabilities stored in the NVD.

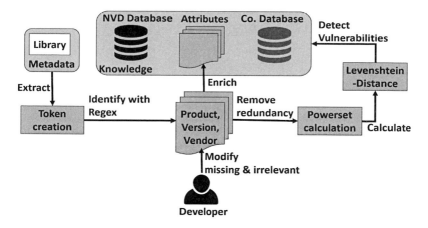

Figure 5-5: Detailed Library Checker Approach [172].

5.3.3 Scope and Limitation for other Programming Languages

A general problem is that software libraries' metadata is not always provided, as previously shown by Java and JavaScript's detailed investigation. Guidelines and specifications exist for almost all programming languages that define the setting of meta-information for libraries. These regulations introduce different attributes that could be part of library information with their distinct priorities—for example, as mandatory and optional. Some specifications do not name any prioritization for them. This makes it difficult to compare the availability of metadata. For most languages, the library name and its version are mandatory attributes. If there is no indication whether information is optional, the attribute is considered compulsory. No of the supposed specifications define any of these attributes as optional. The most demanding programming languages in working life are considered to showcase the limitations of the metadata approach [146].

Regarding the specifications, all programming languages consider the *product name* and *version number* as mandatory. For *PHP* and *JavaScript* there is no attribute containing only the vendor name. In this case, the vendor name could be part of the product name. Again, there is no specific vendor attribute for Python, but it contains the author attribute, which can include the vendor name. All other programming languages considered, contain the vendor as a mandatory attribute or at least not defined as optional. In conclusion, it can be said that theoretically, for all the investigated programming languages, it should be possible to apply the metadata vulnerability checker. The performance of the metadata vulnerability checker probably differs in Java and JavaScript. Particularly whether the optional vendor attribute is set or not can influence the approach's effectiveness. In addition to all the viewed metadata sources, the library name can be an additional source shared with all programming languages. If metadata attributes structure differs between languages, it is not considered within the described analysis. Some languages have all metadata stored inside of library source code files. Others provide internal or external files to provide metadata. Overall, every programming language stores metadata differently due to location and format. To apply the described approach to other languages as Java and JavaScript, wrappers for the metadata are needed. Table 5.4 comprises the comparison results for the metadata of programming languages.

Table 5.4: Comparison of Metadata Availability of Programming Languages [172].

Language	Metadata Attributes	Destination
Java	Name, Version, Vendor	Inside Library, Manifest
C++	Name, Version, Vendor	Library
C#	Name, Version, Vendor	Library
JavaScript	Name, Version, Author, Homepage	Fileheader, package.json
Perl	Name, Version, Author	META.json, META.yml
PHP	Name, Vendor, Version	Composer.json
Python	Metadata-version, Name, Version	pkg-info file

5.4 File Hash Library Checker

Using just these metadata as available in filenames or particular files created for this purpose is susceptible to the targeted dissemination of vulnerabilities. Attackers know that developers search, for example, in the Maven Java software library repository for specific libraries. Therefore, attackers are able to modify a library and add a vulnerability to the regular functionality using the revised version to make systems insecure. They can set the library name similar to the regular software library and upload it to Maven, so that developers think they are using another well-known library instead. Attackers can also use older library versions that might be vulnerable and disguise the real version number to fool developers into a newer version.

This section introduces a hash-based approach to avoid the previously named problems.

Section 5.4.1 provides an overview of the general approach. The remainder of this section explains processes for the hash database creation and applying security checks using these hashes. Both processes are introduced for Java and JavaScript.

5.4.1 General Hash-based Library Checker Approach

An approach that cannot be influenced by maliciously changing the library filename or the metadata file itself is required. Therefore, this section introduces a general approach of building file hashes of libraries and comparing them to detect vulnerabilities. These hashes, also named fingerprints, uniquely identify a file because they are created based on file content.

At first, it is necessary to obtain file hashes of vulnerable libraries. However, the NVD does not provide any file hashes for vulnerable products and does not allow downloading any vulnerable products as a reference. The database only identifies product-specific meta information, which can be used to download the affected libraries using a library repository such as Maven for Java or NPM for JavaScript.

The described approach joins a list of all existing libraries, provided by the library repositories, with the metadata of the vulnerable products expressed by their CPEs. The results are direct URLs to the library JAR-file and provided SHA1 file hashes for Maven. This assignment is subjective, which means that the same URLs cannot be assigned to other product names. For NPM, concrete product names of the vulnerable libraries stored inside of the repositories can be identified.

Suppose some CPEs are incorrect or not filled in completely. In that case, a repository maintainer can set the correct CPEs manually to use the right libraries for vulnerability detection. All vulnerable libraries that do not provide any hash value are downloaded to generate hashes from the retrieved information. Generally, these are JavaScript libraries. NPM provides hashes, but they cannot be used for the later identification of libraries. The generated fingerprints are stored inside of a hash database enriched by additional information of the NVD.

Unique identification is required to identify vulnerable libraries imported in software projects. Again, file hashes for all local libraries within a software project are created. For each of these hashes, a look-up of their fingerprints inside the previously created hash database is made. If the fingerprint is there, then the library is detected as vulnerable. In the end, the results of insecure libraries are reported to the developer. Figure 5-6 outlines the described approach.

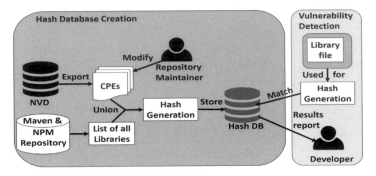

Figure 5-6: Hash Library Checker Approach [119].

5.4.2   Hash Database Creation Process - Java

The center of the described approach is a database composed of hashes of known insecure libraries. The NVD is used to obtain information on reported vulnerabilities of software libraries. To assess its content, the provided JSON data feeds are initially used [120].

Data Export and Preparation

The Maven repository provides a list of all contained software libraries available as a single file or divided into multiple files [11]. These files are binary, but they provide the full groupId, artifactId, and version number as a human-readable string for each library. Listing 5.3 gives a small expression of the file entries.

```
@com.fasterxml.jackson.core|jackson-databind|2.9.0
```

Listing 5.3: Extract from the Maven Binary File [119].

In this example, *com.fasterxml.jackson.core* is the groupId, *jackson-databind* is the artifactId and *2.9.0* is its version number. Both the group and artifactId are used to identify a project. To eliminate duplicates, a set is used containing the concatenated string of the groupIds and artifactIds of all projects, for example, *com.fasterxml.jackson.core/jackson-databind*. This list is used as an export of the maven repository for further processing.

74

For every vulnerable product specific entry, the NVD provides at least one CPE, consisting of the two attributes vendor and product name. These CPEs can be used to identify vulnerable software library products. To combine the data of the different sources, a consistent scheme is necessary. Therefore, to improve a later lookup for specific vulnerable libraries, a CPE-Tree data structure is created. The structure is as follows: a root node connected to all vendors, which in turn branches out into their products. Each vendor only occurs once. Specific product names can be part of multiple distinct vendor nodes. No vendor node can contain more than one product with the same name. The lowest node is the URL node created through the concatenation of the previously explained groupId and artifactId. Regarding other already mentioned constraints, every URL can only occur once. Figure 5-7 shows an example of the search using the tree data structure.

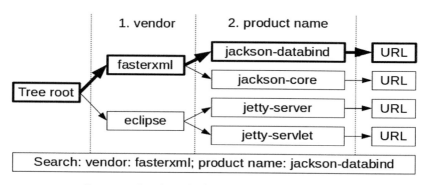

Figure 5-7: Search on the CPE-Tree Data Structure [119].

Union Maven and CPE-Data

For Maven, the vendor is part of the grourpId, but to obtain only the vendor name, any top-level domains must be removed. As a result, there is still a string divided by dots into further attributes. The first substring after the removal is now the vendor. An example is shown in Listing 5.4.

```
com.fasterxml.jackson.core=>fasterxml.jackson.core
```

Listing 5.4: Removing Top-Level Domain from groupId [119].

The artifactId represents the product name within the prepared data structure. The entire process of enhancing the CPE-tree based data structure by using the entire library list of Maven can be described as follows:

```
1. Search for the vendor node assigned to the root node,
for example fasterxml.
      a) Not exist: create the node and select it.
      b) Exist: select the existing node.
2. Check for the previously selected vendor node, whether
product name node exist, for example jackson-databind.
      a) Not exist: create the node and select it.
      b) Exist: select the existing node.
3. Concatenate the groupId and artifactId. Separate them
with a slash /.
      a) Not exist: add a concatenated string as URL for the product name.
      b) Exist: skip entry.
```

Listing 5.5: Process of Removing Top Level Domain from groupId [119].

Within this process, steps one to three are repeated until all libraries of the Maven repository are added to the data structure. For all strings, only lowercase characters are used. If there is a product name that contains hyphens, two product names are inserted: the original with and without hyphens. The goal is to keep the number of false negatives low. This design decision probably also increases false positives.

After this process, the CPE data structure includes all the libraries (Vendor, Product, and URL) of the Maven libraries, with their relative paths given as URLs. Until this step, only relative paths for libraries are known. Now it is necessary to create the full URLs to obtain the exact location of libraries. In November 2020, there are a total of 1,288 Maven repositories that can be used to store a library [117]. Not all libraries must be stored inside of the central Maven repository [107]. Some libraries are stored in multiple repositories, but by default, there is only one primary repository that can be extracted from each individual library's Maven website.

The full URLs are created by the internal *Maven index*. For every previously added vendor, the described approaches prove whether it is present within the index; if not, then the vendor is ignored. Otherwise, all nodes are checked for whether they contain their assigned product name within child nodes. Inside of the Maven index, a product name node contains the full URL, which indicates the library's location in the Maven repository. Each full URL includes both the associated groupId and its artifact Id. The primary repository URL is concatenated with the groupId using slashes / instead of dots . as separators and with the artifactId ending with an appended slash.

Afterward, the hashes can be created for every CPE inside the NVD to have them available for all reported vulnerable libraries. Listing 5.6 shows, among others, an example of a CPE containing the vendor, product name, and a version number. Therefore, the CPE-Tree based data structure enriched with all libraries of the Maven repository is used. At first, for each CPE entry, the vendor is utilized to get that vendor's available product names. In this way, all children of the vendor attribute are checked to see whether they match with the product name. If not, then the specific CPE is rejected as it probably does not contribute to a Java library. If a match is found, all references to the product's assigned URLs are returned. These URLs are links to the root of the maven library repositories containing all available product versions.

```
cpe:2.3:a:fasterxml:jackson-databind:2.9.0:*:*:*:*:*:*:*
```
Listing 5.6: CPE Example jackson-databind [119].

If a software library contains a security flaw, not all versions are affected. Within the CPE, two possibilities can record which versions of a software product are vulnerable. If various versions are affected, then either multiple CPEs, each including the concrete version that is insecure or instead of a single CPE, a placeholder *) for its version is used. For the latter case, additional information to define the affected version range is given. Every library with a version in this range has a security flaw inside. The upper bound of this range is defined by the field *versionEndIncluding* and its lower bound by *versionStartIncluding*. Figure 5-8 shows an example of which library versions are vulnerable within the range of 2.0.0-2.9.10.

Figure 5-8: CPE Versioning Example [119].

As insecure library versions are now known, it is necessary to normalize the library version that does not contribute to the previously introduced semantic versioning concept [137, 138]. This means that every version number containing more or less than three integers divided by dots must be reformed; thus, only three integers remain. For longer strings, the last version number is removed, and for too short ones, a zero is added at the end of the version. Furthermore, non-numeric signs except those with dots are removed. An example is shown in Listing 5.7.

```
3.2.1.2-beta=>3.2.1
```

Listing 5.7: Version Normalization Example [119].

The next step is to download the Maven version page of the software library using the URL inside of the data structure of the concrete products shown in Figure 5-9. All resulting versions that match vulnerable ranges of the library provided by the CPE are considered for further processing.

```
2.0.0/                          2012-03-25 19:11           -
2.0.0-RC1/                      2012-02-19 08:05           -
2.0.0-RC2/                      2012-03-06 07:02           -
2.0.0-RC3/                      2012-03-23 00:19           -
2.0.1/                          2012-04-24 02:18           -
2.0.2/                          2012-05-15 02:16           -
```

Figure 5-9: Maven Version Page Example [119].

Hash Generation

The hyperlinks to which the version numbers refer are the download pages of the Java library JAR-Files for the concrete version number. Besides the .jar file, another file contains the *SHA1* hash of the library. This file is downloaded and the hash is extracted and stored with further meta-information inside the created hash database. Additional data about the vulnerability is exported from the NVD data feeds as CVSS scorings, CVE-ID, and CWE-ID. Rejected NVD entries are not added to the hash database.

```
jackson-databind-2.9.0.jar           2017-07-30 04:22    1328192
jackson-databind-2.9.0.jar.asc       2017-07-30 04:22        473
jackson-databind-2.9.0.jar.md5       2017-07-30 04:22         32
jackson-databind-2.9.0.jar.sha1      2017-07-30 04:22         40
```

Figure 5-10: Maven Hash Download Example [119].

78

5.4.3   Hash Database Creation Process - JavaScript

For the Node Package Manager, less data is required to identify a library. Therefore, only a single package name is used, which is once given by the package author. After a name is assigned once, it cannot be used anymore by other products. This name is the product name string used to uniquely identify a library. Further vendor information is disregarded. The central part of enriching the hash database with JavaScript library hashes is similar to the previously explained Java process in Section 5.4.2. However, the difference is that the procedure for JavaScript is applied to NPM instead of Maven. The previously explained data scheme is not required for using this process.

Similar to Maven, NPM also provides a list containing all available package names in the repository [122]. The CPE product name is used to identify the package names for vulnerable libraries. To identify potential false positives, the vendor of the CPE is also extracted. If a match of a package name in the NPM list and a CPE product name of the NVD is found, whether the vendor from the same CPE occurs in any hyperlink of a given NPM-package website is verified. These URLs are created by adding the package names to the prefix *https://www.npmjs.com/package/*, which forms the full URL (for example, *https://www.npmjs.com/package/xcode*). The hypothesis is that if the same vendor is found, the product is correct. A vulnerability inside the NVD is reported about the product xcode from the vendor apple. The package name xcode also stands for a JavaScript library, for which the first pass of the described approach would decide that it is a vulnerable library by only considering the product name. Checking the hyperlinks occurring on the NPM package website for the vendor, it indicates that the potentially vulnerable library probably could be a false positive. This is because the vendor does not appear in any hyperlink. Indeed, this statement is might not always be true. Therefore, another field in the hash database is created, which indicates that the value is probably a false positive. This heuristic reaches a precision of 86% when checking 100 libraries manually.

Manual checking of JavaScript, showed that the vendors inside of the CPE are usually equal to the product name of the CPE. Otherwise, it is often the case that the vendor starts with the package name, which is concatenated with *_project*, *js* or *.js*. Therefore, it is assumed that the CPE indicates a vulnerability of an NPM library by skipping further assessments to identify false positives.

For libraries that are identified as vulnerable, they have to be downloaded to generate the required library hashes. NPM provides two different approaches to downloading a package expressed by the commands *npm install* and *npm package*. Through the install command, all dependencies required for the appended package are resolved as well. The package command only downloads the compromised tarball (.tar) archive, which is significantly faster. By downloading 100 random packages, *npm pack* only requires five minutes, while using the NPM install command requires 30 minutes. Furthermore, through installing dependencies, there is also the risk of installing malicious packages. In contrast, the *npm pack* command minimizes the risk because the code is stored in an archive file and cannot execute until the extraction.

Furthermore, the *npm pack* command supports the download of multiple packages using a single command, which is impossible with *npm install*.

If a single library version is vulnerably attributed to a CPE, it is downloaded through the *npm pack [name]@[version] –ignorescripts* command. Therefore, the product name and version are extracted from the CPE. For CPEs that contribute to version ranges of libraries, the available package versions on NPM are requested by the *npm view [name] versions* command. Over time, these versions could change because new releases and versions of products emerge. If suitable versions between the CPE and available library version are found, the specific tarball packages are downloaded again.

On the one hand, all packaged tarball archives provide an SHA-512 hash signature. On the other hand, they cannot be used to identify a library inside projects because they differ regarding the content of installed packages in any Node.js project. A reason is that the installed packages have larger package.json files than the packed tarball archives. This is because the installed libraries also contain hidden files created during the installation and, sporadically, an internal *node_modules* directory containing dependencies that are not present in the packed tarball itself.

Hash Generation Node.js

Another approach is required to compute the hashes of the content of the archive and later for the used libraries in Node.js projects. To generate the hashes of tarballs, they are extracted to a temporary directory. Every file except the *package.json* file and the hidden files, beginning with a dot ., are recursively hashed. All files from that archive are hashed within this recursion in all nested directories except the *node_modules* directory.

Every hash signature created this way is saved into a temporary text file. That file's content starts with the tarball's full library name followed by the preliminary created file hashes, each added in a single newline. After all files in that directory are hashed, the text file containing all hashes is also hashed. This hash identifies the library content of its NPM package. This procedure is also used for hashing installed libraries within Node.js projects. Furthermore, the hashes are added to the hash database and enriched with the additional metadata CVE ID, CWE ID, and CVSS of the NVD's vulnerability entry. Finally, all temporary files are deleted. This process ends with the last checked CPE of the NVD. After applying this process, the hash database is enriched with all vulnerable JavaScript library hashes combined with the same available NVD Data as used earlier for the Java libraries. As a selected hash function, the BLAKE2B-512 is used because of its high performance [12, 13].

Hash Generation Standalone JavaScript

Different versions are available for standalone JavaScript libraries, as previously mentioned, the *minified* ones 5.3. Because of many online minification tools, there are several different versions of minified libraries. Hence, attributed to the chosen algorithm, there are quite a few different hashes for them. For also capturing standalone JavaScript libraries, just the minified versions provided by NPM are supported within this approach. Therefore, the single library file is again hashed by the *BLAKE2B-512* hash algorithm. The retrieved hashes are again enriched with the NVD's metadata as CVSS, CVE-ID and CWE-ID. The minified library versions are downloaded in the same way as before described with the normal versions. Partially developers not provide them in their repositories, which means not for all exist a signature inside of the hash database.

5.4.4 Library Hash Checker for Projects

For hash-based vulnerability detection of vulnerable software libraries, the previously described hash database is required. This detection differs considering the available project types and its containing files. It distinguishes between projects containing Java and JavaScript Standalone Files, Maven and NPM Projects. Figure 5-6 visualizes the vulnerability detection process using the previously created hash database for libraries used in projects.

Java and JavaScript Standalone Hash Checker

Iteratively, every directory inside of the project root is recursively searched for any JAR and JavaScript files.

For Jar files, the hashes are created with the SHA1 encryption algorithm, which is also used to generate the Maven repository signatures for file verification.

JavaScript file signatures are generated with the BLAKE2B-512 algorithm instead since it is also used before to fill the hash database. Within this algorithm, there is no difference made between checking for JavaScript minified libraries or normal versions. Therefore, every time a JavaScript library hash is checked, it serves for both minified and original versions.

The generated hash signatures of project files are checked against the preliminary generated hashes of vulnerable libraries stored within the database. The results are presented to the developer. For every matching hash, a vulnerable library is detected inside of the approved project.

Maven Project Hash Checker

Maven projects are identified by the search for a pom file in the project directory root. From this file, all Java libraries are fetched through the command *mvn dependency:list*. Thereby a list is created containing all used libraries and their required dependencies. These libraries are stored within a Maven repository stored on the local device. The precise library location in that repository can be ascertained by the groupId and the artifactId of its maven dependency. For example, for the artifactId *jackson-databind* with its assigned groupId *com.fasterxml.jackson.core* and version number *2.11.3* its relative location would be */.m2/ repository/com/fasterxml/jackson/core/jackson-databin/2.11.3/jackson-databind-2.11.3.jar*. The dots in the groupId are replaced by the platform-dependent file separator.

Again, for all derived Jar files, the hashes are created with the SHA1 encryption algorithm, which is also used to generate the Maven repository signatures for file verification. Afterward, they are looked up for the hash entries of vulnerable Java libraries stored in the hash database.

NPM-Project Hash Checker

A Node.js project is identified by searching the directory for a node_modules directory. If this directory is available, the algorithm described in Sec. 5.4.3 3 is applied on each NPM module inside of the node_modules directory. They are stored in separate directories.At the end, all resulting signatures are checked for their occurrence in the hash database.

5.5 Related Work

This study relates to previous work and research results with a major focus on static library and code inspections, metrics comparison for valid security determination, as well as the fundamental idea of active risk exposures support during the software development process.

Hovemeyer et al. [64]] implemented an automatic detector for a variety of bug patterns found in Java applications and libraries. The authors showed, that the effort required to implement a bug pattern detector tends to be low, and that even extremely simple detectors find bugs in real applications. Since security fragments and exposures rely on code idioms, this thesis aims for an adapted solution that inspects libraries before compilation and supports the developer in writing more secure software.

Hoepman et al. [63] mentioned that giving access to open-source security fragments might seem counterintuitive, but in fact, it presents the highest security. The authors discovered that opening the source code of existing systems first increases their exposure because information about vulnerabilities becomes available to attackers. Moreover, fixes will quickly be available so that the period of increased exposure becomes shortened. This is especially beneficial if open-source libraries can help with extension methods to identify weak spots in new development projects.

Software metrics can help developers choose libraries that are most appropriate for their needs. De la Mora et al. [34] established a library comparison based on several metrics extracted from multiple sources such as software repositories, issue tracking systems, and QA websites. The authors consolidated all information in a single website, where developers can make informed decisions comparing libraries' metrics from several domains. De la Mora's methodology in combination with security approaches, for example, the Open Web Application Security Project (OWASP) [48], provides a necessary base for establishing proactive development support for anyone interested in improving security development.

Likewise, static code and library analysis is considered for this dissertation, following as previous studies by Giffhorn et al. [52] and Louridas et al. [103]. Their primary has solely been on static code checking in action. Louridas created an Eclipse plugin, which contains a wide range of analysis techniques such as dependence graph computation, slicing, and chopping for sequential and concurrent programs, computation of path conditions, and algorithms for software security. The author's plugin analyzes Java programs with a broad range of slicing and chopping algorithms and uses accurate algorithms for language-based security to check applications for information leaks. Such processing, in combination with the metrics comparison strategy, will make coding more secure.

To distinguish between the introduced approach and previous research, this dissertation concentrates on the software developer's support while using secure libraries and public and privately available vulnerability databases such as the NVD, CVE, and company internal databases. The libraries' metadata is broken down into meaningful attributes that are used to uniquely identify the libraries.

The OWASP Dependency-Check developed by Long et al. [102, 101] provides a Java command-line interface, a Maven plugin, an Ant task, and a Jenkins plugin for detecting vulnerable software libraries within projects. Their approach is similar to the introduced metadata library checker described in this thesis. The authors also used the dependencies in software projects and meta information from the manifest file to identify vulnerabilities among them. They leveraged the CPE data of the NVD datafeeds to detect vulnerable libraries. For a concrete identification, they also used vendor, product, and version of each library. Their tool utilizes NPM Audit API, the OSS Index, RetireJS, and Bundler Audits to fulfill a security check. Long et al. did not process each library individually, as is done within the described metadata library checker. Only dependency files and the manifest for Java libraries were considered to apply security checks. Besides the manifest file of Java libraries, the metadata library checker also considers filenames as well as the block comments inside the .js files of each distinct library. Long et al. planned to create a hash database for future analytical purposes by only providing signatures for often used Java libraries. This approach has already been taken via the described hashed library checker introduced in this thesis with a larger scope for all vulnerable libraries listed in the NVD for both, Java and JavaScript.

Oftedal [131] introduced a JavaScript library checker named Retire Js to detect vulnerabilities in web applications. To apply their security checks, they provided a command-line application, grunt plugin, burp plugin, OWASP Zap plugin, and a web browser extension for Chrome and Firefox. The authors approach compares a small non-exhaustive list of vulnerable NPM-packages with the dependencies of projects stored in the package.json and package-lock.json file to detect vulnerabilities. This list includes over 400 JavaScript and node packages. In comparison to Oftedal, this thesis supports the recognition of almost all existent vulnerabilities stored in the NVD.

Chapter 6

Identification of Vulnerabilities in Source Code

It is possible to check the security of a software library with the use of the NVD. This can be accomplished using the introduced approaches, such as checking the available meta-information (Ch. 5). For detecting vulnerabilities within source code, this procedure is impossible because inside of the NVD vulnerabilities are listed as product-specific. Chapter 4.2 describes the creation of a Security Code Knowledge Base consisting of code fragments extracted from community websites such as Stack Overflow and GitHub. This knowledge base is used by a code clone detection approach to reveal vulnerabilities in source code. In this manner, the solution of RQ2 is addressed in this chapter: *"How can the extracted community knowledge be used for heuristic security checks on source code artifacts to identify vulnerabilities?"*.

When using the code clone detection to identify vulnerabilities, challenges arise, which are described in 6.1. The general approach to detect vulnerabilities within source code is described in Section 6.2. For applying security checks on source code, the Java and JavaScript programming languages are considered, as described in Section 3.3. Language-dependent aspects are explained, and their differences are shown in Section 6.3. Section 6.4 introduces the considered clone detection approach and shows its limitations. Necessary adaptions are explained for using the clone detector for vulnerability identification within source code. Heuristics are developed to tackle some of the mentioned challenges. The heuristics are described in Section 6.5. The related work attributed to detecting vulnerabilities in source code is compared against this dissertation's approach in Section 6.6.

6.1   Challenges

While it is possible to enter library names directly into search engines of vulnerability databases to obtain appropriate findings, this is extremely difficult for source code fragments. Specific method names syntactically given by a programming language can be used to find vulnerabilities, but not all can be identified in this manner. Many vulnerabilities only emerge from an incorrect combination or missing statements, such as in the case of the known *Buffer Overflow* error. In this case, the method which reads the buffer has not to be vulnerable. A check for the buffer size is required to end in a secure code fragment before reading it.

Many tools exist to tackle this problem of automatically checking source code for specific purposes. For example, there are currently many security checkers that detect vulnerabilities in source code. Many merely check predefined patterns for specific vulnerabilities. Furthermore, code clone detection approaches can find duplicated code fragments within a project, which can be used for refactoring and to find code clones between two projects. The second option is also occasionally used to detect clones in projects concerning a vulnerable reference [94, 95]. For the present dissertation, the idea is to use a good-performing clone detection approach combined with the previously created community knowledge database about security and investigate its performance in detecting security vulnerabilities while utilizing the database.

As mentioned, several methods for clone detection exist with different approaches, each with their own strengths. Not every approach can detect all the code clone types, one to four. Therefore, it is not generally recommended to use a clone detector supporting all clone types for vulnerability detection, because not all types would deduce that duplicates of vulnerable references are also insecure. Their relevance decreases by the value of types—for clones that are more similar to the original, their chance of also detecting vulnerabilities by finding a clone increases. This is only true if it is known that the used reference contains a security flaw. For Types 1 and 2, the potential similarity is the highest; therefore, they are the most suitable types for detecting vulnerabilities. These types do not occur so often, like Type 3 clones, because they only allow minor changes such as in variable names, whitespaces, and comments. This means that the support of Type 3 clones during the detection increases the chance of matches because there are, to a defined extent, additional statements allowed to count as duplicates. The last are Type 4 clones, which express semantically equivalent code but can be completely distinct regarding syntax. When discussing vulnerabilities, usually specific components and methods are implemented with a security flaw, which makes Type 4 clones not practically relevant for vulnerability detection. Therefore, a code clone detection approach providing the detection of Types 1 to 3 is required.

The capability of detecting Type 3 clones invites another problem. It can be a significant benefit to consider clones of Type 3, but this can also result in many false positives. A *Buffer Overflow* weakness can be securely patched by a single *if* statement, which still counts as a Type 3 clone of the vulnerability. Therefore, it would be a false positive for the vulnerability detection using a code clone detector, which can detect Type 3 clones. Thus, heuristics are applied to reduce the miss-classification of vulnerabilities for securely patched code. Thus, it is necessary to improve the identification of insecure code fragments using code clone detectors.

Furthermore, the granularity of code clone detectors can be set differently. The range starts with an upper abstraction as project-based and ends in a lower granularity such as line-based detection. Therefore, clones can be found between projects but also between two simple strings or lines of code. For a higher granularity, the chance to find clones seems to be lower than between simple lines of code within a project. In contrast, it is highly probable that single lines of project files are equal but using this granularity for vulnerability detection is infeasible. Code fragments with vulnerable code also contain lines of code that are not insecure by viewing them individually. Therefore, this can highly influence the ability to detect clones. However, on Stack Overflow and GitHub, the major identification of vulnerabilities is within code fragments added by a commit or posted through security-inexperienced users on Stack Overflow. This granularity best suits a block or method-based clone detector, which determines the method level within the code clone detection for this thesis. As argued before, vulnerabilities can occur in insecure implementations of concrete components or methods, reinforcing this design decision.

6.2 General Approach

The developed approach involves the following four steps: *Pre-Processing*, *Code-Processing*, *Clone Detection combined with Heuristics* and *Reporting*. Pre- and Code-Processing both consist of the three sub-processes Parsing, Tokenization and Indexing. The only difference is that there is the NVD metadata linking interleaved within the token-building process for the Security Code Knowledge Base. The abstract process is visualized in Figure 6-1.

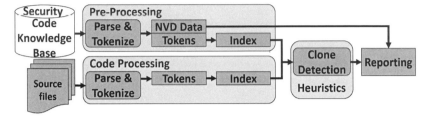

Figure 6-1: Security Code Clone Detection Approach Overview [170].

The pre-processing goal is to transform source code fragments with its security-related meta information within a format accessible by the code clone detector. During the parsing, all contained methods and constructors are identified. A file containing the used tokens as variables, method names, parameters, operators, and more, is created for each vulnerable code fragment. To interleave these token information to security-related metadata, a bookkeeping file is created consisting of CVE-ID, CWE-ID and, if available, links to code fragments that express an example of a security-patch or an exploit. These additional code examples will provide developers a better understanding of the security warnings themselves to be able to subsequently remove the vulnerabilities. The pre-processing procedure's outcome is the indexed tokens interleaved with the available security-related metadata for the processed vulnerable code fragment. The bookkeeping information file is linked to the previously generated tokens by the assigned index. The pre-processing must be repeated each time the Security Code Knowledge Base changes, for example, by the consequence of newly identified and added vulnerable code fragments to that repository.

The code processing is similar to the pre-processing, but it aims at the project source code instead of the Security Code Knowledge Base. The generated tokens thus express every single method and constructor inside of files within the project root path. Regarding that process, the same Parse, Tokenize, and Index processes occur, but there is one thing missing: the bookkeeping information and its links to the tokens.

If vulnerabilities are present, then they are detected during the code clone detection. For all methods and constructors existing in the source files of a project, their similarity to code fragments for which a vulnerability is known is calculated. During this procedure, the created tokens for both: code fragments from the project and those stored in the reference knowledge base are used to identify potential duplicates, which are also named clones. For two fragments that exceed a predefined degree of similarity, they are detected as code clones. That is, if a methods code clone of a project corresponds to any stored fragment in the knowledge base containing a vulnerability, then it is possible that also the project code is vulnerable. To improve this prediction, heuristics are used, which should prevent false positives among the security alerts. These heuristics can improve the performance expressed by metrics such as precision and the recall introduced within Section 2.6. The developed heuristics are described in detail within Section 6.5. To provide additional information to the detected vulnerabilities, the stored meta information from the NVD and examples of code fragments that express their security patch and exploit are presented as outcomes for developers.

6.3   Java vs. JavaScript Source Code

Programming languages can be distinguished in their specifications, structures, and syntax. Some hierarchical abstraction concepts provide sequences of the computational logic within languages as functions and routines [156]. Strachey [156] defines a function as a complicated sort of expression that produces a value. Furthermore, a routine contains sequences of commands. Therefore, these concepts somehow express the computational logic of software. For some languages, the program logic is encapsulated in specific methods such as Java [59] However, these concepts of functional units aiming to fulfill particular tasks also partially exist in other programming languages. Within this thesis, the focus is on the Java and JavaScript programming languages. Therefore, their differences concerning the goal of code clone detection are discussed in this section.

Every variable in Java must be declared by providing one datatype as, for example *String*, *Integer*, *int*, *double* or by own created types. Hence, it is impermissible to create a variable if the datatype is not set. A Java program's start of execution is always the *main* function. A further design constraint is that all executable code must be placed within method bodies [59]. It is not possible to declare a new function inside of another. Therefore, the code clone detection's design decision only considers the Java programming language methods because their execution can make a program insecure. To be more precise, the granularity is set to method level. This means that other source code artifacts as variable declarations outside of methods, imports and class names are not considered for the clone detection. Listing 6.2 shows a small example of a Java class.

In comparison to Java, JavaScript supports a more flexible syntax [70]. For JavaScript variables can be declared by the keywords *def*, *let* and *const*. It is therefore unnecessary to set any data type, though it is possible if desired. JavaScript also provides functions that contain executable source code, but it is possible to place this code outside of method bodies. All executable source code does not have to be part of any class or function. The code can be placed anywhere inside of a *.js* file. For JavaScript, a primary function as in Java is not required unless coded accordingly. Furthermore, a function can be defined as a variable, which is also not possible within Java. On top, there are closures, which are functions that are returned by others as a return. These functions inherit from the outer, giving them access to the variable definitions inside of its defining function but not vice-versa. This means that variables have a longer lifetime than within the scope they are defined, which is different to Java. Therefore, closures are made available to any scope outside the outer function [174]. Conclusively, a method- or function-based granularity for the code clone detection would not consider the whole available executable source code. Hence, for this dissertation, the clone detection is similar to method-based but with the difference of additionally building blocks of the executable code placed in closures and the code between functions. This is defined as block-based granularity. Each code fragment between other functions is therefore considered as a new block. That way, existing functions count as dividers for the block creation. An example of building blocks within JavaScript code is shown in Figure 6-2.

6.4   Code Clone Detection Approach and its Limitations

In the survey of code clone detection approaches, Sheneamer et al. [150] compared specific clone detectors. Only the two, SourcererCC [144] and CCFinderX [81], of these clone detectors are applicable for colossal data sets contain 100 million lines of code (LOC). The plan is to use an information system with big data content of vulnerable source code snippets for the described approach. Therefore, this capability is essential to be able to process a steadily increasing database. The source code of both, the SourcererCC and the CCFinderX,

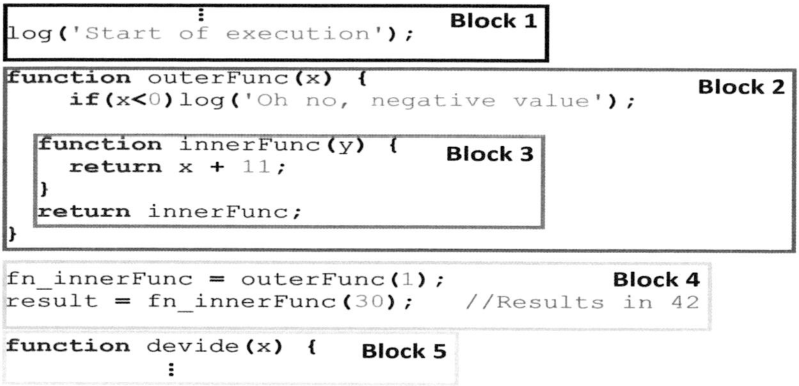

```
               ⋮
log('Start of execution');        Block 1

function outerFunc(x) {
    if(x<0)log('Oh no, negative value');    Block 2

    function innerFunc(y) {      Block 3
       return x + 11;
    }
    return innerFunc;
}

fn_innerFunc = outerFunc(1);            Block 4
result = fn_innerFunc(30);      //Results in 42

function devide(x) {    Block 5
            ⋮
```

Figure 6-2: Block Building Example JavaScript.

is publicly accessible. Furthermore, for distinct programming languages, the SourcererCC reaches the best recall. In conclusion, reasoned to its benefits, the SourcererCC is used as a base for the approach described in this dissertation.

The SourcererCC [144] is a state-of-the-art token-based code clone detector for detecting duplicates within Type 1 to 3 clones. It performs on large-scale project repositories while providing high precision and recall.

To quantitatively infer whether two code fragments are code clones, a similarity function is applied that returns the non-negative degree of sameness between code fragments. This function can be configured by adjusting a given threshold θ, which specifies the lower limit of similarity that must be reached for two code fragments to be considered code clones. In other words, it is a percentage value that represents how many tokens at least should be shared by two different code fragments to be identified as code clones. For each clone detection applied to two methods, the similarity value achieved is returned. Listing 6.1 shows the formal definition of the described similarity measurement.

```
1  Given two projects Pₓ and Pᵧ, f as similarity-function and
2  θ as threshold, the aim is to find all code block pairs Pₓ,ᵦ
3  and Pᵧ,ᵦ such that f(Pₓ,ᵦ, Pᵧ,ᵦ) ≥ ⌈θ * max(|Pₓ,ᵦ|, |Pᵧ,ᵦ|)⌉
```

Listing 6.1: Formal Description of the Similariy-function of the SourcererCC [170].

SourcererCC uses an overlap similarity function induced by the intuitively capturing notion of overlap among code fragments. To compare two code fragments to each other, they are tokenized and stored within a set beforehand, which is similar to the previously explained notation of the *Bag of Words* from NLP. This means that the set contains the names and counted occurrences of tokens.

Nevertheless, token-based code clone detectors such as the SourcererCC follow the two primary steps: indexing and clone detection. Within the indexing phase, code fragments will be tokenized, and for the resulting tokens, indexes will be created to enable faster detection of matches among them.

6.4.1 Adaption of the SourcererCC

The tokenizer delivered with the SourcererCC supports Java, C, and C# programming languages. Since this dissertation focuses on Java and JavaScript, the tokenizer was replaced by a newly created one. Thereby, the tokenizer format is adapted to a custom representation, which also interleaves the metadata about security with the tokens of code fragments. This information allows the tracing back to the underlying vulnerability of the code fragments represented by the tokens of the referenced security knowledge base.

Before the tokenizer can be applied, source files must be parsed to obtain software artifacts of source files such as method names and constructors. For parsing the code, a Java and JavaScript parser are used. For each identified method and constructor, a new list of tokes is generated for every created block. Therefore, all whitespaces, operators, and comments are ignored. Meanwhile, to interleave the metadata about vulnerabilities with the tokens, all required information is extracted from the knowledge base. The custom-created tokenizer generates two output files: one containing all token lists for the methods, and the other consisting of meta-information about the vulnerabilities, using the previously named bookkeeping information. Specific entries are interleaved by the indexes created for each token list.

To illustrate this process, Lst. 6.2 shows a Java example code fragment before the pre-processing takes place.

```
public class TokenizerExample
{
    private boolean isEven(int n)
    {
        int two = 2;
        return n % two == 0;
```

```
7       }
8 }
```

Listing 6.2: Example: Java Input Source Code for Tokenizer [170].

During the tokenization, the number of appearances for each token is counted, and both, the token and the appearance are added to the output. Therefore, a token-file contains all occurred datatypes, method, and variable names, as well as the provided return values that are named and counted. For Java, a method granularity is chosen regarding the named reasons. In contrast, for JavaScript, a block-based granularity is selected as argued in Sec. 6.3 because of the absence of the restriction to place source code logic only in methods. For other programming languages, it might be possible that another granularity level like file-based is required. For the previously shown code fragment, its token file output is shown in Listing 6.3.

```
1 {0,private,2,boolean,isEven,int,two,n,return}
```

Listing 6.3: Tokens of Code Listing 6.2 [170].

The publicly available software of the SourcererCC is implemented to detect only intra-project clones, which are clones within a specific project. In contrast, this dissertation aims to detect inter-project clones since the plan is to use the created Security Code Knowledge Base as a reference for finding duplicates between the project source code and vulnerable code fragments. A presentation of the described intra- and inter-clone detection is shown in 6-3. In the left part of the figure, the representation of inter-project clones is visualized. The figure shows the detection of code clones within code fragments stored in two different projects, or in the case of this dissertation, a project and the reference knowledge base. The visualization of intra-project clones is placed in the right part of the figure, which presents the detection of clones within the same project's code fragments. In this way, the fragments can be placed in different files.

This can be expressed more formally as follows:

```
1 Let (a₀,...,aₙ) and (b₀,...,bₘ) with n,m ∈ ℕ code fragments, for
2 which aᵢ ∈ A and bⱼ ∈ B with i,j ∈ ℕ.
3 Inter-Project Clone: aᵢ ≃ bⱼ
4 Intra-Project Clone: aᵢ ≃ aᵢ₊₁
```

Listing 6.4: Inter and Intra Project Clones.

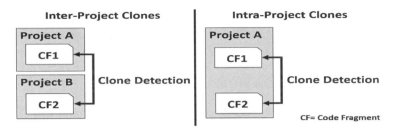

Figure 6-3: Security Inter and Intra Project Clones.

For this thesis, the focus is on pairs of code fragments (a_i, b_j) being code clones. Therefore, the SourcererCC was adapted to support the detection of inter-project clones.

Furthermore, the original SourcererCC can only assign a single clone to a code fragment. However, there is the possibility that a code fragment is similar to multiple fragments. Therefore, the clone detector was modified to store all detected clones of each code fragment to further process all potential clones for later applied heuristics.

6.5 Heuristics

For vulnerability identification using clone detection approaches, problems such as false positives are required to be addressed for receive more suitable results. A false positive for the clone detection is, for example, when securely-patched code fragments are detected as vulnerable because the difference from the source code of a vulnerability is minimal, so both: the vulnerable and the securely patched version are similar to each other. In particular, for the clone detector supporting Type 3 clones that are leveraged to disclose insecure source code, an enrichment of the approaches is required. Furthermore, the code clone detection tends to falsely predict code fragments with fewer lines of code as getter and setter methods as duplicates, especially if a lower threshold value is used. It is vital to prevent wrong vulnerability detection results because afterward, they must be viewed manually by developers or security experts. If too many incorrect results are shown, the trustworthiness of the vulnerability detectors can be reduced for users [179, 33]. An overwhelming number of incorrect results can lead to the disuse of the tools altogether. Therefore, heuristics can be used to reduce the increase in false positives. A heuristic is generally explained in Section 3.5.

Numerous interdisciplinary strategies exist to measure the similarity between two objects [35, 145, 155]. Often the two of them, *Jaccard Index* and *Salton's Cosine*, are frequently compared regarding their different capabilities within a variety of tasks, but it is remained inconclusive [35, 145, 155]. Both follow their own similarity computation and can retrieve good results. These approaches are enriched to form some heuristics for improving the identification of similar code fragments to each other while considering security. Thereby, tokens provided for the clone detection are processed.

This section introduces the *Jaccard-Index* and *Salton's Cosine* computation. Furthermore, general heuristics partly compared with their similarity computation are introduced named *Borderline*, *Patch-Comparison* and the *Weighting of Tokens*.

6.5.1 Jaccard-Index

The *Jaccard-Index* [35] is often used before to calculate similarities between two citations, texts or documents [155, 61]. Initially, it was introduced for the similarity analysis of citation and co-citations. Generally, it abstracts distribution of data and only considers the numbers of entries in two sets, their intersection, and their sum. Through the use of sets, the frequency of tokens is disregarded. Therefore, the similarity S_{ij} of source code using the Jaccard index is calculated by intersecting generated token sets of two code fragments divided by all individual tokens not shared in both sets. This is represented by the following equation. The similarity S_{ij} of two code fragments always results in a value between zero and one $\in \mathbb{Q}_0$.

$$S_{ij} = \frac{tokens_{ij}}{(tokens_i + tokens_j - tokens_{ij})} \tag{6.1}$$

- S_{ij} = Denotes the similarity of token for two code fragments.

- $tokens_{ij}$ = Token number contained in both token sets of code fragment i and j.

- $tokens_i$ = Token number only contained in token set of code fragment i.

- $tokens_j$ = Token number only contained in token set of code fragment j.

- Denominator = Contains all individual tokens that are not shared by the two token sets of code fragments.

6.5.2 Salton's Cosine

As previously mentioned, *Salton's Cosine* [145] and the *Jaccard-Index* [35, 61] largely share the same purpose, and both are often applied with the same goal of similarity determination [155]. The cosine has more of a geometrical nature, which measures the similarity between two vectors by focusing on the angle where the two meet. Within this approach, the frequency of tokens is considered. The vectors size is n-dimensional where n defines the number of tokens in the union of both code fragments. Furthermore, they are ordered in a shared and fixed arbitrary manner. Thereby, each element of the vector is represented by a zero or one, respectively, on whether the correlating code fragment contains the token at that position. Cosine's result again is a value between zero and one $\in \mathbb{Q}_0$. To explain the computation of similarity more textually, the result is computed by the inner product of two vectors representing code fragments i and j divided by the product of their lengths. The equation of Salton's Cosine is represented as follows:

$$S_{ij} = \frac{tokens_{ij}}{\sqrt{tokens_i^2} * \sqrt{tokens_j^2}} \qquad (6.2)$$

6.5.3 Patch-Comparison

As previously mentioned, there is a problem within the clone detection of securely-patched and vulnerable code fragments as their difference can be just a few added lines to check concrete conditions as the buffer size before its read. To minimize false positives for the vulnerability detection for these securely-patched code fragments in projects I developed in collaboration with a master's thesis the *Patch-Comparion* heuristic [27]. It is implemented as simple as it sounds. After the clone detection identified a fragment as vulnerable, again the similarity of the vulnerable code to the project code is calculated by the Jaccard index and Salton's cosine. Beside that also the similarity between an example patch of the vulnerable reference and the project code is computed. In the end, it is checked which similarity regarding the project code fragment is higher, to the vulnerable or securely-patched code. If the similarity to the patched code fragment is higher, then the project clone is seen as secure, and the result can be ignored for the vulnerability detection. This approach can only be applied if next to the vulnerable code fragment; there also is a patched one stored inside of the security knowledge base. The described approach is shown in and Unified Modeling Language (UML) Activitydiagram in Figure 6-4.

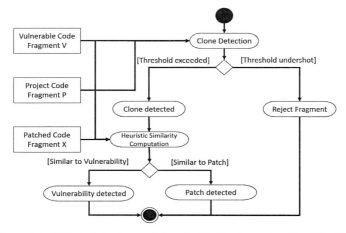

Figure 6-4: UML Activitydiagram Integrated Patch-Comparison Heuristic [27].

6.5.4 Weighting of Tokens

For this measure, the goal is the same as the Fix-Comparison heuristic to better distinguish between vulnerabilities and security-patched code fragments after the clone detection. Again, the Jaccard index and Salton's cosine are utilized. Within this heuristic, the tokens are enriched with weightings, according to their probability to be part of a patch or a vulnerability. Tokens that probably are more often part of a patch are considered more valuable to detect a security-patch and vice-versa for a vulnerability. Furthermore, this procedure shall reduce the non-security-related matches because of the consideration of code fragments, with fewer lines of code (LOC) because they tend to be more often predicted as false positives during the code clone detection, especially if a lower threshold is used. Thereby, sometimes two methods can be detected as duplicates if they include a similar method header. This statement is underpinned by the Inverse Document Frequency (IDF), which measures the significance of a word or, in the modification for this dissertation's approach, tokens inside a set of code fragments [99]. The IDF equation is shown in the following:

Table 6.1: General Tokens of Code Fragments in the Security Knowledge Base [27].

Token	IDF
void	0.1677
new	0.3010
vulnerable	0.3182
String	0.3895
public	0.4813
return	0.4943
if	0.5814
null	0.6803
0	0.7118
int	0.7456

$$IDF = \log_2 \cdot \frac{N}{DF} \tag{6.3}$$

The document frequency (DF) describes, therefore, the number of code fragments in which concrete tokens occur. Thereby, N is the number of all considered fragments. This means the more code fragments have a concrete token, the more general it is. If the similarity of two code fragments can only be retrieved on such general tokens, the similarity considering the Jaccard index and Salton's cosine would be reduced to the use of weightings. This approach can be modified such that for these cases, a threshold θ is not reached anymore, which means that a duplicate is not detected. A smaller IDF means that tokens are more general. It can take values between zero and one $\in \mathbb{Q}_0$

To receive a list of general tokens, they are for each application of the vulnerability detection automatically calculated based on the code fragments stored in the Security Code Knowledge Base. Thereby, the introduced IDF is utilized. Table 6.1 summarizes the top ten frequently occurring Java tokens with their calculated IDF.

This table contains intuitive tokens that could have been predicted before as general as *void*, *String*, *public*, *return* and *int*. In addition, there are also terms that are reasoned to the design decision of the security knowledge base. To retrieve out of Stack Overflow executable code, method headers containing *vulnerable* as placeholder for method names are created. This relies on the fact, that posted code is not always part of a method or class. In the considered code fragment *new* is used to initially create object instances beside that *null* and *0* are often used as default values.

Table 6.2: Patched Tokens of Code Fragments in the Security Knowledge Base [27].

Token	Substraction result	IDF
try	11	0.335
if	11	0.335
catch	10	0.369
1	8	0.461
new	7	0.526
null	7	0.526
String	6	0.614
throw	6	0.614
for	6	0.614
is	6	0.614

Furthermore, the second goal for this heuristic is to identify whether a code fragment tends to be a security-patch. Thereby the IDF is used to identify terms that occur more likely within a security patch. As described before, the Security Code Knowledge Base is used too, to identify affected terms. Therefore, the frequency of vulnerable and security-patched code fragments for the programming language Java are identified independently by the IDF. As a second step, the frequency of vulnerable tokens identified as IDFs are subtracted from the security-patched IDFs. To then draw conclusions about the IDF, the product of their occurrences with a pre-computed constant *0.055* are calculated. The process of calculating this constant is described in detail in Appendix A.5. The results are shown in Table 6.2, which summarizes the top-ten frequent Java tokens addressed as a result of occurrences and their calculated IDFs in security-patches.

For the results summarized in the previous table, a base of 179 vulnerable and 120 security-patched code fragments were used. The results show that often-occurring tokens are in this case those that aim to prevent exceptions and manage specific conditions such as *try, catch,throw* and *if*. Tokens that are within the first view that are somewhat confusing are *1* and *is*. After further manual investigation, they are attributed to SQL-Injection patches. Prepared statements can then be used to set variables inside of a query string. The vulnerability is that only string concatenation is used instead of therefore envisaged prepared statements. The *1* defines thereby the first parameter set within such a query. The token *is* is often used by a short variable name for input-strings. Furthermore, it is used in error messages catched by a throw as shown in a excerpt of a code fragment in Listing 6.5.

```
1  // don't allow updating system user
2  if (user.getId() == User.UID_SYSTEM) {
3      throw new PermissionDeniedException("user id : " + user.getId() +
4      " is system account, update is not allowed");
5  }
```

Listing 6.5: Code Fragment Example with *is* Token [27].

To combine the weightings of general and security-patch tokens with the previous explained Jaccard index and Salton's cosine the calculations are adopted.

The Jaccard index is modified so that the equation contains the weighting of tokens in its counter. If many tokens are contributed to general or security-patched ones, the weightings reduce the similarity value between the two code fragments. Thereby, code fragments that do not reach the predefined thresholds are not longer detected as duplicates of vulnerabilities. Without considering weights, a value is increased by one for all shared tokens in both code fragments. The change now is that the value is increased by the weights, if existent, otherwise by one. This equation is a modification of the known weighted Jaccard index [71]. The regular implementation of the Jaccard is not used, because it is to similar to the weighted cosine which is applied in this dissertation's approach. The used equation is shown in the following.

$$Jaccard_{modified} = \frac{weight(tokens_{ij})}{(tokens_i + tokens_j - tokens_{ij})} \qquad (6.4)$$

The *weigthed Salton's Cosine* is often used within the Information Retrieval [130]. For the computation also the *weights* of general and security-patched tokens are used. Thereby, they will multiplied by the occurrence for each of its tokens. If tokens not occurring in the list of frequent tokens, they get assigned a weight of one. This equation is shown in the following.

$$Cosine_{weighted} = \frac{tokens_{ij} * weights_{ij}}{\sqrt{tokens_i^2 * weights_i} * \sqrt{tokens_j^2 * weights_j}} \qquad (6.5)$$

102

6.5.5 Borderline

These heuristics are based on the previously explained knowledge base creation process. Sometimes it is difficult to decide about the suitability or security relevance of code fragments meaningfully. Therefore, an additional entry called *Borderline* inside of the internal database is created, which indicates whether for a code fragment a final decision cannot or difficulty be made regarded to these problems. This is a subjective attribute established by the individual opinion from a repository maintainer during the verification of extracted security-related code fragments. Some code is probably not good suited for the code clone detection, which is also identified by this Boolean attribute. In sum, a code fragment seen as borderline meets at least one of the following conditions:

- **Ambivalent classification:** The decision of whether a code fragment represents a vulnerability is ambivalent. The fragment could contain a vulnerability, but the repository maintainer cannot make a concrete decision.

- **Integrity:** Code seems to be not complete. Therefore, not the whole content of a vulnerability is reflected.

- **Context-dependent:** Code might be very dependent on the context to be declared as vulnerability.

- **Few lines of code:** A very short code fragment that tends to produce false positives. For example, fewer than 50 symbols that represent the extent of a getter method.

- **Security patch insecure:** The security patch appears not to close a vulnerability.

After a clone with these fragments is detected, it is proven whether the reference is a borderline clone. Maybe duplicates to the borderline vulnerable code fragment do not represent a security flaw meaningfully. If the attribute is set, then the probability increases that a clone's recognition can lead to a false prediction. This way, the heuristic can be combined with others to decrease the prediction value to a fixed proportion. This value must be equal for all fragments because it can only be true or false. No difference is made between code fragments that have this attribute assigned to true. This heuristic aims to identify code clone matches that are false predictions based on unsuitable fragments.

6.6 Related Work

Vulnerability detection using clone detection. The clone detector ReDeBug [72] is language agnostic and uses a syntax-based pattern matching approach. ReDeBug can recognize some type 3 clones, but not type 2 clones or clones with short code modifications. The approach aims to achieve a low false positive rate, that could harm the recall. VulPecker [93] is a tool-based approach that detects vulnerabilities in software. The VulPecker considers a learning phase and a particular selection algorithm to identify vulnerabilities. This approach can detect Type 1, Type 2 and some Type 3 clones [96] in C/C++ code. CLORIFI [94] combines static and dynamic analysis to detect vulnerabilities. The approach identifies vulnerabilities by using clone detection and a token-based algorithm. The use of concolic testing reduces false positives in vulnerability detection. The clone detection described in this dissertation is mostly complementary to the presented ones. The approach focuses on striking the right balance between precision and recall, using a clone detector that allows processing large amounts of program code while being language independent.

Static analysis for security. The approach described in this thesis can be considered as a static analysis technique that can uncover vulnerabilities without executing the application at hand. Such design-time based approaches have been successfully used to identify vulnerabilities, sometimes even better than dynamic techniques such as penetration testing [147]. Most techniques have focused on detecting specific vulnerabilities based on hard-coded patterns, such as used for recognizing SQL injections [100] and buffer overflows [180]. Fischer et al. [46] used static analysis to investigate the extent to which Android apps are affected by vulnerabilities caused by copying code snippets from stack overflow.

Code clone detection. There are several approaches to detecting code clones with distinct capabilities. These approaches have a different level of granularity, such as code lines, tokens, nodes of abstract syntax trees or nodes of a program dependency graph.

In their survey, Sheneamer et al. [150] distinguish the following main classes of approaches.

Text-based techniques identify code clones based on the text's similarity accessible in the textual content of code fragments [16]. The approaches are able to process type-1 clones in a language-independent manner. Lexical techniques are also called token-based clone detection techniques [81, 144]. All source code is divided into sequences of tokens converted.

104

Afterwards, the approach detects clones by checking two token lists for their correspondence. Several state-of-the-art techniques belong to this class of code clone detection approaches. Token-based clone detection is one of the best-performing of these techniques. They can recognize different code clone types with higher recall and precision than the textual clone detectors. Syntactic techniques are either metric-based or tree-based. Tree-based techniques parse the source code in abstract syntax trees and detect code clones using tree-matching algorithms [21]. Metric-based techniques create for each code fragment to be considered for the clone detection a metric vector and compare them to find clones [109]. Examples of metrics used are the number of declaration statements, loop statements, executable statements, conditional statements, return statements, function calls, and parameters. Semantic techniques recognize two code fragments with the same computational logic but differ in terms of syntax as a Type 4 clone already mentioned [89]. Semantic techniques are separated into graph-based and hybrid techniques. Graph-based approaches use a graph to represent a program's data and control flow, for example, a program dependency graph. The hybrid techniques are a combination of several methods that can solve problems encountered with individual tools and approaches.

Sheneamer et al. [150] mentioned that of these clone detectors, Sourcerer CC and CCFinderX are applicable for colossal data sets containing 100 million lines of code (LOC). For our approach, scalability and good recall are key requirements. For this dissertation, the plan is to use information systems with big data content of vulnerable source code snippets. Therefore, this capability is significant for us. The source code of the SourcererCC is publicly accessible and the code of the CCFinderX is not. Furthermore, for distinct programming languages, the SourcererCC reaches the best recall.

To distinguish between the introduced approach and the related work approaches mentioned above, vulnerability detection is integrated into Eclipse as a plug-in. This thesis aims to reach a high recall value to guarantee that as many security flaws as possible will be detected. Moreover, the revealed weaknesses are enriched with knowledge from the CVE.

Chapter 7

Prototypical Implementation

The approaches described above were implemented within three different tools. They differ due to their aims: creating a security knowledge base (Appendix A.6) and applying security checks based on community knowledge. The tools were employed to enable the technical validation of the approaches and conduct the case studies. For the case studies, security checkers are used, which are introduced in this chapter.

7.1 Security Checker Eclipse Plugins

For support during the software development for secure applications, security checks are directly integrated within the integrated development environment (IDE). This has the benefit of developers not having to work with other software. Developers can be directly supported within a familiar environment. The tools build on Eclipse user interface mechanisms. Already existing views and editors are enriched with new features. Several perspectives for summarizing the vulnerability warnings and managing the basic data are provided. There are two separate plugins, a library checker and a security code clone detector, and each can be used independently. The plugins are designed to process in the background and not disturb developers during the software implementation.

7.1.1 Eclipse Library Checker

The prototype of the library checker implements the described approaches for identifying vulnerable software libraries used within projects. Again in collaboration with a master's thesis, I developed the plugin [173]. Therefore, each library is analyzed for security directly after its import into a project. If a vulnerable library is detected, the present library files are highlighted with a color from the common vulnerability scoring system (CVSS) severity range, as described in Sec. 2.3.1. A numeric severity score is represented by the following colors: red (10–7.0), orange (6.9–4.0) and yellow (3.9–0.0) within the *"Package Explorer"* view (Point 1 in Figure 7-1). This color-coding directly enables file-specific feedback in the familiar view of the development environment. The specific severity values enrich the view of the library file names. The *"Library View"* shows all identified tokens for a library filename (Point 2 in Figure 7-1). Library View also enables the ignoring of libraries or the modification of metadata used to find insecure software libraries. The adoption of metadata-tokens is necessary for the case where a library does not provide enough metadata to uniquely identify it. The ignoring of libraries feature is also required because of vulnerabilities that are irrelevant for developers or projects. All detected vulnerabilities within libraries are summarized in the *"Vulnerability View"* (Point 3 in Figure 7-1). Furthermore, a *"Vulnerability Blacklist"* view lists all ignored libraries for the vulnerability detection (Point 4 in Figure 7-1). Another window called *"External Database List"* enables the addition of other vulnerability databases as internal company collections that can be used besides the NVD to identify insecure libraries.

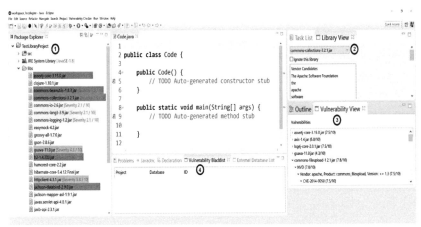

Figure 7-1: GUI Library Checker Eclipse Plugin [172].

7.1.2 Eclipse Code Clone Detection

To check written source code for insecure code fragments, I developed in collaboration with a master thesis another eclipse plugin [23]. Suppose a vulnerable code fragment inside of a file is detected. In that case, the source files are highlighted with a color representing the CVSS severity: red (10-7.0), orange (6.9-4.0), yellow (3.9-0.0), or gray (no scoring available) within the *"Package Explorer"* view (Point 1 in Figure 7-2). The highest-scoring among the vulnerabilities contained in the code fragments was concatenation to the filename. The reason is that this is probably the most critical vulnerability to close because it has the highest Severity Scoring assigned by the NVD. The text editor (Point 2 in Figure 7-2) was adopted for implementing source code. The affected code fragments are highlighted according to the same severity of available CVSS. This enables the precise localization of vulnerable methods or blocks in source files. The *"SCCDetector - Clone Results"* view summarizes detected vulnerabilities in all project files (Point 3 in Figure 7-2). This visualization enables an overview of all present vulnerabilities in the source code files. Furthermore, it is possible to obtain detailed information about selected vulnerabilities by the right-click drop-down menu of the previously introduced view. The details are shown in *"SCCDetector - Vulnerable Details view"* (Point 4 in Figure 7-2).

These details comprise the published date; last modified date; a short summary from

Figure 7-2: GUI Security Code Clone Detector Eclipse Plugin [170].

the NVD; the affected method name; links to an exploit example; and a security patch, if available. The details can help to understand the vulnerability itself to finally close it with a code modification via a security patch.

7.2 JIRA Security Checker

In collaboration with several bachelor and master theses, I created a security plugin to add security perspectives to the project management framework JIRA [5, 23, 27, 119, 173]. To preserve short feedback cycles on potential vulnerabilities within the implementation of supposed completed tickets, the plugin supports the sprint-specific feedback on vulnerabilities.

Within a ring chart (Point 1 in Figure 7-3), each ring visualizes the vulnerabilities detected in the realized sprints. Security flaws are attributed to their CVSS value as expressed by the following color distribution: red (10-7.0), orange (6.9-4.0), yellow (3.9-0.0), gray (no scoring available), green (no issues detected) and white (ignored by member). A full ring with 360 degrees represents all contained files committed within the time frame of a sprint inside a git repository. The proportion of vulnerable and secure files is thereby visualized.

This chart's center shows the sprint name, severity, number of affected libraries, source files, and total files within the selected area (Point 2 in Figure 7-3). The center summarizes details of the selected sprint and expresses the visualized percentage values as file numbers. The chart also indicates whether the commits done during specific sprints contain vulnerabilities, which can lead to manual checks of vulnerability detection results.

At the right side of the figure, a color legend (Point 3 in Figure 7-3) and the selectable sprints (Point 4 in Figure 7-3) are shown.

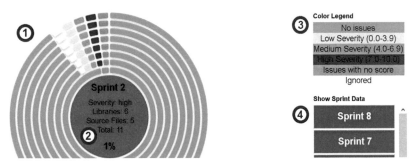

Figure 7-3: JIRA Ringchart Extract Security Checker Plugin [5].

To obtain detailed information about detected security flaws, a table view summarizing results used is shown in Figure 7-5. Vulnerabilities in libraries (Point 1 in 7-5) and source files (Point 2 in 7-5) are shown in different tables. Vulnerabilities lists information about affected filenames, CVE-ID, CWE-ID, and their CVSS. The second enhances this information by the affected function name, its located line range, the reference filename in the repository, and as well as the affected function name and its located lines. Thereby, the CVE-ID, CWE-ID and if a reference is obtained from Stack Overflow, they are linked to the original website posts. This information shall help to better understand the security flaws and the reasons for vulnerabilities detected.

If project members ignored a vulnerability, it is shown in the CVSS column. Furthermore, an entered ignore message can be seen by clicking on the "ignored by" link or the dialogue bubble symbol concatenated to the right. This is necessary for communicating about ignoring decisions made.

Furthermore, filter mechanisms enables it to configure the visualization to vulnerabilities affecting specific files, containing vulnerabilities with concrete CVE or CWE IDs or within a severity scoring range (Point 3 in 7-5).

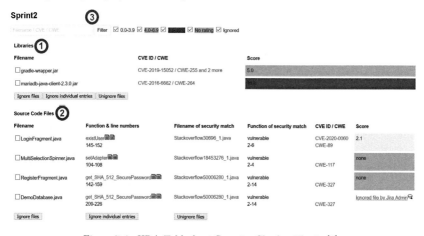

Figure 7-4: JIRA Tablechart Security Checker Plugin [5].

Another view shows a detected code vulnerability at the source code level within a side-by-side view with the affected project file (Point 1 in 7-5) and the vulnerable reference (Point 2 in 7-5). Affected clones are highlighted in the color of the severity of CVSS: red (10-7.0), orange (6.9-4.0), yellow (3.9-0.0), or gray (no scoring available). This view enables analyzing specific vulnerability findings in detail at the source code level.

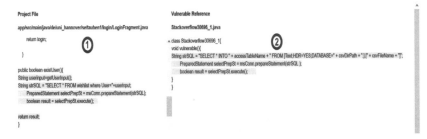

Figure 7-5: JIRA Side-by-Side View Extract Security Checker Plugin.

Chapter 8

Technical Validation

This chapter describes the technical validation of the concepts introduced in Chapters 4 - 6. The validation is divided into three parts: *Security Knowledge Base creation, Library Checker* and *Security Code Clone Detection.* The performance of the classification approaches is investigated by metrics introduced within the information retrieval described in Section 2.6. Therefore, precision, recall, the F1-measure, and accuracy are considered. The result tables show the best values in each column or for code clone type specific results within each row in bold.

The evaluation steps are separated into three sections: Security Knowledge Base creation (Sec. 8.1), Library Checker (Sec. 8.2) and Security Code Clone Detection (Sec. 8.3). Each step begins with explaining the validation setup and continues with the results and their discussion. All steps end with the identification of threats to validity.

8.1 Security Knowledge Base Creation

For the Security Knowledge Base Creation, the identification of security-related code fragments and their classification in vulnerable, patch, and exploit code is introduced in Ch. 4. These approaches' performance is measured according to the previously introduced metrics precision, recall, F1-measure, and accuracy.

8.1.1 Identification of Security-Related Code Fragments

To identify security-related content on Stack Exchange, algorithms introduced in Sec. 4.2.1 and 4.2.3 were used. The algorithms comprise a keyword-based search and machine learning algorithms combined with NLP techniques. A balanced training set containing question and

Table 8.1: Performance of Classifiers Measured by 10-Cross Validation [92].

Approaches	Precision in %	Recall in %	F1-Measure in %	Accuracy in %
Naive Bayes	89.9	89.1	89.5	89.5
Multinomial Naive Bayes (2/3-gram)	91	86.2	88.6	88.9
Naive Bayes (2/3-gram)	68.5	87	76.7	73.5
Support Vector Machine	**97.5**	85.5	91.1	91.6
SMO	94.1	93	93.5	93.6
LSTM (Stack Overflow)	90.6	85.5	88	88.5
LSTM (Google News)	95.9	**95.9**	91.3	93.7
CNN	94.9	94.5	95.2	95.2
ULMFiT	96.5	95.6	**96.1**	**96.1**

answer pairs, including their comments from Stack Overflow, is used to train the classifiers. Therefore, 4,475 question and answer pairs discuss security-related content and the same number of posts represent no relevant security content. The data sources are described in Section 4.2.2. For the machine learning algorithms, K-Cross Validation is used to measure their performance. Thereby, 90% of the data is always used for training and 10% for validation. This division is called 10-Cross Validation. The splitting is made randomly for the overall data samples. For keyword-based searches, no learning is required; therefore, only the terms are used to classify the whole data set. In this section, the results and their discussion are presented. Table 8.1 summarizes the received performance of the classifiers.

Regarding the previous results, almost all classifiers receive appropriate performance to identify security-related content based on the training and validation set. Moreover, all classifiers except the Naive Bayes classifier with 2 and 3 grams get a value above 85% for all metrics, which is probably sufficient for the task of identifying security-relevant content on Stack Overflow. This minimum of 85% is significantly higher than the value of dumb classifiers (50%) [91]. In general, the new learning procedure called ULMFiT delivers the best results for accuracy, recall, and F1-measure. In addition, the precision is close to the SVM (1% less), which reaches the best value. In average across all performance mertrics, the ULMFiT classifier reaches the best results. Due to the cross validation results, it is possible to use text classification to decide whether posts discuss security-related content.

The previous validation is based on the training set; therefore, the performance is only measured on the containing data and the vulnerabilities discussed therein. Therefore, the cross validation is enriched by manual validation. An adequate sample size is required that represents the entire data set. Generally, the risk of non representative results can be mitigated by higher sample sizes [17]. If manually validating all results often requires a lot of work and is, therefore, more likely to be avoided. To receive a good sample set based on all existing question-answer tuples on Stack Overflow (134881), a suitable sample size of 166 is calculated by the Cochran's sample size calculation [28]. Thereby, the sample has a 99% precision with an abbreviation of approximately ±10%. The set is again balanced regarding security-relevant and non-relevant posts. The security-related posts are retrieved through a search for security-relevant terms as contained from attack strategies retrieved of the CWE and general terms as insecure. The validation set is created to consider as many different kinds of vulnerabilities as possible. Figure 8-1 shows a diagram containing security flaws categorized regarding their weakness and reasons derived from post content as texts and code fragments. The Other category summarizes vulnerabilities for which the community did not name any reasons. Again, the unrelated security posts do not consider any of these terms mentioned in Sec. 4.2.2 for creating unrelated security samples.

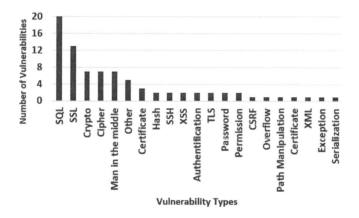

Figure 8-1: Vulnerabilities in the Manual Validation Set [92].

Additionally, the performance of ten security experts that they receive within the task of finding security-related content on Stack Overflow is added [169]. To contribute to this experiment, all the subjects have to deal with security for one semester or a half year at least. Thereby, also the work with the NVD, cryptography or other security-related topics are considered. Furthermore, the study of a security-related course for one semester enabled

115

Table 8.2: Number of Subjects Related to Their Security Experience [169].

Experience (Years)	0.5	1	2-4	18
Number of Experts	1	4	4	1

Table 8.3: Performance of Classifiers Measured by Manual Validation [169, 92].

Classifier	P %	R %	F1 %	A %	Security-related	Non Security-related
Security Experts	76	-	-	-	95	140
Keyword-based	100	69.9	82.3	84.9	15611	1342630
Naive Bayes	86.8	71.1	78.2	80.1	211847	1144393
Multinomial Naive Bayes (2/3-gram)	89.2	69.9	78.4	80.7	135959	1220281
Naive Bayes (2/3-gram)	69.5	79.5	73.2	72.4	**602657**	753583
SVM	94.6	62.7	73.5	79.5	56011	**1300229**
SMO	93.7	**89.2**	**91.4**	91.6	192303	1163937
LSTM (SO)	95	69.7	79.7	82.5	115016	1241220
LSTM (GN)	93.3	67.5	78.3	81.3	93290	1260532
CNN	92.5	74.7	82.7	84.3	132347	1223889
ULMFiT	100	84.2	**91.4**	**91.9**	88715	1255166

potential volunteers to participate in this experiment. Eight of the participants worked before with CVE-IDs. Their security experience varies from six months to 18 years. Table 8.2 summarizes the number of subjects who contributed to their years of security experience.

The experts had 17 minutes because this was the longest time the software needed for the same task. Within the experiment, the recall, F1-measure and accuracy could not be measured. Otherwise, the task would have been too limited and the natural use of the search engine in Stack Overflow could not be guaranteed. Appendix A.8.1 include the document handed out to access the demographic information and that describing the task. According to their task, the number of security-related posts reflects the true positives and the non-related false positives. All performance results using the manual validation set are presented in Table 8.3.

For manual validation, which aims to cover diverse vulnerability types, the Naive Bayes classifier again received the worst precision with 2/3-grams. This is the only classifier that received worse results than the security-experts. Therefore, all other text classifiers received better precision than the subjects. The ULMFiT delivers the best results again, according to precision, F1-Measure and accuracy. For the recall the SMO is better and in contrast to the F1, they received almost the same results. In average, the ULMFiT reaches the best results of classifiers due to all metrics. The results of the cross validation and the manual validation set are close to each other. This emphasizes that already the previous used data is suitable to show the performance of classifiers. However, there are differences according to the variety of vulnerability types, which are more widespread in the manual validation set. The validation results show, that the most text-classifiers reach very good performance values. These results are probably good enough to find security-related content on code communities as Stack Overflow. Therefore, the ULMFiT classifier reaches a perfect precision of 100%, which means that all posts identified as security-related, belong to that class. Within the identification of security-related posts contributing source code, the precision metric is prioritized. Due to the large amount of data, it is not important to obtain all representations of individual vulnerabilities. When one is detected and added to the Security Knowledge Base, security code clone detection can detect vulnerabilities that are similar to that code fragment.

8.1.2 Classification of Security-Related Code Fragments

To distinguish between security-related code fragments, a subset of these classifiers is used (Sec. 4.3). Thereby, the classifiers are investigated due to their performance of differentiating between vulnerabilities, security-patches and their exploits. The distinction of security-related code fragments is inevitable for using security-related code fragments as reference for detecting vulnerabilities with the code clone detection. For creating a training and validation set, 200 randomly picked posts classified as security-related by the keyword-based approach are manually assigned to the named classes introduced in Section 4.2.2 [169]. Again the 10-Cross Validation is used whereby always 90% of the data is used for training and 10% for validation. The sets are created by randomly picking data out for creating the validation set. The text classifiers are compared against security experts. Therefore, the performance of security experts by manually classifying 33 pre-selected Stack Overflow posts in vulnerable, security-patch and exploit information is measured. The posts represent almost balanced data among the three types (Appendix A.8.4). A tool is created to log their results during classification (Appendix A.8.3). The participants had no time limit for the task. The results are summarized in Table 8.4.

Distinguishing security-related data automatically into subcategories as vulnerable, security patch, and exploit appears to be more difficult than detecting posts about security in general. For almost all classifiers, the average values of metrics are lower. In conclusion,

Table 8.4: 10-Cross Validation: Classification Results for all Information Types [169].

Classifier	Vulnerability				Patch				Exploit			
	P %	R %	F1 %	A %	P %	R %	F1 %	A %	P %	R %	F1 %	A %
Security Experts	**78**	58	61	68	**78**	65	70	**72**	82	**68**	**72**	**76**
Keyword-based	54	**98**	70	52	59	**88**	**71**	63	**100**	50	67	75
Multinomial Naive Bayes	69	77	**73**	**72**	52	48	50	52	36	40	38	35
Naive Bayes (2/3-grams)	61	70	65	62	55	52	53	55	45	50	47	45
SMO	61	64	62	61	52	44	48	52	0	0	-	30
LSTM (SO)	68	65	66	67	61	66	63	62	53	65	57	54
LSTM (GN)	57	48	52	53	41	45	43	58	40	60	48	49
ULMFiT	59	65	62	60	60	61	60	60	37	40	38	40

there is a tendency for text classifiers to distinguish between these categories. Some approaches receive a better precision than dumb classifiers (50%) [91]. Therefore, the security experts reach better results for the precision within vulnerability and security-patch assignment. For exploits, the keyword-based classifier surpasses the subjects regarding precision. The results show that the text classifiers retrieve better results for recall and F1-measure in the task of identifying information about vulnerabilities. To choose a winner as the best-performing text classifier for this task is difficult. Thereby, it can be done concerning the priorities that be made for the categorization. For this task, the recall is probably required if the goal is to find more representations of each class. Therefore, the keyword-based classifier performs the best. Due to the low precision results for vulnerable and security-patch content, much rework is required to obtain in a result set consisting of only correct classified posts and code fragments.

Although some approaches are designed to perform well with less domain-specific training data, the number of training samples is probably too low to retrieve meaningful results. Due to the low number of posts that are probably containing exploit code fragments on Stack Overflow, the class of exploits is disregarded for further evaluation. To enhance the previous evaluation in the context of data, 1872 secure and 1872 randomly picked vulnerable posts from the whole data described in Sec. 4.2.2 is used to distinguish between secure and vulnerable code fragments. Thereby, 10-Cross Validation is used for the machine learning classifiers. A split of 90% for training and 10% for validation is considered.

Moreover, a keyword-based classifier is used without the need for training. The complete

Table 8.5: Performance of Classifying in Secure and Vulnerable Measured by 10-Cross and Manual Validation [92].

Classifier	Vulnerable				Secure			
	P %	R %	F1 %	A %	P %	R %	F1 %	A %
Keyword-based	43.8	17.9	24.8	47.5	48.5	**77.9**	59.8	47.5
Multinomial Naive Bayes (2/3-gram)	69.7	68.5	69.2	69.4	69	70.2	69.6	69.4
Naive Bayes (2/3-gram)	68.6	61.9	65.1	66.7	65.1	71.5	68.2	66.7
SVM	64.7	**79.8**	71.5	68.1	**73.5**	56.3	63.7	68.1
SMO	68.3	68.9	68.6	68.4	68.5	67.8	68.1	68.4
CNN (SO)	**73.3**	73.3	71.8	**72.3**	71.2	71.3	71.3	**72.3**
ULMFiT	72.2	72.4	**72.3**	72.1	72.1	71.8	**71.9**	72.1

data is used to measure its performance. All in Sec. 4.3 terms are utilized for this purpose. Therefore, the vulnerability class is represented by only using specific terms. All others belong to the class of secure included with exploit and security-patch terms.

For this validation, the single Naive Bayes approach is not considered because combined with 2/3-Grams, it performed better, regarding F1-measure, for identifying security-related content on Stack Overflow presented in Section 8.1.1. For CNN compared to LSTMs, it is the same. Only CNN's combined with a Word2Vec trained by security-related Stack Overflow posts is used. Thereby, CNN's learning the domain-specific knowledge for posts tackling security purposes. The results are presented in Table 8.5.

In total, the classifier results are improved by using more training-data for distinguishing between vulnerable and secure post content. The secure posts represent somehow content about security-patches. In detail, they provide secure code fragments of specific security concerns. Conclusively, the best classifier due to precision is the CNN with Word2Vec trained on Stack Overflow posts. For both types, the network receives the best results across all metrics. The ULMFiT and CNN (SO) classifier, exceed for all performance metrics values above 70%. Hence, both can be identified as suitable classifiers for the task of distinguishing between vulnerable and secure post content of security-related Stack Overflow posts. Nevertheless, no approach reaches a 100% precision, which means that manual rework is still required. In contrast to the validation that distinguishes between vulnerable, security-patched and exploit information, the classifiers deliver more suitable results for a first categorization. The assignment should be reviewed by security experts afterwards.

8.1.3 Threats to Validity

Wohlin et al. [175] defined types of threats to validity for empirical software engineering research. The threats for the validation of the security knowledge base creation are listed and assigned to that types as follows:

Construct: Each approach is validated based on a single configuration and a combination of various natural language processing mechanisms. Not all potential classifiers and all configurations could be considered. Hence, it cannot be guaranteed that they are the best choice for all classification tasks applied. In the literature recommended machine learning approaches that are used before for text-classification purpose are considered to reduce this threat.

Conclusion: The manually created validation sets can be subjectively influenced, because they are organized by hand. This threat is mitigated by the design decision of considering a widespread range of vulnerability types (CWE-IDs) within these sets.

The bigger training sets majorly contain cryptographic posts and code fragments. Thereby it is possible that the classifiers can only identify cryptographic and not as described security-related content. The small validation set is created with the goal of containing a wider range of sample data. Thereby, it could be shown, that the algorithms could also classify noncryptographic content correctly as security-related.

Besides approaches that need less training data as usual as Word2Vec and ULMFiT, neural networks require many training data to learn domain-specific knowledge. The sample size for training and validating the classifiers to distinguish between vulnerable, securely-patched and exploit posts might be too small. Due to the nature of occurrence for exploit code the sets have less samples to train and validate a classification meaningfully. To remove this threat, the differentiation of vulnerable and secure code fragments is investigated with a bigger training and validation set.

External: The approaches of identifying security-related content and distinguishing between vulnerable, securely patched and exploit code bases on Stack Exchange content. By applying the investigated approaches on other community knowledge sources as GitHub, they might be perform differently. For the accessing of content on other platforms further interfaces have to be created.

8.2 Library Checker

For identifying vulnerable libraries, the approaches introduced in Ch. 5 are used. Their evaluation is divided into two parts: Java and JavaScript. For the performance evaluation of the metadata and hash-based approach, these are compared with other state-of-the-art vulnerability detectors for software libraries. The metadata library checker provides therefore three different configurations with distinct goals: high precision for reducing the number of incorrect error notifications, high recall for finding as most vulnerable libraries as possible and a combination of both which takes a loss in recall and precision to keep the combination of both metrics as good as possible. The configurations differ regarding how version ranges and update types of CPEs are considered (Appendix A.4). If, for an insecure library, at least one vulnerability is detected by the approaches, it counts as true positive for the vulnerability detection.

8.2.1 Java

For measuring the performance of the detection of insecure Java libraries the hash-based and the metadata library checker were compared against the OWASP Dependency Checker (OWASP D.C) [102]. To obtain a suitable validation set, the top depended upon libraries from any Maven repository in March 2020 are utilized. To retrieve a balanced set with a total of 40 secure and vulnerable libraries, older versions of libraries are used to obtain some with security flaws within. For newer versions, their vulnerabilities are ordinarily patched. Thereby, to enriching the set with secure libraries, 20 other most popular Maven Java libraries with the newest main versions are utilized. One reason for the use of popular libraries is that more developers are probably using them than others. The resulting set of software libraries is listed in Table 8.6, whereby the library names are concatenated with their CVE-ID if they are vulnerable.

The tools classify the same libraries to have a base for comparison. Their performance is measured by feeding the libraries into the tools. Table 8.7 summarizes these results.

Note that the metadata library checker is surpassed by the hash-based approach and the OWASP dependency checker (D.C.) among all metrics. Both reach the same performance for all metrics. But the hash-based library checker compares files based on hashes and not on metadata, which is an improvement because it cannot be tricked by metadata manipulation.

Table 8.6: Software Library Validation Set for Java [119].

Vulnerable Library [CVE-ID]	Secure Library
Apache Commons-beanutils 1.8.3 [CVE-2014-0114]	Assertj-core 3.15.0
Apache Commons-collections 3.2.1 [CVE-2017-15708]	Clojure 1.10.1
Google Guava 11.0 [CVE-2018-10237]	Apache Commons-io 2.6
Apache Groovy-all 1.7.0 [CVE-2016-6814]	Apache Commons-lang3 3.9
Apache Httpclient 4.3.1 [CVE-2015-5262]	Apache Commons-logging 1.2
FasterXML Jackson-databind 2.9.0 [CVE-2019-17267]	Easymock 4.2
Jackson-mapper-asl 1.9.1 [CVE-2019-10172]	Google Gson 2.8.5
Jetbrains Kotlin-stdlib 1.3.0 [CVE-2019-10101]	H2database H2 1.4.200
Apache Log4j 1.2.9 [CVE-2019-17571]	Hamcrest-core 2.2
Apache Log4j-core 2.0.1 [CVE-2017-5645]	Hibernate-core 5.4.12.Final
QOS Logback-classic 1.0.0 [CVE-2017-5929]	Jaxb-api 2.3.1
QOS Logback-core 1.0.0 [CVE-2017-5929]	Joda-time 2.10.5
Apache Maven-plugin-api 3.0.4 [CVE-2013-0253]	Json 20190722
Oracle Mysql-connector-java 8.0.11 [CVE-2018-3258]	Junit 4.12
Squareup Okhttp3 3.0.1 [CVE-2016-2402]	Lombok 1.18.12
Plexus-utils 2.0.0 [CVE-2017-1000487]	Mockito-core 3.3.0
Retrofit 2.0.0 [CVE-2018-1000850]	Scala-library 2.13.1
Spring-core 3.0.0 [CVE-2011-2894]	JavaX Servlet-api 4.0.1
Spring-web 4.0.0 [CVE-2014-0225]	Slf4j-api 1.7.30
Spring-beans 2.5 [CVE-2010-1622]	Testng 7.1.0

Table 8.7: Java Library Vulnerability Detection Validation Results [119].

Approach	Precision	Recall	F1-Measure	Accuracy
Meta Precision	71.4	25	37	57.5
Meta Recall	65.4	85	73.9	70
Meta Combined	77.8	35	48.3	62.5
Hash checker	100	95	97.4	97.5
OWASP D.C. [102]	100	95	97.4	97.5

8.2.2 JavaScript

To identify the quality of metadata and hash-based library checker approach's performance, they are compared with other JavaScript security checker as Retire.js [131] and the build-in NPM version [123]. Thereby, a validation set containing 15 vulnerable libraries and 20 secure libraries retrieved from the top 20 most popular NPM libraries are utilized. Here it is the same as the performance measure for Java library checker - the vulnerable libraries do not use the newest versions because the vulnerabilities are mainly closed. The validation set is shown in Table 8.8.

Again, for ascertaining the validation results, a confusion matrix is created. Through the use of containing values, the performance metrics are computed. For the metadata library checker considering JavaScript libraries, the three configurations are evaluated: high precision, high recall and combined. The results are shown in Table 8.9.

According to the results, the metadata library checker (Meta) performs better than for Java libraries (Tab. 8.7). It can reach a precision and recall of 100%, but in different configurations. The best performance considering all metrics among all library checkers received the hash-based approach. It surpasses other tools as Retire.js and the built-in

Table 8.8: JavaScript Libraries Validation Set [5].

Vulnerable Library [CVE-ID]	Secure Library
general-file-server 1.1.8 [CVE-2018-3724]	Lodash 4.17.15
libnmap 0.4.10 [CVE-2018-16461]	Chalk 3.0.0
waterline-sequel 0.5.0 [CVE-2016-10551]	Request 2.88.2
mathjax 2.7.3 [CVE-2018-1999024]	Express 4.17.1
angular-http-server 1.9.0 [CVE-2018-3713]	Commander 4.1.1
reduce-css-calc 1.2.4 [CVE-2016-10548]	Moment 2.24.0
Serve-static 1.0.0 [CVE-2015-1164]	Debug 4.1.1
Mustache 2.2.0 [CVE-2015-8862]	Prop-types 15.7.2
Negotiator 0.6.0 [CVE-2016-10539]	React-dom 16.13.0
Mqtt 2.0.0 [CVE-2016-10910]	Async 3.2.0
Node-jose 0.9.2 [CVE-2018-0114]	Fs-extra 8.1.0
Pidusage 1.1.4 [CVE-2017-1000220]	Bluebird 3.7.2
Decamelize 1.1.0 [CVE-2017-16023]	Tslib 1.11.0
Converse.js 2.0.4 [CVE-2017-5858]	Axios 0.19.2
Uri-js 2.1.1 [CVE-2017-16021]	Uuid 7.0.1
	Underscore 1.9.2
	Vue 2.6.11
	Classnames 2.2.6
	Mkdirp 1.0.3

NPM library checker. Furthermore, it is working on file content and not on metadata as others. Overall, the developed hash-based library checker reaches better results than other state-of-the-art tools or at least the same performance. In terms of performance metrics, recall is prioritised for vulnerability detection in project source code, as any missing security alert can result in a insecure project due to a single overlooked vulnerability.

8.2.3 Threats to Validity

Wohlin et al. [175]] listed threats to validity of the empirical software engineering research. In the following the identified threats of the library checker validation are introduced and assigned to threat types.

Conclusion: The imbalance nature of the test set for detecting vulnerabilities within JavaScript libraries can influence the performance values. Furthermore, all the used test sets did not reflect the occurrence of vulnerable and secure software libraries in the real world. All validation sets are almost balanced. This is inevitable to show the performance for detecting vulnerabilities.

Internal: The used Java Run-time Environment version is not considered for the vulnerability detection. Some libraries invoke a security flaw in specific Java versions and are unaffected in others. As consequence, this can result in wrong error notifications for secure libraries. Therefore, the approaches consider the manual checking of vulnerability detection results by developers and security-experts.

Construct: Utilized metrics and the chosen process of fingerprint generation are remarkable for the performance. Maybe other strategies deliver better results than the chosen. To select valid hash algorithms, the same as provided by the fingerprints of the Maven repository or recommended by different performance aspects within the literature are utilized.

External: Without adaption, the approaches are not applicable to other programming

Table 8.9: JavaScript Library Vulnerability Detection Validation Results [119].

Approach	Precision	Recall	F1-Measure	Accuracy
Meta Precision	100	80	88.9	91.4
Meta Recall	78.9	100	88.2	88.6
Meta Combined	78.9	100	88.2	88.6
Retire.js [131]	100	73.3	84.6	88.6
NPM [123]	100	86.7	92.9	96.5
Hash-based	100	93.3	**96.5**	**97.1**

languages as Java or JavaScript. Wrapper for other languages to identify software libraries uniquely must to be created. A chance that further attributes are more suitable to identify libraries in other languages is possible. Furthermore, the hash creation might be done differently. To mitigate this threat, the investigation of identifying vulnerabilities for two programming languages is done.

8.3 Security Code Clone Detection

In the past, other work compared different state-of-the-art code clone detectors regarding their performance [150]. An evaluation of in the dissertation's approach used code clone detector without modifications is already done by Sajnani et al. [144]. The SourcererCC performed the best according to recall for Type 1 to 3 clones and for precision it receives the second-best results behind iClones [57]. Instead of iClones the SourcererCC can process 100 million lines of code where the iClones tool already has problems with 1 million lines of code. Thereby, the effectiveness of the SourcererCC for the general clone detection purpose is already measured. The evaluation in this dissertation considers the validation of the SourcererCC for vulnerability detection purposes.

For the clone detection, there are θ-threshold values which represent somehow the previously introduced configurations: high precision (θ=8.0), high recall (θ=3.0) and their combination (θ=5.5). A higher threshold identifies that a code fragment has to be more similar to another fragment to still count as a clone.

The heuristics introduced in this thesis are developed to be programming language independent. To measure their performance, they are in detail validated for the programming language Java. For JavaScript, only the performance evaluation considering security is conducted without the use of heuristics.

8.3.1 Java

At first, the clone detection performance for identifying vulnerable code fragments is determined. To improve the approaches capability to distinguish between securely patched code fragments and vulnerable ones, heuristics are used (Sec. 6.5). Thereby, it is proven whether the heuristics can reduce wrong matches with code fragments that are too short or somehow unrelated clones to specific vulnerable reference code snippets. These heuristics are applied

125

after a regular match for the clone detection is found.

For better considering the suitability of heuristics to solve the previously named problems occurring during the clone detection, the new metric *Specificity* to measure their performance is introduced in the following:

- **Specificity:** The *Specificity* is also known as true negative rate. It shows the ratio of items that are considered as not relevant results to all items that are irrelevant. For the vulnerability detection within code fragments, this is the ratio of fragments that are truly considered as not being vulnerable to all other not relevant or secure fragments. Therefore, the denominator contains the wrongly identified vulnerabilities, which do not contribute to them. This value can take place between zero and one. Classifiers or heuristics receiving this value close to one are probably more meaningful than others. Because it shows how good the heuristics can detect not relevant items for the classification purpose.

$$Specificity = \frac{TN}{TN + FP} \tag{8.1}$$

To identify the suitability of heuristics, their evaluation is done in three iterations. Within the first all introduced heuristics are used and their results are equally weighted interpreted to decide about the security of a concrete code fragment. Only the borderline heuristic is assigned the double weight because I and a collaborating master's thesis student assumed that this heuristic performs the best attributed to the preliminary pre-work done to enable their apply [27]. Furthermore, the θ-threshold is set to 3.0 as it is used for the recall configuration to receive many matches. Thereby, code fragments can match multiple vulnerabilities in the security knowledge base. Iteration two now aims to change the utilized weights for heuristics according to heuristics' individual performance to identify such false predictions. To consider the named problems of clone detection regarding vulnerability detection, specificity and recall are used. Therefore, the average values of recall and specificity for security patches and unrelated matches are normalized taken for the weights.

The θ-threshold is adapted to 2.5 because in iteration one a vulnerability was already disregarded by the clone detector so that the heuristics cannot be applied. Furthermore, to increase the precision code fragments are now matching only to the best suitable vulnerability in the reference security knowledge base. For iteration three, the recall is prioritized for a new weight calculation of heuristics, to find as many vulnerabilities as possible. Thereby, the recall weights are doubled. Furthermore, dumb classifier [88] heuristics are ignored, which receive less than 50% precision.

To form a suitable validation set, vulnerabilities found with the approaches described in Sec. 4 are utilized. Thereby, the vulnerabilities are obtained in half from Stack Overflow and in the other of GitHub. To tackle different problems of vulnerable clone detection, the code fragments have different sizes. In this way, small fragments (less than 150) can be can be distinguished from medium-sized (up to 600) and large-sized code fragments (more than 800 symbols). These fragments are symbols including comments, but token-based clone detectors do not consider them. Therefore, the number of tokens are also provided in Table 8.10.

All 10 vulnerable code fragments also offer security-patches that close them. To check the capability of detecting vulnerabilities according to clone Types 1 to 3, vulnerabilities and security-patches types two and three were manually created. Additionally, a different Type 3.5 expression was created, which contains the double of changes concerning clone Type 3. Type 1 clones are the same retrieved fragments and are the base of the type creation. For Type 2 clones, the names of tokens are changed. If a variable occurs multiple times, the same value is always assigned. Within Type 3 clones, statements were added or removed. For that operation, probably secure statements were used by accessing files from top GitHub projects that have not changed over a long time.

In summary, the validation set comprises 40 vulnerable and 40 securely-patched code fragments expressed within Type 1 to 3.5. During vulnerability detection, the secure code fragments should not be detected because they are false predictions. The validation set is balanced regarding secure and insecure fragments, as shown in Table 8.10.

Table 8.11 summarizes the results of using the SourcererCC for vulnerability detection, whereby iterations one to three represent the enrichment of the vulnerability clone detection with heuristics.

The results show that the combination of introduced heuristics could enrich the performance values. Already *Iteration 1* with equal weights for each heuristic improves almost all performance metric values for every clone type. Only the borderline heuristic delivered

Table 8.10: Security Code Clone Detection Validation Set 1 [27].

Vulnerabilitytype [CVE-ID]	# Symbols	# Tokens
XML External Entities [CVE-2017-9096]	411	19
Cross Site-Scripting (XSS) [CVE-2015-3654]	424	19
SQL-Injection	565	52
SQL-Injection	215	22
Missing Password Key Derivation	142	12
Risky Cryptographic Algorithm	110	6
Cross Site-Scripting (XSS)	1005	64
Permissions, Privileges and Access Control [CVE-2011-3190]	5424	275
Information Leak [CVE-2013-1926]	117	6
Permissions, Privileges and Access Control [CVE-2014-0050]	889	65

bad results (Appendix A.7); therefore, it was ignored for Iteration 3. Using the remaining heuristics improved the security code clone detector (SCCD) performance for all clone types among all performance metrics. In this manner, a perfect recall for clone Types 1–3 could be reached with a high precision above 90%. The origin approach has problems detecting similar code fragments of clone Types 3–3.5 with a higher threshold value $\theta > 3.0$. A drawback of using a low threshold of 3.0 or lower is the relationship between recall and precision. A lower threshold enable the recognition of clones for high clone types but reduces in the same way the precision. The accuracy varies among clone detector thresholds and clone types. Depending on the code clone type, the accuracy is reduced to values between 44.4 and 61.5%, which leads to many false recognition's during vulnerability detection. With heuristics, it can be shown that the security clone detector's weakness can be mitigated with improved recall. The recall is improved because the clone detector was modified to store all clone results found by the clone detector and the heuristics can therefore process them. The original code clone detector has a single clone as output, which can also filter out correct results. The accuracy is improved, which reflects the proportion of correct classifications. Overall, enriching the clone detector with the developed heuristics improves the vulnerability detection remarkably.

As already mentioned, the strength of heuristics can be highlighted by the specificity for the vulnerability detection. Table 8.12 shows the heuristic performance for specificity unrelated matches (S(U)), specificity patches (S(P)), recall, and precision for iteration 1-3. These performance values are calculated across all clone types. Unrelated matches are

128

Table 8.11: Security Code Clone Detection Heuristics Validation Results (Set 1) [27].

Approach	T	TP #	FP #	TN #	FN #	P %	R %	F1 %	A %
SCCD θ =3.0	1	9	10	0	1	47.4	90	62.1	45
	2	8	10	0	2	44.4	80	57.1	40
	3	8	8	2	2	50	80	61.5	50
	3.5	8	5	5	2	61.5	80	69.6	65
SCCD θ =5.5	1	9	7	3	1	56.3	90	69.2	60
	2	8	7	3	2	53.3	80	64	55
	3	6	1	9	4	85.7	60	70.6	75
	3.5	0	0	10	10	-	0	-	50
SCCD θ =8.0	1	9	4	6	1	69.2	90	78.3	75
	2	8	1	9	2	88.9	80	84.2	85
	3	0	1	9	10	0	0	-	45
	3.5	0	0	10	10	-	0	-	50
Iteration 1	1	**10**	6	4	**0**	62.5	**100**	76.9	70
	2	**10**	1	9	**0**	90.9	**100**	95.2	95
	3	9	1	9	1	90	90	90	90
	3.5	5	1	9	5	83.3	50	62.5	70
Itoration 2	1	**10**	4	6	**0**	71.4	**100**	83.3	80
	2	9	1	9	1	90	90	90	90
	3	9	1	9	1	90	90	90	90
	3.5	6	1	9	4	85.7	60	70.6	75
Iteration 3	1	**10**	1	9	**0**	**90.9**	**100**	**95.2**	**95**
	2	**10**	1	9	**0**	**90.9**	**100**	**95.2**	**95**
	3	**10**	1	9	**0**	**90.9**	**100**	**95.2**	**95**
	3.5	**9**	1	9	**1**	**90**	**90**	**90**	**90**

identified clones by the clone detection but are not related to the reference code fragment's vulnerability. During the validation, it could be noticed that many short methods invoke these unrelated matches. S(U) shows the percentage of unrelated matches that were correctly recognized by the clone detection and deliver therefore no security-notifications. S(P) is the percentage of patches that were correctly identified as such.

Table 8.12: Performance of Heuristics for the Security Code Clone Detection (Set 1) [27].

Approach	Types	Total #	Target #	Actual #	S(P) %	S(U) %	R %	P %
Iteration 1	Vulnerabilities	40	40	34				
	Patches	40	0	9	77.5	67.5	85	79.1
	Unrelated	157	0	51				
Iteration 2	Vulnerabilities	40	40	35				
	Patches	40	0	7	82.5	**99.1**	87.5	83.3
	Unrelated	340	0	**3**				
Iteration 3	Vulnerabilities	40	40	**39**				
	Patches	40	0	**4**	**90**	98.8	**97.5**	**90.7**
	Unrelated	340	0	4				

The results show that the combination of heuristics could remove many matches of the code clone detection during each iteration. Thereby, iteration 3 reaches the best performance values regarding precision and recall. For patches, the heuristics perform with a specificity of 90% for iteration 3, which is very good. This means that up to 90% of the patches could be detected as such and thus not lead to false alarms in vulnerability detection. For the unrelated matches, 98.8% could be filtered out by the heuristics. These are false alarms that the code clone detector is producing without using heuristics. Iteration 2 reaches a slightly better S(U) of 0.3% but for Iteration 3, both, precision and recall are improved.

Another small validation set is used to prove whether the previously calculated weights are also suitable for unseen data. The remaining data samples are utilized that were not already employed in the prior validation set retrieved by Viertel et al. [170] and remain as a suitable representation of the vulnerabilities. Therefore, the validation set 2 contains eight vulnerabilities for which the clone Types 1 to 3 exist. The validation set comes with security patches, that are, therefore, not separated into different clone types. The vulnerabilities within the second validation set are listed in Table 8.13.

For further validation, the heuristic weights previously computed are investigated with the use of validation set 2. For another comparison, the modified SourcererCC (SCCD) used

Table 8.13: Security Code Clone Detection Validation Set 2 [27].

Vulnerabilitytype [CVE-ID]	# Symbols	# Tokens
XML External Entities [CVE-2017-9096]	396	25
Path Traversal [CVE-2007-5461]	673	32
Information Leak [CVE-2013-1926]	633	34
Path Traversal [CVE-2009-2693]	2096	138
Improper Access Control [CVE-2016-6723]	312	29
Cross Site-Scripting (XSS) [CVE-2010-4172]	301	14
Exposure of Sensitive Information [CVE-2016-3897]	323	27
Permissions, Privileges and Access Control [CVE-2011-3190]	846	33

heuristics against the performance to detect vulnerabilities without them. Results are listed in Table 8.14.

The results for unseen data show that using the heuristics with the weights identified earlier again the developed heuristic approach achieves better performance than applying only the clone detector. The approach enriched with heuristics performs the best within iteration 3. For Type 1-2 clones, it reaches perfect values for all metrics. For Type 3 clones, the recall is slightly lower as the for the clone detector $\theta = 3$, but in contrast to the other metrics, the heuristic approach received much better results. In general, the developed heuristics in this thesis can improve the security code clone detection considering all metrics

Table 8.14: Security Code Clone Detection Validation Results (Set 2) [27].

Approach	T	TP #	FP #	TN #	FN #	P %	R %	F1 %	A %
SCCD θ =3.0	1	8	8	0	0	50	100	66.7	50
	2	8	8	0	0	50	100	66.7	50
	3	8	8	0	0	50	100	66.7	50
SCCD θ =5.5	1	8	7	1	0	53.3	100	69.6	56.3
	2	8	7	1	0	53.3	100	69.6	56.3
	3	3	7	1	5	30	37.5	33.3	25
SCCD θ =8.0	1	8	3	6	0	72.7	100	84.2	82.4
	2	3	3	6	5	50	37.5	42.9	52.9
	3	0	3	6	8	0	0	-	35.3
Iteration 2	1	8	4	4	0	66.7	100	80	75
	2	8	4	4	0	66.7	100	80	75
	3	6	4	4	2	60	75	66.7	62.5
Iteration 3	1	8	0	8	0	100	100	100	100
	2	8	0	8	0	100	100	100	100
	3	7	0	8	1	100	87.5	93.3	93.8

like precision, recall F1-measure and accuracy measured for almost all clone types.

8.3.2 JavaScript

To validate the implemented modification of the security code clone detector to the JavaScript programming language, the three configuration thresholds with their distinct goals are considered: high precision (θ=8.0), high recall (θ=3.0) and their combination (θ=5.5). To create a suitable validation set, existing vulnerabilities on GitHub are retrieved by searching for concrete CVE-IDs. The found vulnerable code fragments count as type one code clone. To generate other types, JavaScript code obfuscation tools are used. For type three, new statements are added or existing were removed, which does not contribute to the vulnerability. Additionally, for all 20 detected vulnerable code fragments, their fixes are created through GitHub and a web-based search for removing the concrete vulnerabilities if not provided. The validation set of vulnerabilities is presented in Table 8.15.

For every code clone type, the performance is measured by considering the same security patched code fragments. Therefore, to compute the approach's performance, each type is

Table 8.15: Security Code Clone Detection JavaScript Validation Set [5].

CVE-ID	Vulnerabilitytype (CWE-ID)	#S	#T
CVE-2019-11358	CWE79: Cross-site Scripting	1011	72
CVE-2017-2445	CWE79: Cross-site Scripting	235	33
CVE-2017-1000042	CWE79: Cross-site Scripting	274	27
CVE-2014-7192	CWE94: Code Injection	281	18
CVE-2014-7192	CWE94: Code Injection	418	34
CVE-2018-3754	CWE89: SQL Injection	289	13
CVE-2018-16462	CWE77/78: (OS) Command Injection	241	11
CVE-2016-3714	CWE20: Improper Input Validation	533	47
CVE-2018-3750	CWE20: Improper Input Validation	1582	120
CVE-2007-3670	CWE79: Cross-site Scripting	296	25
CVE-2017-16088	CWE610: Externally Reference	660	60
CVE-2017-11895	CWE119: Improper Restriction Buffer	908	69
CVE-2014-0046	CWE79: Cross-site Scripting	846	78
CVE-2018-3774	CWE918: Server-Side Request Forgery	573	20
CVE-2018-11093	CWE79: Cross-site Scripting	938	57
CVE-2017-7534	CWE79: Cross-site Scripting	584	29
CVE-2019-7167	CWE-754: Improper Exception Conditions	3968	602
CVE-2015-1840	CWE200: Exposure Sensitive Information	3970	319
CVE-2015-7384	CWE-400: Resource Consumption	1407	112
CVE-2019-10744	CWE20: Improper Input Validation	99	11

Table 8.16: Security Code Clone Detection JavaScript Validation Results [5].

Configuration	T	TP #	FP #	TN #	FN #	P %	R %	F1 %	A %
	1	**20**	20	0	**0**	50	**100**	**66.7**	**50**
SCCD θ =3.0	2	**20**	20	0	**0**	**50**	**100**	**66.7**	**50**
	3	**17**	20	0	3	45.9	**85.**	**59.6**	**42.5**
	1	**20**	20	0	**0**	50	100	66.7	50
SCCD θ =5.5	2	16	20	0	4	44.4	80	57.1	40
	3	1	20	0	19	4.8	5	4.9	2.5
	1	20	**16**	**4**	**0**	**55.6**	100	**71.4**	60
SCCD θ =8.0	2	2	**16**	**4**	18	11.1	10	10.5	15
	3	0	**16**	**4**	20	0	0	-	10

evaluated individually within a balanced validation set of 20 samples containing vulnerable and securely-patched code fragments. The results are summarized in Table 8.16.

Comparing these results to those retrieved for the Java programming language shows that they are close to each other. Both get problems to detect clones of type 3 for higher θ thresholds without the use of heuristics. Using the clone detection for vulnerability identification purposes can result in incorrect warnings due to the low precision of approximately 50% close to dumb classifiers [91]. Hereby, using the previously introduced metrics, the performance probably could also be improved. Thereby, an assumption is that also the precision can be improved by keeping the recall.

In total, it can be noted that the SourcererCC itself provides a code clone detection approach, which can be used with a lack of precision and recall for vulnerability detection. It's apply on type 1 clones delivers more suitable results than to others. The introduced heuristics in this dissertation can improve such token-based clone detectors with the purpose of vulnerability identification. Utilizing these clone detectors for a vulnerability detection purpose ends in many false warnings without using in this dissertation introduced heuristics. Again, the recall is prioritised for vulnerability detection in project source code. Any missing security alert can result in a vulnerable project due to a single overlooked vulnerability.

8.3.3 Threats to Validity

To consider the validity of the applied validation, the types of threats to validity of the empirical software engineering research defined by Wohlin et al. [175] are utilized. They are identified as follows:

Construct: There is a wide range of existing heuristics that can be used for comparing two items as for example code fragments. It is possible, that the utilized heuristics perform not the best for the comparison of source code fragments or tokens. Besides the invented strategies widely established approaches for comparing two items are used to reduce this threat impact.

The heuristics are developed to be clone detector independent but receive probably similar results for token-based approaches. This is not measured by the described validation. To address this problem, the design of the heuristics was chosen so that the heuristics can be applied to sets of tokens that can be created independently of the clone detection process.

Conclusion: Only a small set is considered to measure whether calculated weights of heuristics also performing well for unseen data. Probably the second validation set is to small for a meaningful conclusion.

The heuristics are developed to be programming language independent but for validating the combination of clone detectors only Java is considered. Maybe the heuristics perform differently for other languages. The heuristics can be applied on a individual set of tokens, which should be programming language independent.

Internal: During the vulnerability detection, the Java Run-time Environment version and the individual library version used within source code fragments are not considered. Some code fragments are only insecure within specific Java versions and by the use of concrete library versions. This issue can be solved by the manual prove of developers or security experts considered in the described approach.

It is imaginable that other code clone detection approaches are more suitable to detect vulnerabilities within code fragments than token-based clone detection. This is an aspect for future investigation. For the selection of clone detection approach, the literature was analyzed for a good performing clone detector that meets appropriate characteristics.

Construct: The SourcererCC's performance is controlled by it's configuration as the θ-threshold adjustment. Maybe there is a better configuration then the utilized ones. To mitigate this threat, the clone detection is executed with different θ-thresholds. Afterwards, the best performing which show different results are selected.

Chapter 9

Case Study: Applying Security Checks Based on Community Knowledge to Software Projects

The approaches developed in this thesis described in Chapters 5 and 6 are based on community knowledge about security. Vulnerability detection in code requires a security knowledge base consisting of security-related code fragments. This creation process is described in Chapter 4. Chapter 7 shows the prototypical implementation used within the case studies. All the underlying approaches are technically validated in Chapter 8. This chapter describes the conducted case studies with different goals. Section 9.1 considers research question 2.1 and shows the feasibility of using community knowledge for security checks. Section 9.2 and 9.3 also address research question 2.1 and also consider research question 2.2 and the recording of user satisfaction. Due to my observation and the requested changes by participants, these case studies improve the functionality and usability aspects of the implemented prototypes. Each case study section ends with associated threats to validity.

9.1 Security Knowledge Base Validation

This section describes the validation of data provided about vulnerabilities in software projects stored inside the security knowledge base. The discussed vulnerabilities that have CVE-IDs are used to check whether the projects' security flaws can be detected where they were discovered using the reference data. Therefore, the developed code clone detection approach is leveraged. If the vulnerabilities could not be retrieved by automated approaches, the reasons were manually investigated.

9.1.1 Methodology

The security knowledge base contains reference code fragments of 179 Java vulnerabilities, wherein 39 provide CVE-IDs in discussions on Stack Overflow or in commit messages on GitHub. This means that these 39 IDs describe product-specific security flaws reported to the NVD. Since the example code fragments are retrieved from community knowledge, there is a chance that they were wrongly assigned to the CVE-IDs by community members. To validate whether the code fragments express the vulnerabilities related to the mentioned CVE-IDs, verification was conducted of whether the vulnerabilities can be detected in the origin projects. The described code clone detection approach uses the extracted reference code fragments. For each vulnerable code fragment, the occurrence of clones is only checked within the project versions that should contain the security flaw. The clone detection results are then manually checked. The fragments are partially edited during the revision of a repository maintainer before adding the code fragments to the knowledge base. Only the code that is relevant for the vulnerability remains. A vulnerable fragment in the repository might be different in contrast to the one within the source. Perhaps the difference is too significant, so that the fragments can no longer be recognized as clones. If the clone detection does not find a fragment with a high recall configuration (θ=3.0), the reason is manually investigated. Therefore, the NVD description is read and the project source code files of referencing projects are scanned manually for the fragment's occurrence. The deduction of whether the correct code fragments were detected was completed by two security experts.

9.1.2 Results and Discussion

For 32 of 39 projects, inferences could be made by using originated projects referenced by the CVE-ID within the NVD. For the other seven, the origin projects could not be retrieved but projects containing similar code to the CVE-ID expressing the same kind of vulnerability or importing components of the referenced projects as libraries were used. An example of that is the JBoss application server, which internally uses the Apache Tomcat server. The results of the case study are shown in Table 9.1. The table displays the CVE-ID, the originated project (with its version), and information whether vulnerabilities could be detected by the clone detection (SCCD) manually or not at all.

Results show that 35 of the vulnerabilities could be detected within the origin projects

Table 9.1: Knowledge Base Vulnerabilities Detected in the Origin Projects by SCCD.

CVE-ID	Product	Version	Found by
CVE-2015-5262	Apache HttpComponents HttpClient	4.3.5	SCCD
CVE-2012-5783	Apache Commons HttpClient	3.1	Manual
CVE-2007-5461	Apache Tomcat	6.0.14	SCCD
CVE-2016-5007	Spring Security	4.1.0	SCCD
CVE-2014-0119	Apache Tomcat	7.0.20	SCCD
CVE-2016-3092	Apache Commons Fileupload	1.3.1	SCCD
CVE-2013-4415	Spacewalk / RHN Satellite	2.0.2	SCCD
CVE-2017-9096	iText	4.2.1	SCCD
CVE-2014-7810	Apache Tomcat	8.0.15	SCCD
CVE-2017-0554	Android	5.1.1	SCCD
CVE-2014-3004	Castor	1.3.2	SCCD
CVE-2014-3595	spacewalk-java	2.0.2	SCCD
CVE-2014-3654	spacewalk-java	2.0.2	SCCD
CVE-2014-3654	spacewalk-java	2.0.2	SCCD
CVE-2016-6813	Apache CloudStack	4.9.0.0	SCCD
CVE-2015-3252	Apache CloudStack	4.5.1	Manual
CVE-2008-1947	Apache Tomcat	5.5.26	SCCD
CVE-2011-2481	Apache Tomcat	7.0.16	SCCD
CVE-2015-5174	Apache Tomcat	7.0.64	SCCD
CVE-2010-4172	Apache Tomcat	7.0.4	SCCD
CVE-2017-13158	Android	5.1.1	SCCD
CVE-2014-0050	Apache Commons FileUpload	1.3	SCCD
CVE-2016-6723	Android (Proxy Auto Config)	5.1.0	Manual
CVE-2011-2204	Apache Tomcat	5.5.33	SCCD
CVE-2011-3190	Apache Tomcat	7.0.20	SCCD
CVE-2015-5174	Apache Tomcat	7.0.20	SCCD
CVE-2009-2693	Apache Tomcat	5.5.26	SCCD
CVE-2017-0846	Android framework (clipboardservice)	5.5.1	SCCD
CVE-2011-1582	Apache Tomcat	7.0.13	Manual
CVE-2013-1926	IcedTea-Web	1.0.1	SCCD
CVE-2006-2806	Apache Java Mail Enterprise Server	2.2.0	SCCD
CVE-2016-5725	JCraft JSch	0.1.54	SCCD
CVE-2011-0706	IcedTea-Web	1.0.1	SCCD
CVE-2015-3839	Android	5.1.1	SCCD
CVE-2016-3897	Android	5.1.0	SCCD
CVE-2011-1475	Apache Tomcat	7.0.11	SCCD
CVE-2015-3251	Apache CloudStack	4.5.1	SCCD
CVE-2013-2250	Apache Open For Business Project	12.04.01	SCCD
CVE-2016-3919	Linux kernel	-	SCCD
CVE-2011-2526	Apache Tomcat	5.5.33	SCCD

using clone detection and the provided security knowledge base. Four code fragments could not be found by the clone detection but were instead discovered manually. This is because the reference code fragments were too different from those provided by the origin projects, which also contain secure code parts removed from the knowledge base's fragments. Therefore, by using the reference for the vulnerability detection, 35 of 39 vulnerabilities could be detected within the origin projects. This shows that vulnerability detection based on community knowledge is possible. However, this does not mean that the mentioned approach cannot find the other four vulnerabilities within other projects. For example, if the methods in other projects do not containing as many tokens as in their origin, the vulnerabilities can also be detected. Furthermore, the security knowledge base is not limited to these 39 vulnerabilities. In total, 179 code fragments express vulnerabilities that are supported by the mentioned approach for Java. For JavaScript, the security knowledge base provides 59 vulnerable code fragments and 26 security-patches.

9.1.3 Threats to Validity

In the following section, threats are listed and annotated with the types of threats to validity by Wohlin et al. [175] introduced in Section 2.7.

Internal: The obtained code fragments and the assignment of CVE-IDs is made by the community members. These assignments sometimes could be incorrect but are included within the 39 samples investigated in this study as they fit my investigation.

External: This study considers only Java code fragments. For JavaScript and other programming languages, the community knowledge about security—and consequently the study's results—applied to code fragments might differ from the findings obtained in the described case study. Therefore, other programming languages are out of scope for this thesis and were not entirely investigated.

Credibility: The manual proof of a single security issue identified by a person is quite subjective. To tackle this issue, a second security expert investigated the deduction of vulnerability identification. Thus, the results are not only based on the opinion of one person. Nevertheless, it is possible that their opinions do not reflect the general view.

9.2 Applying Jira Security Checker to Real Projects

This chapter describes the application of the developed JIRA plugin and its results based on approaches to real projects carried out by a small-sized software company. Within this study, the JIRA plugin was used by teams during the software development of two different projects. The goal is to show whether the security checker can detect vulnerabilities in real software projects. Furthermore, its utility and usability regarding user satisfaction are considered. Identification of user satisfaction was qualitatively obtained through interviews with the project leader, who expressed the team's overall feedback.

9.2.1 Projects

A small-sized software house with 41 employees developed the projects. Their focus is on developing software to control human resources. Therefore, they consider web-based and mobile application technology. Their projects are developed through an agile software development process using Scrum [149]. The development is divided into sprints that have a dynamic time frame from one to four weeks. The company scheduled daily scrum meetings. At the end of each sprint, developers applied a retrospective analysis of the completed sprint.

Both projects used the JIRA management framework to organize their project development. The developers applied for a review at the end of each release. During the preparation of the projects, the team sizes varied from 3–6 people. Employees assigned to the projects had different tasks as developers, quality assurance, or project lead. They used the version management system Git for storing files and source code belonging to the projects. The team is widely geographically distributed, with the project lead in Germany and developers and software testers in Spain. During COVID-19, they worked from home offices. The source code languages used within the projects can be induced by the file extensions shown in Figure 9-1.

The projects' programming languages were mainly PHP and JavaScript, whereby most files have the file extension .js. During this case study, the security analysis was supported only for the Java and JavaScript programming languages. The projects contained a framework of reusable PHP components with a php dependency checker for identifying vulnerabilities.

9.2.2 Methodology and Change Requests

Input from stakeholders was obtained with the intent of adjusting the software to customer needs. Academic research has often been criticized as having little or no impact on practice [14]. Therefore, the *Action Research* (AR) method was utilized to receive feedback from

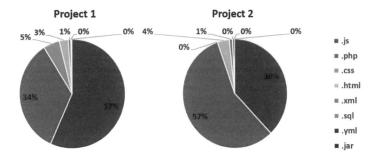

Figure 9-1: File Extensions that Express Programming Languages.

practitioners [19]. AR helps identify functionality that has not been implemented as well as the usability and user satisfaction of software. Therefore, a case study to improve the developed JIRA plugin was conducted using the AR method.

To summarize the case study details, they are described based on the bullet points listed by Medeiros dos Santos and Travassos [40] for distinguishing between AR methods. The case study was organized within an AR model. One to multiple AR cycles can be applied. For this study, however, only one cycle was used, as has been identified for most projects [40].

The center of this case study is a prototype supporting security checks in JIRA. The prototype was handed out to two teams who developed two different software applications. The case study was conducted for six months, where interviews with the project lead were conducted every three months to receive feedback on using the plugin. The research process was divided into five phases: (1) diagnosing, (2) action planning, (3) action taking, (4) evaluating, and (5) specifying learning [19].

1) **Diagnosing:** Identification of the primary research problems allows a hypothesis to be formed for validation during the research process.

2) **Action Planning:** Identifies concrete actions to solve the research problems. This planning targets the future research state and the changes that will achieve it.

3) **Action Taking:** Implements the planned actions of phase two.

4) **Evaluating:** Evaluates the outcome of the applied action.

140

5) **Specifying Learning:** As a formally undertaken phase, specifying learning reflects the identification of new knowledge that can be obtained through the applied process.

Figure 9-2 shows the described AR process applied to the developed prototype. The center represents the JIRA plugin prototype.

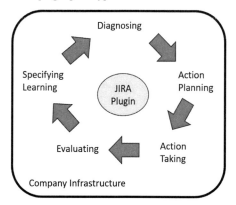

Figure 9-2: Adapted Action Research Cycle [19].

The focus of AR is to identify required functionality and user satisfaction to adjust the developed approaches and make them usable for practitioners. The approaches are then implemented in a JIRA plugin. The case study was initialized by the researcher within a corporate company of Leibniz University in Hannover.

In the following subsections, the specific steps applied for each action research phase are explained.

1. Diagnosing

An issue is that the approaches developed in this dissertation had only theoretically investigated or evaluated within the technical validation. The methods had not previously applied to real projects. Therefore, a hypothesis that the developed software approaches can be applied to real projects to identify vulnerabilities was created and investigated. To validate this hypothesis, the developed JIRA plugin was handed out to two project teams. During the software development, both projects used the provided plugin for a period of approximately three months. Developers could continuously use the plugin during the software development. Every week, a security analysis was applied once to keep the vulnerability data up

Table 9.2: Changes Identified as Relevant During Case Study.

Changes	Before	Change to
1	Vulnerabilities are only be visualized within the commited sprints.	All present vulnerabilities that still exist within sprints are shown.
2	Insecurities cannot be ignored or set to a done state.	Vulnerabilities can be ignored and commented.
3	Missing view of affected vulnerable source code.	Side-by-side view contains matched lines of project and reference code.
4	Vulnerability detection can only check the "master" branch.	Vulnerability detection supports now all project branches.
5	JIRA Projects can have only a single Git repository.	Multiple repositories can now be added to a single JIRA project

to date. Furthermore, both teams viewed the vulnerability results during the retrospective analysis at the end of each sprint. These are considered together with all participating team members. To receive feedback about the utility and usability of the plugin, an interview with the project lead who expressed the opinion of developers was conducted.

2. Action Planning

Through the interviews applied in the first phase, some usability problems and functional needs were identified. Based on the feedback, a plan for making the plugin more responsive to practitioners' needs was made. For example, adding new or modifying currently implemented features was considered. As an example, only one Git repository can be assigned and checked for vulnerabilities for each JIRA project. However, the company's projects had multiple Git repositories belonging to the same project listed in JIRA. Therefore, the planned action was to modify the software to support the security analysis of multiple Git repositories belonging to the same project. Table 9.2 shows software changes due to the interviews from the AR case study as applied to the security analysis of the projects.

3. Action Taking

In this phase, the prototype was modified and implemented in the organization for the two projects. The teams were then able to use the plugin with added modifications. After using the prototype for a further three months, qualitative feedback from the project lead expressing the practitioners' opinions was received again through interviews.

4. Evaluating

After the action-taking phase, a reflection on the received feedback could be done to plan for additional modifications in further AR cycles. For this case study, however, only one cycle was conducted.

After implementing the requested changes, one requirement remained, yet was not implemented within the plugin—another view that could compare sprints. According to the diagram type visualizing the results, it appeared that the vulnerabilities were increasing for outer sprints. The explanation was that the outer rings were becoming larger. The idea behind that design decision was that vulnerabilities found in later sprints are more costly. Therefore, their priority to be removed increases across the number of sprints. A new view would enable an even representation of all sprints. The change request was not considered, however, because of the late request for the change and the advantages of the currently used ring chart. Moreover, the teams enjoyed the idea and the use of the plugin. The project lead expressed this opinion in the final interview.

5. Specifying Learning

For future projects, some of the identified changes can already be considered. For example, the support of adding multiple repositories to projects. This is possible but was, in theory, not considered beforehand. Otherwise, there is no additional knowledge that could be obtained.

It can be noted conclusively that the developed plugin better fits user needs following the case study. It was shown that the approaches can also be applied to real projects developed by a software house. The software company would like to use the plugin during the development of other projects.

9.2.3 Vulnerability Results

Within this case study, security was not a hard requirement. Therefore, the project members did not remove any of the detected vulnerabilities of the JIRA plugin. After six months of study, the vulnerabilities detected by the tool were manually verified for their validity and impact. Therefore, the specific CVE-IDs of vulnerable software libraries are listed by their assigned CWE-IDs in Table 9.3. The code clone detection did not find any insecure code fragments for Java or JavaScript.

Table 9.3: Vulnerabilities Detected in Real Software Projects.

		Project 1	
Library name	**CVE-ID**	**CWE-ID**	**CVSS**
mixin-deep	2019-10746	88: Argument Injection	7.5
mixin-deep	2018-3719	20: Improper Input Validation, 471: MAID	6.5
elliptic	2020-13822	190: Integer Overflow	6.8
minimist	2020-7598	20: Improper Input Validation	6.8
serialize-javascript	2020-7660	502: Deserialization of Untrusted Data	6.8
lodash	2020-8203	770: Allocation of Resources Without Limits or Throttling	5.8
lodash	2018-3721	471: MAID	4
faye-websocket	2020-15133	295: Improper Certificate Validation	5.8
sockjs	2020-7693	20: Improper Input Validation	5
sockjs	2020-8823	79: Cross-site Scripting	4.3
webpack-subresource -integrity	2020-15262	345: Insufficient Verification of Data Authenticity	5
url-parse	2020-8124	20: Improper Input Validation	5
jquery	2007-2379	-	5
webpack-dev-server	2018-14732	20: Improper Input Validation	5
express	2014-6393	79: Cross-site Scripting	4.3
echarts	2020-2193	79: Cross-site Scripting	3.5
echarts	2020-2194	79: Cross-site Scripting	3.5
		Project 2	
Library name	**CVE-ID**	**CWE-ID**	**CVSS**
jquery	2007-2379	-	5
echarts	2020-2193	79: Cross-site Scripting	3.5
echarts	2020-2194	79: Cross-site Scripting	3.5

The only vulnerabilities that could be detected in the two real projects were third-party library induced vulnerabilities. For Project 1, the dependencies on external libraries were made by the references to the dependent libraries. This means that only the dependencies that were required to use the libraries contained vulnerabilities. However, these dependencies can also make the projects insecure.

A total number of dependencies on 1,060 different libraries were detected, wherein 111 dependencies on 13 libraries were responsible for making the project insecure. Within Project 2, only two libraries were detected as vulnerable from the direct dependencies of the project. Both projects were, therefore, vulnerable to XSS. If security was more important for the projects, plugin users would be made aware of the contained vulnerabilities that could probably be removed.

This study shows, that vulnerabilities in real projects could be detected by using community knowledge about security. The real projects could use the security checker plugin to access the security of files within projects.

9.2.4 Threats to Validity

Types of threats to validity are listed by Wohlin et al. [175]. Identified threats for this case study were introduced and assigned to these types.

External: The case study was conducted on two projects within a single company. The company itself and its employees have their own workflow and type of software management for projects. Perhaps some of the identified functional requests and user feedback from this study do not contribute to requirements of other practitioners. Some functional changes may not be relevant for others and the results and functional needs identified in this case study could differ when applying findings to other companies' projects. To mitigate this threat, the study was conducted with two projects developed by different teams.

The results of the conducted case study are probably not generally valid. Other programming languages possibly require other features and functionalities when analyzing them for security. During this case study, the application of developed approaches on real projects containing JavaScript and, partially, Java, could be guaranteed.

Conclusion: The projects did not have any requirement for security and therefore, they did not remove vulnerabilities. This fact could also limit the value of feedback regarding the security checker plugin. Furthermore, developers may not have completely used the plugin. To tackle this problem, the vulnerability results were presented to the attending team members during the retrospective after each sprint.

The projects were developed with PHP and JavaScript programming languages. For PHP, no vulnerability detection was implemented. Therefore, not all potential vulnerabilities could be detected.

Construct: The team's opinion is expressed only within interviews with the project lead. This scenario might possibly influence the results. Perhaps interviews with all individual employees would deliver different results.

Again to obtain insights of other team members, the project lead collectively viewed the vulnerability results with attending team members of the retrospective analysis.

9.3 Applying Eclipse Security Checkers within an Experiment

This section describes a quantitative case study to receive feedback about the use of implemented tools and compare the performance as well as the time effort in contrast to manual security checks. Surveys were used for collecting the data. The subjects executed both manual and tool-based identification of vulnerabilities among potential Java software artifacts. The experiment was divided into two parts, considering software libraries (.jar) and source files (.java).

9.3.1 Methodology

For checking insecure software libraries, the NVD was used by the tools and as part of the manual task. The same technique was done for the task of identifying vulnerable code. Additionally, a small sample set of six insecure code fragments was employed to give users a sample CVE-ID expression in source code. This excerpt of the security knowledge base was also used by the security code clone detector tool. Therefore, the subjects applied the task of identifying vulnerabilities in four software libraries with four code fragments used for both parts: manual and tool-based vulnerability detection. Within both sets of experimental data, half was insecure and the other half did not contain any vulnerabilities according to the NVD on 11 February 2019. The data shown to the subjects is summarized in Table 9.4.

The subjects were graduate students and researchers recruited from the Leibniz Universität of Hannover. Half of the volunteers had been hired for part-time jobs as software developers in addition to their studies. Fourteen subjects participated in the described experiment, and were not selected for their security expertise. The volunteers filled out a survey to assess their demographic information and obtain their general opinions and recommendations for the plugins (Appendix A.9). Through the use of a Likert scale [6], almost the half (43%) had prior knowledge about security and at least 29% were neutral to that knowledge. This finding means that participants with security knowledge and without were asked for their opinions and had their performance measured by the experiment. The user groups investigating security issues were divided into experienced and inexperienced subjects, which is valuable in obtaining diverse data. All subjects were briefly instructed on the use of the NVD and were allowed to ask questions. Furthermore, they could attempt to use the NVD search engine to obtain their first impressions of the engine.

To prevent a learning curve from library checks according to source code analysis from use of the NVD, half of the subjects started with library checks and ended with code security checks. The remainder completed the experiment vice versa. The time was measured within each step to later compare the performance for the manual and automated security checks. Furthermore, each subject's results and decisions were documented by themselves for further investigation of incorrect decision-making.

During their tasks, participants had to identify vulnerabilities for the specific library versions, though for the source code fragments, no versions were obtained. Therefore, versions are only considered for libraries and not for source code fragments to receive accurate results.

Table 9.4: Source Code Fragments and Software Libraries for the Experiment.

Software Libraries			
CVE-ID	**Product**	**Version**	**CVSS**
Secure	daytrader	2.1.7	-
CVE-2014-0107	xalan	2.7.0	7.5
Secure	xstream	1.4.8	-
CVE-2008-6504, CVE-2007-4556, CVE-2011-2088	xwork	2.1.1	6.8
Source Code Fragments			
CVE-ID	**Product**	**Version**	**CVSS**	**#S**
CVE-2008-2086	Java Web Start	5.0	9.3	1770
Secure	-	-	-	1147
Secure	-	-	-	570
CVE-2017-0846	Android framework (clipboardservice)	5.0	5	669

9.3.2 Results and Discussion

The efficiency of using the tool-based approach as an eclipse plugin and the manual identification of vulnerabilities in libraries and source code differ. The performance results are presented according to precision (P), recall (R), F1 measure (F1), and accuracy (A) in Table 9.5. These metrics are identified for each task where they are computed by considering a total of 56 classifications for all participants. Considering the subjects' security knowledge, there could be no performance difference identified compared to inexperienced users by the experiment results.

In the manual task of vulnerable library identification, the subjects used 33 CVE-IDs,

Table 9.5: Experiment Performance Results for each Task.

Vulnerability Identification				
Task	P	R	F1	ACC
Manual Lib	100	64.3	78.3	73.2
Tool-based Lib	100	**66.7**	**80**	**75**
Manual Code	62.2	82.1	70.8	66.1
Tool-based Code	**100**	**100**	**100**	**100**
Consequence Identification				
Task	P	R	F1	ACC
Manual Lib	100	**64.3**	**78.3**	**73.2**
Tool-based Lib	100	18.5	31.3	46.3
Manual Code	56.8	75	64.6	58.9
Tool-based Code	**92.6**	**89.3**	**90.9**	**91.1**

which cannot be used to decide about a library's security. The subjects' correct classifications for nine software libraries were only based on incorrect CVEs. Some CVEs of libraries with similar names were incorrectly considered as the investigated libraries. The earlier tool using the metadata approach (Sec. 5.3) could not detect the vulnerable library *xstream* in version *1.4.8* without user interaction. The hash-based approach (Sec. 5.4) detected the remaining library as insecure. Additionally, the performance using the tools for the vulnerability detection was better, considering all performance metrics, than the subjects' manual classification. Therefore, users always trusted the classification made by the tools even if they had previously recognized them differently during the manual checks.

For the deduction of consequences with respect to attack strategies for that are vulnerabilities susceptible to, in average of all metrics the subjects receive better results for the manual library checks. The deduction for tool-based and the manual task reaches both a perfect precision. This means that each consequence could be correctly derived for tools and during the manual task, but only the use of the NVD allows more consequences to be identified. Due to the consequence identification, the tool-based approaches surpasses the results of manual source code checks for all metrics.

The time each user needed to identify libraries as insecure was measured for each task. The results are summarized in Table 9.6.

The time results show that the tool-based approaches were superior to manual tasks. For the library vulnerability detection, the tool-based approaches only need approximately 1/3 of the median time as the manual. The vulnerability detection in source code only needs approximately 1/6 of the time required for the manual task.

148

Table 9.6: Experiment Time Results for each Task.

Task	Time (Minutes:Seconds)		
	Average	Median	Range
Manual Lib	14:07	14:10	**07:04-25:31**
Tool-based Lib	**6:38**	**4:42**	2:19-35:25
Manual Code	13:05	12:08	06:14-28:55
Tool-based Code	**2:28**	**2:01**	**0:53-4:40**

Through the surveys conducted, feedback about the usability of the findings and remarks for the improvement of the plugins were obtained. Only bug fixes for visualization issues could be identified. In the cake diagram shown in Figure 9-3, the general opinion about the ease of security checks from using the plugins is visualized.

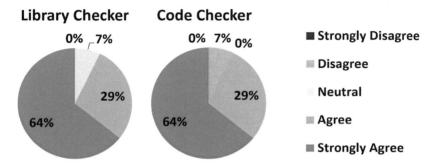

Figure 9-3: Opinion: Ease of Plugin Use.

The diagram shows that the plugins ease the application of security checks for libraries and source code artifacts compared to manual vulnerability detection. Only one volunteer did not confirm this statement.

9.3.3 Threats to Validity

Wohlin et al. [175] listed threats to validity types for empirical software engineering research. The identified threats are introduced within this section and addressed to the types.

Internal: Security results obtained from this case study are highly restricted to the small number of investigated code fragments and software libraries. This limitation derives from the time required to investigate the security of each artifact. It is possible that the results are different and more meaningful when considering more artifacts for security checks.

Construct: The same vulnerabilities were considered for both manual and tool-based security checks. A learning curve could not be permitted yet probably occurred. To remove this threat, the experiment should have been extended with more security checks, which would have exceeded the required time.

Conclusion: Due to the recruitment of volunteers at the university, only students and researchers participated in the described case study. If this case study would have been conducted with practitioners who are employed on a full-time basis, then the results might have differed. However, almost the half of the participants had a part-time job as software developer, which reduces the relevance of this threat.

Chapter 10

Conclusion

Security has become vital for organizations. Developers as yet do not have the necessary expertise to meet the requirements for security [2]. The security community knowledge has increased over time as developers become overwhelmed by a mass of information. It is challenging to find and select the correct security information for applying vulnerability checks to software.

This thesis's contribution is the identification of security-related community knowledge on websites such as Stack Overflow or GitHub and storing it in a security knowledge base containing code fragments of vulnerabilities, their security-patches, and exploits. Moreover, this dissertation develops heuristic approaches to using community knowledge to apply auto-mated security checks. Two eclipse plugins and a JIRA plugin were implemented to actively support developers during the implementation of secure software.

10.1 Addressed Challenges

Challenge 1.1 - Identify sources of reusable security knowledge: Stack Overflow, which is the current source developers use for software implementation assistance, was identi-fied as a relevant source for security knowledge as well [2]. Furthermore, developers mention specific CVE-IDs of vulnerabilities within the comments on GitHub, making it a lucrative data source. Furthermore, the use of those sources shows that security knowledge in the form of source code fragments can be retrieved. Furthermore, NVD and CWE already store security information in a textual manner, which can enrich the previously obtained knowledge of coding communities.

Challenge 1.2 - Identify security knowledge: The technical validation of artificial intelligence approaches combined with natural language processing shown in Ch. 8 reveal that this challenge can be solved by leveraging the introduced approaches. In particular, textual information can be used to classify code fragments as security-related, which expressing the community's security knowledge, considering algorithms with good performance according to precision, recall, F1-measure, and accuracy.

Challenge 1.3 - Distinguish security information into three classes - vulnerabilities, patches, or exploit: To solve this issue, the same text classification approaches used to identify security-related information are utilized. The knowledge of whether the community can identify a code fragment as a vulnerability, a security patch, or an exploit is used. For classifying information by exploit code, supervised machine-learning algorithms are infeasible because of the low number of discussions available on Stack Exchange. Better results can be retrieved by simply distinguishing between vulnerable and secure posts that discuss security-related content. This is shown by the technical validation (Ch. 8).

Challenge 1.4 - Store security knowledge in a reusable manner: Natural text is difficult to reuse for applying security checks within source code. For checking external libraries, the textual representation of data such as that provided in the NVD can be used. To automatically access the community's security knowledge, a security knowledge base consisting of code fragments was developed representing vulnerable, security-patch, and exploit representations. To enrich the knowledge base with additional information extracted from the NVD and CWE, an SQLite database (Appendix A.6.1) was created inside the root of the developed knowledge base. The SQLite database stored CVE-IDs, CWE-IDs, relationships between vulnerable code fragments and paths to their security-patches, and exploits. The case studies conducted (Ch. 9) and the technical validation (Ch. 8) show that the data is stored in a machine-reusable manner.

Challenge 2.1 - Reuse security knowledge on reported vulnerabilities
and Challenge 2.2 - Security checks for different source code artifacts: As relevant artifacts, software libraries and source code were identified. Different methods are introduced for both artifacts in this dissertation. A technique to reuse the textual representation of security knowledge stored in the NVD on vulnerabilities metadata combined with file hashes is used to identify insecure software libraries. To fulfill security checks within source code, a state-of-the-art code clone detection approach named SourcererCC was modified and enriched by heuristics. Both approaches received reliable results according to metrics precision, recall, F1-measure, and accuracy.

10.2 Answers to Research Questions

The stated research questions relevant for this dissertation are answered in this section.

Research Question 1: Can security knowledge be semi-automatically extracted from coding communities?

This thesis (Sec. 8.1.1) shows that the security knowledge represented by the contributions of Stack Exchange community members on Stack Overflow and GitHub can be semi-automatically extracted. This is done by supervised machine learning and keyword-based classifiers. The best text classification algorithm reaches a precision of 96-100% for identifying security-related content. Since there is the possibility of not achieving a perfect precision, a manual revision is necessary to ensure that all retrieved content is genuinely security-related. This represents a superior results; however, depending on the validation set, there is the chance that a perfect precision of 100% is not reached. The results show, that the text classifiers surpasses security experts, when performing the same task.

Research Question 1.1: Can security information be semi-automatically differentiated into vulnerabilities, patches, and exploits?

To apply the code clone detection to identify vulnerabilities in combination with the obtained community knowledge about security, it is necessary to distinguish between types of security-related information. This dissertation (Sec. 8.1.2) has shown that text classifiers using natural language processing can distinguish between the types of vulnerable, security-patch, and exploit information. The use of supervised learning is difficult for exploit information because it rarely occurs on Stack Exchange. Again, manual rework is required to obtain perfect precision. The classifiers reached 61-100 % for distinguishing between vulnerabilities, security patches, and exploit codes depending on the respective types. For differentiating among vulnerable and secure post content, the best classifier performed with a precision above 73 %. Again manual reviewing results is required to obtain perfect results.

Research Question 2: How can the extracted community knowledge be used for heuristic security checks on source code artifacts to identify vulnerabilities?

Textual security-related information stored in the NVD can be used in a simple string comparison enriched with heuristics or file hashes to identify vulnerable software libraries (Ch. 5). To the author's knowledge, it is currently impossible to simply reuse textual information to apply security checks within source code. A code clone detection approach is utilized to detect code fragments that are similar to vulnerable source code that probably also invokes a security issue (Ch. 6). To enhance this procedure, further heuristics are compared according to their performance. Both approaches received good values for the performance metrics including precision, recall, F1-measure, and accuracy (Ch. 8).

Research Question 2.1: How valuable is the use of community knowledge about security in detecting vulnerabilities?

On the one hand, the RQ is answered by this study (Sec. 3.4.1) verifying whether the community has positive security knowledge within a sample set of 1429 security-related posts. The verification revealed that the community could recognize vulnerabilities in posts or provide secure source code fragments. This study shows that approximately 73 % of the community had positive security knowledge according to the investigated post content. On the other hand, RQ 2.1. is answered by the application of tools to real projects described within the conducted case studies (Ch. 9) and the technical validation (Ch. 8) that is also based on community knowledge. Due to the case studies, 35 of 39 vulnerabilities could be detected by using community knowledge within the projects being listed within the NVD. Furthermore, in two real projects, vulnerabilities were detected based on community knowledge about security.

Research Question 2.2: How useful are the developed approaches for detecting vulnerabilities?

This research question is addressed by the case studies conducted on real projects carried out by a software company. Feedback from interviews and a quantitative survey were assessed following an experiment with students (Chapter 9). Results show that users of the tools were remarkably satisfied due to the automated nature, functionality, and time-saving of the approaches compared with manual security-checks. Furthermore, the approaches could be applied to find vulnerabilities in two real software projects.

10.3   Limitations of Heuristic Security Knowledge Checks

The introduced approach leverages community knowledge expressed by vulnerable code fragments combined with code clone detection to identify insecure source code snippets. Theoretically, this procedure can consider code fragments, including contextual information regarding vulnerabilities expressed by the source code. If the context is not part of the vulnerability itself, however, or too much context-relevant code is added to the reference source code, then the code fragments are inflated so that fewer matches to the reference code fragment can be detected. Therefore, within this thesis, the decision was made to place only the parts relevant for the vulnerability inside the security knowledge base code fragments. Consequently, no contextual information (or reduced contextual information) for vulnerability detection was considered.

A further problem is the recognition of vulnerabilities spread over multiple methods and classes. According to the developed approach's decision regarding design, the chosen approach might only detect those vulnerabilities that are included in a single block or method.

One further limitation is that only reported and known vulnerabilities can be detected. It is impossible to find new security flaws that are completely different from previously known and discussed vulnerabilities. The approaches based on community knowledge have been discussed and reported on publicly available platforms. Furthermore, the approaches are limited to the security knowledge of the community. This means that if code fragments on Stack Overflow or GitHub are not identified by the community as vulnerable, then the text classifiers for the security knowledge base creation could not classify the code fragments as vulnerable.

10.4   Future Work

During the research for this dissertation, other topics to consider in future studies have been raised. For example, a challenge is detecting vulnerabilities spread over multiple methods and classes using code clone detection. Therefore, further research is required to solve that concern.

An idea that emerged is to use vulnerable code fragments for different programming languages interchangeably to detect clones in an independent programming language . Therefore, a token-based clone detector is probably not the best choice. Perhaps the technique of program dependency graph clone detection can be used to better investigate the method. This raises the question of whether other clone detection techniques possibly perform better for detecting vulnerabilities within source code, which can also be part of future research.

The supported languages within the security knowledge base can be enriched by further samples of already-considered programming languages such as Java and JavaScript. The number of supported languages can be enriched, which is already done by PHP and Python, but is not described within this dissertation.

The assignment of CWE-IDs must be done manually to entries inside of the security knowledge base introduced in this dissertation. Therefore, the introduced text classifiers can also be investigated to automatically assign CWE-IDs based on natural language texts of user contributions.

Another remaining problem is that the security checks are almost context-independent, which can cause flawed results when detecting vulnerable code clones. Many factors can make a code fragment vulnerable, which depend on the context of use. For example, comparing password strings with the *equal* method in Java is vulnerable to timing attacks. Other string comparisons with this method, however do not result in a vulnerability.

Appendix A

Appendix

A.1 Preliminary Publications

- Fabien Patrick Viertel, Oliver Karras, and Kurt Schneider: Vulnerability Recognition by Execution Trace Differentiation.
  IN: 2017 ACM/IEEE International Symposium on Software Performance (SSP), 2017. [171]

  This paper describes a tool-based approach named FOCUS+ to detect security incidents by execution trace monitoring and its analysis. To recognize such anomalies, the difference of traces of regular software and other executions are conducted where it is known that no malicious action occurs. If some difference is detected, then a security incident probably can be identified. The affected code lines from execution traces that vary are highlighted to developers or security experts for further analysis. The location in the source code can then be determined by the use of execution traces generated by software at run-time.

  After a difference is detected, the approaches of security checking introduced within this dissertation can be applied in the resulting source code to enhance the warnings provided. General information about the vulnerability can be given, such as CVE-ID, CWE-ID, and a sample code to patch it securely, if available.

- Fabien Patrick Viertel, Fabian Kortum, Leif Wagner, and Kurt Schneider: Are third-party libraries secure? a software library checker for java.
  IN: 13th International Conference on Risks and Security of Internet and Systems (CRISIS), Springer, Cham, 2018. [172]

Within this work, a tool-based approach using metrics to identify vulnerabilities in Java software libraries is presented. Metadata such as the library filename and the content of the manifest file is utilized to draw conclusions about the library and its version. To detect vulnerable software libraries, the NVD is scanned for matches due to the metadata of preliminarily identified libraries. To actively support developers during software development, the approach was implemented in an eclipse plugin.

The paper describes a first version of the metadata library checker approach described in this dissertation.

- Fabien Patrick Viertel, Wasja Brunotte, Daniel Strüber, and Kurt Schneider: Detecting Security Vulnerabilities using Clone Detection and Community Knowledge.
  IN: International Conference on Software Engineering and Knowledge Engineering (SEKE2019), pages 245-324, 2019. [170]

  This work describes a keyword-based approach to identifying security-related content contributed on Stack Exchange, to which the Stack Overflow website belongs. The textual description within posts is employed. Furthermore, the security-related content is distinguished between vulnerable, security-patch, and exploit information using machine-learning approaches. Source code that is contributed in the same way is also considered to belong to one of the three previously identified information types. As a result, a knowledge base is created containing security-related code fragments usable for vulnerability detection with clone detectors.

  The identification of security-related content and storing this information in a security code knowledge base are the first steps in the approach described in this thesis to make community knowledge accessible for automated security-checking approaches.

- Fabien Patrick Viertel, Wasja Brunotte, Yannik Evers, and Kurt Schneider: Community knowledge about security: Identification and classification of user contributions.
  IN: 15th International Conference on Risks and Security of Internet and Systems (CRISIS), 2020. [169]

  This work describes a keyword-based approach to identifying security-related content contributed on Stack Exchange, to which the Stack Overflow website belongs. The textual description within posts is employed. Furthermore, the security-related content is distinguished between vulnerable, security-patch, and exploit information using machine-learning approaches. Source code that is contributed in the same way is also considered to belong to this type of information. As a result, a knowledge base is created containing security-related code fragments usable for vulnerability detection with clone detectors.

The identification of security-related content and storing this information in a security code knowledge base are the first steps in the approach described in this thesis to make community knowledge accessible for automated security-checking approaches.

- Cyntia Montserrat Vargas Martinez, Jens Bürger, Fabien Viertel, Birgit Vogel- Heuser, and Jan Jürjens: System evolution through semi-automatic elicitation of security requirements: A Position Paper.
  IN: IFAC, volume 51, pages 64-91, Elsevier, 2018. [167]

  This position paper describes the enhancement of SecVolution design-time approach by information delivered by security checkers and monitors to consider evolving requirements of automation domain during the software life cycle. Thereby, results of penetration tests and security assessments are inserted into the Security Maintenance Model (SMM) to manage security-related information. As a result of an industrial collaboration, the paper was created.

  This position paper describes somehow the relationship between SecVolution@Runtime and the present dissertation. Security findings during run-time can be enriched by the design-time security-checking approaches introduced within this thesis.

- Jan Jürjens, Kurt Schneider, Jens Bürger, Fabien Patrick Viertel, Daniel Strüber, Michael Goedicke, Ralf Reussner, Robert Heinrich, Emre Taspolatoglu, Marco Konersmann, Alexander Fay, Winfried Lamersdorf, Jan Ladiges, Christopher Haubeck: Maintaining Security in Software Evolution.
  In: Managed Software Evolution, pages 207-253, Springer, 2019.
  Editors: Ralf Reussner, Michael Goedicke, Wilhelm Hasselbring, Birgit Vogel- Heuser, Jan Keim, and Lukas Märtin. [79]

  This book is the outcome of all projects participating in the first or second founding period of the SPP1593, of which SecVolution and SecVolution@Runtime belong. The referenced SecVolution part describes the support for retaining the security of long living systems during the design-time co-evolution. A first concept is presented to support keeping a system secure even if malicious incidents occur during run-time.

- Jan Ole Johanssen, Fabien Patrick Viertel, Bernd Bruegge and Kurt Schneider: Tacit Knowledge in Software Evolution.
  In: Managed Software Evolution, pages 77-105, Springer, 2019.
  Editors: Ralf Reussner, Michael Goedicke, Wilhelm Hasselbring, Birgit Vogel- Heuser, Jan Keim, and Lukas Märtin. [75]

The referenced chapter represents another contribution in the same book involving SecVolution. The identification and externalization of tacit knowledge during the design and run-time of long-lived systems is considered. The SecVolution approach identifies tacit knowledge about security using heuristics, for example, those contained within nonfunctional requirements. Security experts can focus on these requirements for further security purposes.

A.2 Dissertation Context: Research Project SecVolution

This dissertation is an outcome of the research project *SecVolution@Run-Time - Beyond One-Shot Security: Requirements-driven Run-time Security Adaptation to Reduce Code Patching*. The project was founded by the German Research Foundation (DFG) and is part of the priority program (SPP) 1593 *Design For Future - Managed Software Evolution* [141]. The SPP is organized into two founding phases, whereby SecVolution@Run-Time belongs to the second. The preliminary project of the first phase is called *SecVolution – Beyond One-Shot Security: Keeping Information Systems Secure through Environment-Driven Knowledge Evolution*. The DFG scheduled the SPP1593 for a run-time of 6 years and an overall founding of approximately 10 million euro.

SecVolution focuses on evolving security knowledge within the scope of the software projects environment. Information systems occupy the central focus of the research. Some systems might be secure at design time, but may become insecure through the evolving environment. For example, a vulnerability might arise due to evolving technologies or knowledge of new attack vectors. Therefore, a system that was implemented compliant with its security requirements probably becomes vulnerable. An example could be a cryptographic algorithm that is broken by new attack strategies. All systems using the algorithm then become vulnerable.

The basis of the SecVolution concept is the SecReq approach developed in previous work [80]. SecReq considers the reuse of security knowledge during model-based software engineering. With security requirements elicitation and modeling, SecReq supports the analysis of system models. However, the approach cannot manage or use evolving security knowledge. During the SecVolution project, we tried to deal with this issues by monitoring the systems environment.

Static documents such as specifications, laws, and regulations are examples of elements that influence the security of the system environment. Security is also affected by personal knowledge, such as that of white hats or attackers. These factors and more have relevance for the security of a system.

This information is elicited and classified by heuristic approaches whether the obtained data is organized as security context knowledge, an essential security requirement, or merely affects ordinary requirements.

Through the monitoring of new relevant information, a security base (security maintenance model) is enriched. The model contains countermeasures for failed security requirements to restore the security of a system model. The system model is represented as a UMLsec model [78]. UMLsec is an extension to the Unified Modelling Language for enhancing UML models by security related information. Furthermore, this information can be used for model-based security engineering purpose.

A security expert can invoke changes within the design time and enrich the security maintenance model with certain measures. The general concept of the SecVolution approach is shown in Figure A-1. For its visualization, the Flow notation is used [148]. SecVolution considers the information flow and distinguishes between fluid and solid communication (dashed and continuous arrows). The sources can be verbal communication with people or specific documents, such as specifications.

As mentioned, in the first founding period, the core of the research was the continuous provision of secure systems during the design time. With SecVolution@Run-time, the concepts were enriched by approaches considering run-time. The idea is to monitor a system during execution, applying run-time countermeasures if an anomaly or a security incident is detected. The countermeasures facilitate other choices rather than a system shutdown

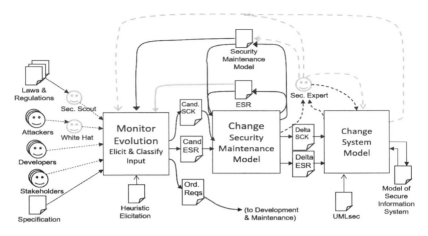

Figure A-1: Overview of the SecVolution Approach Using the FLOW Notation [148, 75].

as the only result of an intrusion. Furthermore, a small run-time patch that automatically deactivates some functions could be an alternative. A quality model (Q Model) can help in decision-making about potential consequences. For this case, the countermeasures again are stored in a run-time security maintenance model (RSMM). This allows the introduced preliminary model to be enriched by run-time information and countermeasures. A security expert can assist in deciding upon specific reactions to detected anomalies. Concrete findings are identified by heuristic indicators or recorded videos. The videos can show specific attacks presented by a security expert, which stores execution traces as a byproduct. These videos and findings can later be used to remove the vulnerabilities during design-time adaption. The explained approach is visualized in Fig. A-2, where the orange rectangle highlights the process of SecVolution phase 1.

This thesis introduces general approaches required to enrich the information about detected security incidents using community knowledge. Available security knowledge is semiautomatically identified and extracted within a unified structure from the largest coding community websites such as Stack Overflow or GitHub. This knowledge is represented by security-related code fragments as the expression of a vulnerability, its security-patch or exploit. After a security incident occurs and is somehow located by a project monitor, security checkers can deliver more specific information about vulnerabilities inside of software components or source code. Thereby, additional context information is delivered as CVE-

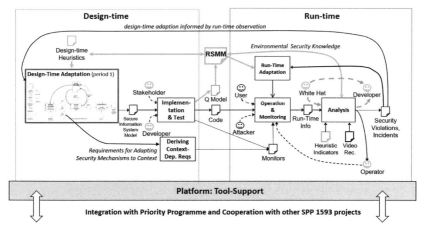

Figure A-2: Overview of the SecVolution@Run-time Approach Using the FLOW [148, 79].

and CWE-IDs if available in the security code repository or the utilized databases. Furthermore, countermeasures can be provided as security-patched code fragments discussed on coding community websites. Developers are able to address and analyse vulnerabilities encountered at runtime in design time by using the information provided by the security checkers. The developed approaches for security knowledge enrichment and security auditing are implemented in a Java application, in Eclipse plugins and in a JIRA plugin.

A.3 Java Libraries used for Manifest-File Analysis

Table A.1: Java Software Libraries Used for Manifest Analysis [172].

With CVE-Entry	Without CVE-Entry
Apache Axis 1.4	JUnit 4.12
Apache Axis2 1.4.1	Scala Library 2.13.0-M2
Apache Commons Fileupload 1.2.1	SLF4J API Module 1.7.25
Apache Commons HttpClient 3.1	Guava 23.0
Jetty 4.2.27	Apache Log4j 1.2.17
Jetty 6.1.0	Apache Commons IO 2.5
javax.mail 1.4	javax.mailapi 1.5.6
Apache OpenJPA 2.0.1	Apache Commons Logging 1.2
Apache Struts 1.2.7	Logback Classic Module 1.2.3
Apache Struts2 Core 2.1.2	Clojure 1.8.0
Apache Xalan-Java 2.7.0	SLF4J LOG4J 12 Binding 1.7.25
XStream 1.4.8	Mockito All 1.10.19
OpenSymphony XWork 2.1.1	Mockito Core 2.10.0
Spring Security Core 4.2.0	Servlet API 2.5
Elasticsearch 1.4.2	Apache Commons Lang 2.6
Apache Commons Collection 3.2.1	Apache Commons Lang3 3.6
Jackson Databind 2.9.1	javax.servlet-api 4.0.0
	Clojure Tools.nrepl 0.2.13
	Apache HttpClient 4.5.3
	Daytrader-EJB 2.1.7
	Clojure Complete 0.2.4

A.4 Metadata Library Checker Configurations

The configurations including their filter criteria are summarized in Table A.2.

Table A.2: Metadata Library Checker Configurations [173].

Configuration	Criteria
High Recall	CPE Version="Any" and ="NA" included. Update attribute is not considered.
Combined	CPE Version="Any" is ignored. Update attribute is now considered.
High Precision	Filters of combined configuration enriched by CPE Version="NA" is ignored.

164

A.5 Calculation Heuristics

A difference is seen between the file number of vulnerable code and the security-patched code, which influences the height of the IDF. Therefore, a constant is calculated to remove this difference to weight them equally within the introduced heuristic. A calculation is described in this section defining a constant weight value for considering security-patch tokens within the similarity calculation of Jaccard as well as Salton's cosine [27].

An average IDF-value of the first 15 general tokens is calculated. This is shown within the following equation:

$$avgIDF = \frac{\sum_{n=1}^{15} IDF_n}{15} \tag{A.1}$$

Afterwards, the term frequencies of the security-patched tokens are inverted. The more frequent the tokens, the more their weight is reduced. This process is expressed within the following equation:

$$invTF_n = \frac{1}{TF_n} \tag{A.2}$$

Finally, a constant K calculated resulting from the multiplication the same size of the average weights as those of the general terms. The calculation is presented in the following:

$$avgIDF = \frac{\sum_{n=1}^{15} invTf_n \cdot K}{15} \tag{A.3}$$

The former equation converted to K, which is the only unknown variable after the computation of the previous variables. After the computation K results in 0.055 as the average weight for security-patched tokens.

A.6 Prototypical Implementation: Security Knowledge Base Creation

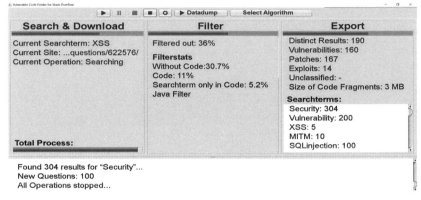

Figure A-3: GUI Security Knowledge Base Creator [169].

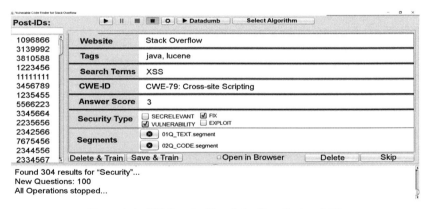

Figure A-4: GUI Security Knowledge Base Reviser [169].

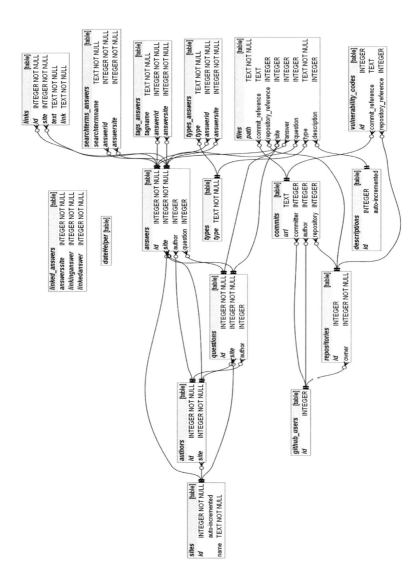

Figure A-5: Database Structure of Security Knowledge Base.

A.7 Heuristic Performances and Iteration Weights

The following heuristic abbreviations are used for the tables included within this section.

- **J:** Jaccard-index

- **C:** Saltons Cosine

- **WJ:** weighted Jaccard-index

- **WC:** weighted Saltons Cosine

- **PJ:** Patch-Comparison combined with Jaccard-index

- **PC:** Patch-Comparison combined with Saltons Cosine

- **WPJ:** Patch-Comparison combined with weighted Jaccard-index

- **WPC:** Patch-Comparison combined with weighted Saltons Cosine

- **BL:** Borderline heuristic

Table A.3 shows the performance values for specificity unrelated matches (S(U)), specificity patches (S(P)) and the recall of each heuristic for Iteration 1. Unrelated matches were considered as clones by the clone detection but are not related to the vulnerability represented by the reference code fragment. During the validation, it could be noticed that many short methods invoke these unrelated matches.

Again, S(U) shows the percentage of unrelated matches, that were correctly recognized as such by the clone detection. S(P) is the percentage of patches, that were correctly recognized as such.

Table A.3: Performance of Heuristics Iteration 1 [27].

M	Heuristics								
	J	**C**	**WJ**	**WC**	**PJ**	**PC**	**WPJ**	**WPC**	**BL**
	%	%	%	%	%	%	%	%	%
R	65	72.5	52.5	67.5	97.5	100	97.5	100	60
S(U)	89.2	66.9	98.1	82.8	38.1	28.6	38.1	38.1	23.6
S(P)	57.6	39.4	69.7	48.5	87.9	97	87.9	97	36.4

The results show, that each heuristic perform differently according to the performance metrics. Furthermore, the borderline heuristic delivers the worst results, which is the reason that the heuristic is ignore within Iteration 3.

Table A.4 summarizes the calculated weights used for every heuristic to predict the final vulnerability detection result.

Table A.4: Weights of Heuristics for all Iterations [27].

Iteration	Heuristics								
	J	C	WJ	WC	PJ	PC	WPJ	WPC	BL
Iteration 1	0.1	0.1	0.1	0.1	0.1	0.1	0.1	0.1	0.2
Iteration 2	0.115	0.10	0.12	0.11	0.12	0.12	0.12	0.13	0.07
Iteration 3	0.117	0.11	0.12	0.112	0.14	0.14	0.14	0.14	0

A.8 Experiment with Security Experts to Identify Security-Related Stack Overflow Posts

A.8.1 Demographic Survey and Search Task

Evaluation von manueller und automatisierter Suche von sicherheitsrelevanten Informationen auf Stack Overflow

Durchgeführt von Fabien Patrick Viertel, Fachgebiet Software Engineering, Leibniz Universität Hannover

Bitte lesen Sie sich diesen Überblick sorgfältig durch. Er dient dazu, das Experiment vorzustellen und Sie auf Ihre Rechte als Proband hinzuweisen. Bei Fragen oder Unklarheiten stehe ich Ihnen gerne zur Verfügung.

Ihre Teilnahme hilft uns, ein Tool zu evaluieren, das automatisch sicherheitsrelevante Inhalte auf der Seite Stack Overflow sucht.

Stack Overflow ist eine Frage-Antwort-Seite für das Thema Programmierung und enthält auch sicherheitsrelevante Codeabschnitte und Informationen.

Sie werden im Rahmen des Experiments 17 Minuten solche Inhalte auf der Seite suchen. Ihre Aktionen werden dabei per Bildschirmaufnahme aufgezeichnet.

Die von Ihnen angegebenen Daten und die Teilnahme am Experiment werden ausschließlich anonym und ohne Rückschlüsse auf Ihre Person ausgewertet. Sie können im Rahmen meiner Doktorarbeit sowie von Publikationen ausgewertet und präsentiert werden. Auch als Bestandteil von Publikationen werden die Daten grundsätzlich vollständig anonymisiert präsentiert.

Bevor das Experiment startet, werden Sie gebeten, ein paar persönliche Daten anzugeben. Diese helfen hinterher bei der Auswertung der Ergebnisse. Dabei geht es vor allem um Vorerfahrung im Software Engineering und der IT-Sicherheit. Die Angabe der personenbezogenen Daten hilft uns bei der Auswertung der Ergebnisse, um beispielsweise den Einfluss von Vorwissen auf Ihre ausgeführten Tätigkeiten zu ermitteln.

Einverständniserklärung zum Experiment zur Evaluation von manueller und automatisierter Suche von sicherheitsrelevanten Informationen auf Stack Overflow

Diese Studie wird im Rahmen der Forschung von Fabien Patrick Viertel zur „Evaluation von manueller und automatisierter Suche von sicherheitsrelevanten Informationen auf Stack Overflow" durchgeführt.

Ich habe den Überblick über das Experiment gelesen und verstanden. Ich nehme freiwillig und ohne Vergütung an dieser Studie teil. Ich habe das Recht, die Teilnahme jederzeit und ohne Angabe von Gründen abzubrechen.

Datenaufzeichnung

Ich wurde darüber informiert, dass während der Studie Daten erfasst, elektronisch zeitlich unbegrenzt gespeichert und zur Auswertung des Experiments herangezogen werden. Die aufgezeichneten Daten werden für die wissenschaftliche Forschung genutzt und ausschließlich anonymisiert ausgewertet. Die Daten werden in wissenschaftlichen Publikationen in anonymisierter Form veröffentlicht.

Auch bei Fragebögen haben Sie gemäß Datenschutz gegenüber dem Informationsträger das Recht auf Auskunft sowie Löschung Ihrer personenbezogenen Daten. Sie können diese Einwilligungserklärung jederzeit widerrufen. Nach erfolgtem Widerruf werden Ihre personenbezogenen Daten gelöscht und für keine weiteren Publikationen mehr verwendet.

Mit den aufgeführten Punkten bin ich

☐ einverstanden.

☐ nicht einverstanden.

Ich habe den Überblick über die Studie gelesen und verstanden. Ich bin mit den aufgeführten Punkten der Einverständniserklärung einverstanden. Ich nehme freiwillig und ohne Vergütung an dieser Studie teil und fühle mich gesundheitlich in der Lage, an der Studie teilzunehmen.

_____

Nachname, Vorname

_____

Ort, Datum, Unterschrift

Fragebogen Personenbezogen

Die Angabe der folgenden personenbezogenen Daten ist freiwillig. Sie helfen mir aber bei der Auswertung der Daten, z.B. bei der Analyse, ob Vorwissen einen Einfluss auf die Ergebnisse hat.

Studiengang (wenn zutreffend): ( ) Informatik (BSc)   ( ) Informatik (MSc)   ( ) _____
Fachsemester: _____   Berufliche Tätigkeit (wenn vorhanden): _____
Seit _____ Jahren

Wenn Student: Ich habe folgende Vorlesungen/Veranstaltungen besucht:

( ) Softwaretechnik   ( ) Softwarequalität   ( ) Kryptographie
( ) Softwareprojekt   ( ) IT-Sicherheit/Security Vorlesung
( ) Andere Veranstaltung(en) im Bereich Softwaresicherheit: _____

Wie viele Jahre Programmiererfahrung haben Sie?

_____ Jahre

Wie viele Jahre Erfahrung im Bereich der Softwaresicherheit haben Sie?

_____ Jahre

Haben Sie bereits Erfahrung im Bereich der Softwaresicherheit bei einem oder mehreren Programmierprojekt(en) oder einer Abschlussarbeit berücksichtigt?

☐ Ja   ☐ Nein

Wenn ja, beschreiben Sie kurz ihre Tätigkeit(en) im Sicherheitsbereich und geben Sie den jeweiligen ungefähren Zeitraum an:

Haben Sie bereits mit CVE-IDs gearbeitet?

☐ Ja   ☐ Nein

Haben Sie die Seite Stack Overflow bereits genutzt?

☐ Ja, regelmäßig (meistens öfter als 1x im Monat)   ☐ Ja, vereinzelt   ☐ Nein

Meine Englischfähigkeiten sind:

☐ Muttersprache ☐ Verhandlungssicher ☐ Fließend ☐ Konversationssicher ☐ Grundkenntnisse

Suche von sicherheitsrelevanten Posts auf Stack Overflow:

Sie werden im Rahmen dieses Experiments die Suchfunktion von Stack Overflow verwenden, um nach sicherheitsrelevanten Posts auf Stack Overflow zu suchen.

Wenn Sie Stack Overflow nicht regelmäßig nutzen, können Sie sich vor dem Beginn des Experiments mit der Suchfunktion und der Unterteilung in Frage, Antwort und Kommentare vertraut machen. Verwenden Sie dabei jedoch noch keine Suchbegriffe aus dem Bereich der Softwaresicherheit.

Es wird Ihre Aufgabe sein, in **17 Minuten** möglichst viele sicherheitsrelevante Posts auf der Seite zu finden. Dabei sollte die Seite nicht verlassen werden und **nur die integrierte Suchfunktion** verwendet werden. Im Rahmen dieser Studie sollen die Funde auf Java beschränkt werden. Um die Ergebnisse entsprechend zu filtern, kann das Java-Tag verwendet werden, indem bei der Suche „**[java]**" vorangestellt wird.

Ein Post ist entweder eine Frage oder eine Antwort. Kommentare zu diesen können Sie dabei ignorieren. Da es oft mehrere Antworten auf eine Frage gibt, kann es vorkommen, dass Sie mehrere sicherheitsrelevante Posts auf der Seite einer Frage finden.

Ein Post gilt als sicherheitsrelevant, wenn er:

- **Code mit einer Schwachstelle** enthält
  oder
- der **Name eines Programms oder einer Bibliothek mit einer Schwachstelle** genannt wird
  oder
- **Code** enthält**, der eine potentielle Schwachstelle schließt**
  oder
- genau **beschreibt, wie eine Schwachstelle zu schließen ist.**
  Diese Beschreibung muss eine Schritt-für-Schritt-Anleitung sein oder es muss zumindest die zu verwendende Bibliothek, Klasse oder Methode ausdrücklich genannt werden
  oder
- **Code, der eine Schwachstelle ausnutzt** enthält
  oder
- genau **beschreibt, wie eine Schwachstelle ausgenutzt werden kann.**

Ob Sie dabei verschiedene Suchbegriffe verwenden oder bei einem bleiben, ist Ihnen überlassen.

Wenn Sie einen sicherheitsrelevanten Post gefunden haben, sagen Sie dies bitte laut und machen kurz eine Kreisbewegung mit dem Mauszeiger über dem entsprechenden Post, damit der Fund auf der Bildschirmaufnahme nachvollziehbar ist. Sie müssen Ihre Wahl dabei nicht begründen, sprechen Sie Ihre Gedankengänge während der Suche aber gerne laut aus.

Vielen Dank für Ihre Teilnahme!

A.8.2 Classification Task

Evaluation von manueller und automatisierter Klassifizierung von sicherheitsbezogenen Informationen

Durchgeführt von Fabien Patrick Viertel, Fachgebiet Software Engineering, Leibniz Universität Hannover

Bitte lesen Sie sich diesen Überblick sorgfältig durch. Er dient dazu, das Experiment vorzustellen und Sie auf Ihre Rechte als Proband hinzuweisen. Bei Fragen oder Unklarheiten stehe ich Ihnen gerne zur Verfügung.

Ihre Teilnahme hilft uns, ein Tool zu evaluieren, das automatisch sicherheitsrelevante Inhalte auf der Seite Stack Overflow findet und diese in Sicherheitslücke, Fix und Exploit unterteilt.

Die von Ihnen angegebenen Daten und die Teilnahme am Experiment werden ausschließlich anonym und ohne Rückschlüsse auf Ihre Person ausgewertet. Sie können im Rahmen meiner Doktorarbeit sowie von Publikationen ausgewertet und präsentiert werden. Auch als Bestandteil von Publikationen werden die Daten grundsätzlich vollständig anonymisiert präsentiert.

Bevor das Experiment startet, werden Sie gebeten, ein paar persönliche Daten anzugeben. Diese helfen hinterher bei der Auswertung der Ergebnisse. Dabei geht es vor allem um Vorerfahrung im Software Engineering und der IT-Sicherheit. Die Angabe der personenbezogenen Daten hilft uns bei der Auswertung der Ergebnisse, um beispielsweise den Einfluss von Vorwissen auf Ihre ausgeführten Tätigkeiten zu ermitteln.

Einverständniserklärung zum Experiment zur Evaluation von manueller und automatisierter Klassifizierung von sicherheitsbezogenen Informationen

Diese Studie wird im Rahmen der Forschung von Fabien Patrick Viertel zur „Evaluation von manueller und automatisierter Klassifizierung von sicherheitsbezogenen Informationen" durchgeführt.

Ich habe den Überblick über das Experiment gelesen und verstanden. Ich nehme freiwillig und ohne Vergütung an dieser Studie teil. Ich habe das Recht, die Teilnahme jederzeit und ohne Angabe von Gründen abzubrechen.

Datenaufzeichnung

Ich wurde darüber informiert, dass während der Studie Daten erfasst, elektronisch zeitlich unbegrenzt gespeichert und zur Auswertung des Experiments herangezogen werden. Die aufgezeichneten Daten werden für die wissenschaftliche Forschung genutzt und ausschließlich anonymisiert ausgewertet. Die Daten werden in wissenschaftlichen Publikationen in anonymisierter Form veröffentlicht.

Auch bei Fragebögen haben Sie gemäß Datenschutz gegenüber dem Informationsträger das Recht auf Auskunft sowie Löschung Ihrer personenbezogenen Daten. Sie können diese Einwilligungserklärung jederzeit widerrufen. Nach erfolgtem Widerruf werden Ihre personenbezogenen Daten gelöscht und für keine weiteren Publikationen mehr verwendet.

Mit den aufgeführten Punkten bin ich

☐ einverstanden.

☐ nicht einverstanden.

Ich habe den Überblick über die Studie gelesen und verstanden. Ich bin mit den aufgeführten Punkten der Einverständniserklärung einverstanden. Ich nehme freiwillig und ohne Vergütung an dieser Studie teil und fühle mich gesundheitlich in der Lage, an der Studie teilzunehmen.

Nachname, Vorname

Ort, Datum, Unterschrift

Klassifizierung der Funde auf Stack Overflow:

Entpacken Sie die Datei *Klassifizierung.zip*.

Das Tool lässt sich danach über die Datei *Klassifizierung.jar* starten. Sollte dies nicht möglich sein, ist vermutlich kein Java oder eine zu alte Version (vor Version 8) installiert. Java 8 auf dem aktuellen Stand finden Sie unter *java.com/de/download*.

Das Tool öffnet automatisch den Fund auf Stack Overflow in Ihrem Standardbrowser.

Die Seite springt dabei direkt zur relevanten Antwort. Diese leuchtet auch kurzfristig orange auf. Falls Sie zu einem Zeitpunkt nicht mehr wissen, welche Antwort gemeint ist, können Sie die Seite jederzeit neu laden. Die Antwort wird dann erneut kurz hervorgehoben.

Ihre Aufgabe ist es, den Inhalt der **betreffenden Antwort und** der **Frage** zu lesen und zu überprüfen, ob dieser in eine oder mehrere der folgenden Kategorien passt. Andere Antworten, Kommentare und verlinkte Inhalte sollen dabei nicht beachtet werden.

Ein Ergebnis soll als **Sicherheitslücke** klassifiziert werden, wenn es

- Code mit einer Schwachstelle enthält
  oder
- der Name eines Programms oder einer Bibliothek mit einer Schwachstelle genannt wird.

Ein Ergebnis soll als **Fix** klassifiziert werden, wenn es

- Code enthält, der eine potentielle Schwachstelle schließt
  oder
- genau beschreibt, wie sie zu schließen ist.
  Diese Beschreibung muss eine Schritt-für-Schritt-Anleitung sein oder es muss zumindest die zu verwendende Bibliothek, Klasse oder Methode ausdrücklich genannt werden.

Ein Ergebnis soll als **Exploit** klassifiziert werden, wenn es

- Code, der eine Schwachstelle ausnutzt enthält
  oder
- genau beschreibt, wie sie ausgenutzt werden kann.

Dabei müssen Sie die Angaben und Aussagen in Frage und Antwort nicht auf Ihre Richtigkeit überprüfen. Gehen Sie davon aus, dass diese korrekt sind.

Das Tool zeigt Ihnen an, welche sicherheitsrelevanten Suchbegriffe gefunden wurden. Dies kann bei langen Posts ggf. helfen, die relevanten Abschnitte zu finden.

Setzen Sie die Häkchen entsprechend und klicken Sie auf „Weiter", um Ihre Wahl zu speichern und mit dem nächsten Fund weiter zu machen.

Insgesamt sind 33 Funde zu klassifizieren. Sie können das Tool jederzeit schließen und zu einem späteren Zeitpunkt fortfahren. Wurden alle Funde bearbeitet, sind in der vom Tool erstellten Datei „SendBack.zip" alle Ihre Antworten enthalten. Schicken Sie diese bitte zurück.

Vielen Dank für Ihre Teilnahme!

A.8.3 Classification Tool

Figure A-6: Tool for Classifying Security-Related Stack Overflow Posts [169].

A.8.4 Stack Overflow Posts Used for Classification

Table A.5: Stack Overflow Posts Used for Classification [169].

SO Post ID	V	P	E	N	SO Post ID	V	P	E	N
2201660	✔		✔		29105936		✔		
3413588		✔			29735658			✔	
5079101		✔			32762093	✔			
8253029			✔		33374690				✔
11009442	✔				33672728	✔	✔		
15446486	✔		✔		34172933	✔			
16438466				✔	34228093		✔		
16623574	✔				34516634		✔		
17651690	✔		✔		35901237	✔	✔	✔	
19061539		✔			38832446		✔		
19677138	✔		✔		38914280		✔		
19974607	✔	✔	✔		39061321	✔			
20627056		✔			44047806	✔	✔		
23263251	✔	✔	✔		44356225				✔
23826921		✔			46904785	✔			
24687457				✔	47655328	✔	✔	✔	
25413017	✔								
Total	9	7	7	2	**Total**	8	9	3	2

A.9 Survey for the Experiment Case Study

Experiment zur Analyse von manueller und automatisierter sicherheitsbezogener Softwarekomponentenprüfung

Durchgeführt von Fabien Patrick Viertel, Fachgebiet Software Engineering, Leibniz Universität Hannover

Bitte lesen Sie sich diesen Überblick sorgfältig durch. Er dient dazu, das Experiment vorzustellen und Sie auf Ihre Rechte als Proband hinzuweisen. Bei Fragen oder Unklarheiten stehe ich Ihnen gerne zur Verfügung.

Ihre Teilnahme hilft uns, die entstanden Security-Plugins zu evaluieren, d.h. Sie im Hinblick auf Nutzen und Effektivität zu untersuchen. Es gibt keine richtigen oder falschen Antworten bzw. Einschätzungen.

Die von Ihnen angegebenen Daten und die Teilnahme am Experiment werden ausschließlich anonym und ohne Rückschlüsse auf Ihre Person ausgewertet. Sie können im Rahmen meiner Doktorarbeit sowie von Publikationen ausgewertet und präsentiert werden. Auch als Bestandteil von Publikationen werden die Daten grundsätzlich vollständig anonymisiert präsentiert.

Bevor das Experiment startet, werden Sie gebeten, ein paar persönliche Daten anzugeben. Diese helfen hinterher bei der Auswertung der Ergebnisse. Dabei geht es vor allem um Vorerfahrung im Software Engineering und der IT-Sicherheit. Die Angabe der personenbezogenen Daten hilft uns bei der Auswertung der Ergebnisse, um beispielsweise den Einfluss von Vorwissen auf Ihre ausgeführten Tätigkeiten zu ermitteln.

Das Experiment findet in zwei Blöcken statt, welche jeweils auf eine Aufgabenstellung bezogen sind. Zum einen sollen Third-Party Libraries auf Ihre Sicherheit bewertet werden. Zum anderen sollen Source Code Ausschnitte auf Ihre Sicherheit bewertet werden. Zu Beginn jedes Blockes, gibt es eine

Einverständniserklärung zur Experiment zur Analyse von manueller und automatisierter sicherheitsbezogener Softwarekomponentenprüfung

Diese Studie wird im Rahmen der Forschung von Fabien Patrick Viertel zur „Analyse von manueller und automatisierter sicherheitsbezogener Softwarekomponentenprüfung" durchgeführt.

Ich habe den Überblick über das Experiment gelesen und verstanden. Ich nehme freiwillig und ohne Vergütung an dieser Studie teil. Ich habe das Recht, die Teilnahme jederzeit und ohne Angabe von Gründen abzubrechen.

Datenaufzeichnung

Ich wurde darüber informiert, dass während der Studie Daten erfasst, elektronisch zeitlich unbegrenzt gespeichert und zur Auswertung des Experiments herangezogen werden. Die aufgezeichneten Daten werden für die wissenschaftliche Forschung genutzt und ausschließlich anonymisiert ausgewertet. Die Daten werden in wissenschaftlichen Publikationen in anonymisierter Form veröffentlicht.

Auch bei Fragebögen haben Sie gemäß Datenschutz gegenüber dem Informationsträger das Recht auf Auskunft sowie Löschung Ihrer personenbezogenen Daten. Sie können diese Einwilligungserklärung jederzeit widerrufen. Nach erfolgtem Widerruf werden Ihre personenbezogenen Daten gelöscht und für keine weiteren Publikationen mehr verwendet.

Mit den aufgeführten Punkten bin ich

☐ einverstanden.

☐ nicht einverstanden.

Ich habe den Überblick über die Studie gelesen und verstanden. Ich bin mit den aufgeführten Punkten der Einverständniserklärung einverstanden. Ich nehme freiwillig und ohne Vergütung an dieser Studie teil und fühle mich gesundheitlich in der Lage, an der Studie teilzunehmen.

_____

Nachname, Vorname

_____

Ort, Datum, Unterschrift

Fragebogen Personenbezogen – vor Experimentstart

Startzeit: Ende:

Die Angabe der folgenden personenbezogenen Daten ist freiwillig. Sie helfen mir aber bei der Auswertung der Daten, z.B. bei der Analyse, ob Vorwissen einen Einfluss auf die Ergebnisse hat.

Studiengang: ( ) Informatik (BSc)   ( ) Informatik (MSc)   ( ) _____
Fachsemester: _____   Berufliche Tätigkeit: _____

Ich habe folgende Vorlesungen/Veranstaltungen besucht:

( ) Softwaretechnik   ( ) Softwarequalität
( ) Softwareprojekt   ( ) IT-Sicherheit/Security Vorlesung

Wie viele Jahre Programmiererfahrung haben Sie?

_____ Jahre

Haben Sie bereits Erfahrung im bereich der Softwaresicherheit bei einem Programmierprojekt berücksichtigt?

☐ Ja   ☐ Nein

Wenn ja, beschreiben Sie kurz ihre Tätigkeit im Sicherheitsbereich?

Meine Englischfähigkeiten sind:

☐ Muttersprache ☐ Verhandlungssiche ☐ Fließend ☐ Konversationssicher ☐ Grundkenntnisse

Bitte geben Sie an, inwiefern Sie den folgenden Aussagen zustimmen.

	5 stimme völlig zu				
	4 stimme eher zu				
	3 weder Zustimmung noch Ablehnung				
	2 stimme eher nicht zu				
	1 stimme überhaupt nicht zu				
Ich habe schon oft im Team Software entwickelt.	1	2	3	4	5
IT-Sicherheit/Security wurde oft im Team mit berücksichtigt.	1	2	3	4	5
Ich habe mich selbst schon oft mit IT-Sicherheit/Security beschäftigt.	1	2	3	4	5
Ich habe schon oft Eclipse als Entwicklungsumgebung genutzt.	1	2	3	4	5
Ich habe Vorwissen in IT-Sicherheit/ Security.	1	2	3	4	5
Meine Java Kenntnisse sind sehr gut.	1	2	3	4	5

Bibliotheken Teil 1:

Drittanbieter Bibliotheken könne ebenfalls Schwachstellen enthalten, sowie der selbst geschriebene Quellcode auch. Bereits bekannte Schwachstellen werden in öffentlich zugänglichen Datenbanken dokumentiert, wie die National Vulnerability Database (NVD)-Datenbank. Wenn Entwickler darüber entscheiden ob Sie eine drittanbieter Bibliothek nutzen möchten, sollte auch die IT-Sicherheit eine Rolle spielen. Die Nutzung einer fehlerhaften Bibliothek könnte das komplette Projekt unsicher machen, sodass ein Angreifer z.b. die Software manipulieren könnte um einen hohen Schaden zu verursachen.

Um zu prüfen wie sicher eine Bibliothek ist, kann unter anderem sämtliches Wissen über bereits bekannte Schwachstellen gesichtet werden. Dies könnte durch Nutzung der NVD Datenbank erfolgen. Möglicherweise ist bereits eine Schwachstelle für eine drittanbieter Bibliothek bekannt, die in ein Projekt eingebunden werden soll. Das entwickelte Plugin führt diese Prüfung automatisiert durch, sobald eine Bibliothek in den Projektordner gezogen wird/importiert wird. Weiterhin kann eine Prüfung nachträglich für bereits importierte Libraries gestartet werden.

Aufgabe: Führen Sie vorerst die Manuelle Prüfung durch, indem Sie das Suchfenster der NVD nutzen um die vier Bibliothek unter den gegebenen Versionen auf Schwachstellen zu prüfen. Um Suchtreffer zu erzielen, macht es meist Sinn vorerst nur nach dem konkreten Bibliotheksnamen zu suchen und bei den Befunden nachträglich zu prüfen ob die jeweilige Bibliothek unter der gegebenen Version betroffen ist. Hierfür haben Sie zunächst 15 Minuten Zeit. Füllen Sie hierfür die folgende Tabelle aus. Sofern eine oder mehrere Schwachstellen in der jeweiligen Bibliothek existieren, geben Sie deren CVE-Identifier an und nennen Sie welche Folgen diese haben. Listen Sie alle zutreffenden CVE-IDs auf. Für eine Nennung der jeweiligen Bibliothek reicht Ihre Nummer aus (1-4). Die zu prüfenden Bibliotheken befinden sich im „Libraries" Ordner des „Studie" Java-Eclipse Projektes. **Bitte prüfen Sie die Artefakte der Reihe nach und schreiben Sie zuerst Ihre Befunde in die Tabelle bevor sie zum nächsten übergehen.**

Bibliotheken: 1.daytrader-ejb-2.1.7.jar, 2.xalan-2.7.0.jar, 3.xstream-1.4.8.jar und 4.xwork-2.1.1.jar.

Bibliothek (1,2,3,4)	Enthält Schwachstelle (Ja/Nein)	Auswirkung der Schwachstelle	CVE-ID falls vorhanden (CVE-XXXX)

Bibliotheken Teil 2:

Aufgabe: Führen Sie nun die automatische Prüfung durch indem Sie die Bibliotheken aus dem Projekt vom Aufgaben Teil 1 in den „Libraries"-Ordner des bestehenden Projektes „Studie LibraryChecker" der anderen Eclipse Instanz kopieren. Starten Sie die automatische Prüfung über den Menüpunkt „Vulnerability Checker"=>"Search" und schauen Sie sich im rechten Fenster „Vulnerabilitiy View" die Informationen der Befunde an. Die Prüfung kann ebenfalls auch nachträglich über das Menü des Plugins gestartet werden. Die Farbe identifiziert wie kritisch eine Schwachstelle ist. Von links nach rechts identifizieren die Farben Schwachstellen mit schlimmeren Ausmaßen (Gelb, Orange, Rot). Sie können ebenfalls auf enthaltene CVE Verlinkungen klicken um weitere Informationen zu den Befunden zu erhalten. Hierfür Haben Sie zunächst 10 Minuten Zeit. Füllen Sie hierfür die folgende Tabelle aus. Sofern eine oder mehrere Schwachstellen in der jeweiligen Bibliothek existieren, geben Sie deren CVE-Identifier an und nennen Sie welche Folgen diese haben. Für eine Nennung der jeweiligen Bibliothek reicht Ihre Nummer aus (1-4). **Bitte prüfen Sie die Artefakte der Reihe nach und schreiben Sie zuerst Ihre Befunde in die Tabelle bevor sie zum nächsten übergehen.**

Bibliotheken: 1.daytrader-ejb-2.1.7.jar, 2.xalan-2.7.0.jar, 3.xstream-1.4.8.jar und 4.xwork-2.1.1.jar.

Bibliothek (1,2,3,4)	Enthält Schwachstelle (Ja/Nein)	Auswirkung der Schwachstelle	CVE-ID falls vorhanden (CVE-XXXX)

Vergleichen Sie nun die Ergebnisse von Aufgaben Teil 1 und 2 miteinander. Stellen Sie unterschiede fest? Was ist Ihnen bei der manuellen Prüfung schwieriger gefallen als bei der automatisierten?

Fragebogen Bibliotheksprüfung – nach Experiment

5 stimme völlig zu					
4 stimme eher zu					
3 weder Zustimmung noch Ablehnung					
2 stimme eher nicht zu					
1 stimme überhaupt nicht zu					
Die Nutzung des Plugins hat mir die Überprüfung der Sicherheit erleichtert.	1	2	3	4	5
Die Sicherheitshinweise des Plugins waren verständlich dargestellt.	1	2	3	4	5
Die Informationen die mir vom Plugin zu den Schwachstellen dargestellt wurden, empfand ich für deren Verständnis hilfreich.	1	2	3	4	5
Das Plugin hat die Entscheidungsfindung bezüglich der Sicherheit erleichtert.	1	2	3	4	5
Die manuelle Prüfung (ohne Plugin) ist leichter durchzuführen als die automatische Prüfung mit Plugin.	1	2	3	4	5
Die manuelle Prüfung (ohne Plugin) ist schwierig durchzuführen.	1	2	3	4	5
Ich würde eher das Plugin nutzen als eine manuelle Prüfung durchzuführen.	1	2	3	4	5

Welche Aspekte am Plugin haben Sie dazu gebracht die letzte Frage so zu beantworten wie Sie es haben?

Wann würden Sie Plugins oder auch andere sicherheitsunterstüzende Software nutzen um die Sicherheit in Ihren programmierten Anwendungen zu erhöhen?

Haben Sie noch weitere Anmerkungen zur Nutzung des Plugins?

Quellcode Ausschnitte Teil 1:

Bei der Programmierung kann es passieren das entstandener Programmcode unsicher ist. Es existieren, als Referenz für eine Sicherheitsprüfung, Verzeichnisse die über schwachstellenbehafteten Programmcode verfügen und genutzt werden können um zu prüfen ob eine Schwachstelle im geschriebenen Programmcode vorliegt oder nicht. Die gemeldet Schwachstelle der Codeausschnitte wird mit einem CVE-Identifier ausgezeichnet. Bei dieser Sicherheitsprüfung gilt: Falls der gleiche oder sehr ähnlicher Quellcode im Referenzverzeichnis enthalten ist, so kann der geschriebene Code ebenfalls über eine Schwachstelle verfügen. Ist ähnlicher Code gefunden, so kann die Suche in der NVD über die CVE-ID durchgeführt werden, mit der der Sourcecode ausgezeichnet ist (siehe Dateiname). Die Nutzung von fehlerhaften Source Code in mindestens einer Komponente eines Projektes, könnte das komplette Projekt unsicher machen sodass ein Angreifer z.B. die Software manipulieren könnte um einen hohen Schaden zu verursachen.

Aufgabe: Führen Sie vorerst die manuelle Prüfung durch indem Sie die Code Fragmente der „Studie.java" Datei des „Studie" Eclipse Projektes nach Schwachstellen prüfen indem Sie die Codeausschnitte mit denen im Ordner „Referenzverzeichnis" vergleichen. Sollten Sie einen Treffer gefunden haben, nutzen sie die referenzierte CVE-ID (Dateiname) um eine Suche auf der NVD auszuführen und weitere Informationen zu der Schwachstelle zu erhalten. Hierfür haben Sie zunächst 15 Minuten Zeit. Füllen Sie hierfür die folgende Tabelle aus. Sofern eine oder mehrere Schwachstellen in dem jeweiligen Codefragment existieren, geben Sie deren CVE-Identifier an und nennen Sie welche Folgen diese haben. Für eine Nennung des jeweiligen Codeausschnittes reicht Ihre Nummer aus (1-4). Die Nummern der Codeausschnitte sind im Kommentar über der jeweiligen Methodendeklaration enthalten. **Bitte prüfen Sie die Artefakte der Reihe nach und schreiben Sie zuerst Ihre Befunde in die Tabelle bevor sie zum nächsten übergehen.**

Codeausschnitt (1,2,3,4)	Enthält Schwachstelle (Ja/Nein)	Auswirkung der Schwachstelle	CVE-ID falls vorhanden (CVE-XXXX)

Quellcode Ausschnitte Teil 2:

Aufgabe: Führen Sie die automatisierte Prüfung durch indem Sie die Codefragmente der „Studie.java" Datei des „Studie" Eclipse Projektes in die „Stuide.java" Datei des „Studie_SCCD" Java Eclipse Projekt kopieren. Speichern Sie anschließend die Datei ab indem Sie auf das Disketten Symbol klicken oder führen Sie die automatische Prüfung der Codefragmente über das Menü aus (SCC Detector=>Scan File). Warten Sie nun bis das Plugin die Prüfung abgeschlossen hat. Nun werden die Codefragmente eingefärbt. Von links nach rechts identifizieren die Farben Schwachstellen mit schlimmeren Ausmaßen (Gelb, Orange, Rot). Sollte eine Schwachstelle gefunden worden seien, so können Sie die Informationen hierzu im unteren Fenster „SCC Detecor – Clone Results" einsehen. Wenn Sie mehr Informationen zu einer Schwachstelle benötigen, klicken Sie mit der rechten Maustaste auf die Ergebnisse und wählen sie „MoreDetails" aus. Falls Ihnen Informationen fehlen um die Schwachstelle zu analysieren, können Sie ebenfalls auf enthaltene Verlinkungen zur CVE Seite klicken. Hierfür haben Sie zunächst 15 Minuten Zeit. Füllen Sie hierfür die folgende Tabelle aus. Sofern eine oder mehrere Schwachstellen in dem jeweiligen Codeausschnitt existieren, geben Sie deren CVE-Identifier an und nennen Sie welche Folgen diese haben. Für eine Nennung des jeweiligen Codeausschnittes reicht Ihre Nummer aus (1-4). Die Nummern der Codeausschnitte sind im Kommentar über der jeweiligen Methodendeklaration enthalten. **Bitte prüfen Sie die Artefakte der Reihe nach und schreiben Sie zuerst Ihre Befunde in die Tabelle bevor sie zum nächsten übergehen.**

Codeausschnitt (1,2,3,4)	Enthält Schwachstelle (Ja/Nein)	Auswirkung der Schwachstelle	CVE-ID falls vorhanden (CVE-XXXX)

Vergleichen Sie nun die Ergebnisse von Aufgaben Teil 1 und 2 miteinander. Stellen Sie unterschiede fest? Was ist Ihnen bei der manuellen Prüfung schwieriger gefallen als bei der automatisierten?

Fragebogen Codeausschnitte – nach Experiment

5 stimme völlig zu					
4 stimme eher zu					
3 weder Zustimmung noch Ablehnung					
2 stimme eher nicht zu					
1 stimme überhaupt nicht zu					
Die Nutzung des Plugins hat mir die Überprüfung der Sicherheit erleichtert.	1	2	3	4	5
Die Sicherheitshinweise des Plugins waren verständlich dargestellt.	1	2	3	4	5
Die Informationen die mir vom Plugin zu den Schwachstellen dargestellt wurden, empfand ich für deren Verständnis hilfreich.	1	2	3	4	5
Das Plugin hat die Entscheidungsfindung bezüglich der Sicherheit erleichtert.	1	2	3	4	5
Die manuelle Prüfung (ohne Plugin) ist leichter durchzuführen als die automatische Prüfung mit Plugin.	1	2	3	4	5
Die manuelle Prüfung (ohne Plugin) ist schwierig durchzuführen.	1	2	3	4	5
Ich würde eher das Plugin nutzen als eine manuelle Prüfung durchzuführen.	1	2	3	4	5

Welche Aspekte am Plugin haben Sie dazu gebracht die letzte Frage so zu beantworten wie Sie es haben?

Wann würden Sie Plugins oder auch andere sicherheitsunterstüzende Software nutzen um die Sicherheit in Ihren programmierten Anwendungen zu erhöhen?

Haben Sie noch weitere Anmerkungen zur Nutzung des Plugins?

Vielen Dank für Ihre Teilnahme!

A.9.1 Code Fragments for the Security Assessment

```
1   package de.luh.se.sccd.plugin.evaluation;
2
3   public class Studie3 {
4       //Vulnerable
5       //CVE-2008-2086
6       private static FileInputStream privilegedOpenProfile(String fileName)
7       {
8           FileInputStream fis = null;
9           String path, dir, fullPath;
10
11          File f = new File(fileName); /* try absolute file name */
12
13          if ((!f.isFile()) && ((path = System.getProperty("java.iccprofile.path")) !=
            null))
14          {
15              /* try relative to java.iccprofile.path */
16              StringTokenizer st = new StringTokenizer(path, File.pathSeparator);
17              while (st.hasMoreTokens() && (!f.isFile()))
18              {
19                  dir = st.nextToken();
20                  fullPath = dir + File.separatorChar + fileName;
21                  f = new File(fullPath);
22              }
23          }
24
25          if ((!f.isFile()) && ((path = System.getProperty("java.class.path")) != null)
26          {
27              /* try relative to java.class.path */
28              StringTokenizer st = new StringTokenizer(path, File.pathSeparator);
29              while (st.hasMoreTokens() && (!f.isFile()))
30              {
31                  dir = st.nextToken();
32                  fullPath = dir + File.separatorChar + fileName;
33                  f = new File(fullPath);
34              }
35          }
36
```

```
67          catch (NumberFormatException e)
68          {
69              // Ignore
70          }
71          if (contentLength > MAX_PAC_SIZE)
72          {
73              throw new IOException("PAC too big: " + contentLength + " bytes");
74          }
75          ByteArrayOutputStream bytes = new ByteArrayOutputStream();
76          byte[] buffer = new byte[1024];
77          int count;
78          while ((count = urlConnection.getInputStream().read(buffer)) != -1)
79          {
80              bytes.write(buffer, 0, count);
81              if (bytes.size() > MAX_PAC_SIZE)
82              {
83                  throw new IOException("PAC too big");
84              }
85          }
86          return bytes.toString();
87      }
88
89      //Secure
90      public static DhcpPacket decodeFullPacket(byte[] packet, int length, int
        pktType) throws ParseException
91      {
92          ByteBuffer buffer = ByteBuffer.wrap(packet, 0,
            length).order(ByteOrder.BIG_ENDIAN);
93          try
94          {
95              return decodeFullPacket(buffer, pktType);
96          }
97          catch (ParseException e)
98          {
99              throw e;
100         }
101         catch (Exception e)
102         {
103             throw new ParseException("DHCP parsing error: %s", e.getMessage());
104         }
105     }
106
107     //Vulnerable
108     // CVE-2017-0846
109     private boolean isDeviceLocked()
110     {
111         boolean isLocked = false;
112         KeyguardManager keyguardManager = (KeyguardManager)
            mContext.getSystemService(Context.KEYGUARD_SERVICE);
113         boolean inKeyguardRestrictedInputMode =
            keyguardManager.inKeyguardRestrictedInputMode();
114         if (inKeyguardRestrictedInputMode)
115         {
116             isLocked = true;
117         }
118         else
119         {
120             PowerManager powerManager = (PowerManager)
                mContext.getSystemService(Context.POWER_SERVICE);
121             isLocked = !powerManager.isScreenOn();
122         }
123         return isLocked;
124     }
125
126
127 }
128
129
```

Bibliography

[1] Yasemin Acar, Michael Backes, Sascha Fahl, Doowon Kim, Michelle L Mazurek, and Christian Stransky. You get where you're looking for: The impact of information sources on code security. In *2016 IEEE Symposium on Security and Privacy (SP)*, pages 289–305. IEEE, 2016.

[2] Yasemin Acar, Christian Stransky, Dominik Wermke, Michelle L Mazurek, and Sascha Fahl. Security developer studies with github users: Exploring a convenience sample. In *Thirteenth Symposium on Usable Privacy and Security ({SOUPS} 2017)*, pages 81–95, 2017.

[3] Mary Cindy Ah Kioon, Zhao Shun Wang, and Shubra Deb Das. Security analysis of md5 algorithm in password storage. In *Applied Mechanics and Materials*, volume 347, pages 2706–2711. Trans Tech Publ, 2013.

[4] Tanvir Ahmed and Anand R Tripathi. Static verification of security requirements in role based cscw systems. In *Proceedings of the eighth ACM symposium on Access control models and technologies*, pages 196–203, 2003.

[5] Amin Akbariazirani. Advancement of security monitoring in jira with javascript support. Bachelor's thesis, Leibniz Universität Hannover, Software Engineering Group, 2019.

[6] Gerald Albaum. The likert scale revisited. *Market Research Society. Journal.*, 39(2):1–21, 1997.

[7] Jeff Altwood and Joel Spolsky. Information Security. https://security.stackexchange.com/, 2009.

[8] Jeff Altwood and Joel Spolsky. Server Fault. https://serverfault.com/, 2009.

[9] Jeff Altwood and Joel Spolsky. Stack Overflow. https://stackoverflow.com/, 2009.

[10] Jeff Altwood and Joel Spolsky. Super User. https://superuser.com/, 2009.

[11] Apache. Maven central index. https://maven.apache.org/repository/central-index.html, 2020.

[12] J. P. Aumasson, S. Neves, Z. Wilcox-O'Haern, and C. Winnerlein. BLAKE2. https://blake2.net/, 2017.

[13] Jean-Philippe Aumasson, Samuel Neves, Zooko Wilcox-O'Hearn, and Christian Winnerlein. Blake2: simpler, smaller, fast as md5. In *International Conference on Applied Cryptography and Network Security*, pages 119–135. Springer, 2013.

189

[14] Salman Azhar, Irtishad Ahmad, and Maung K Sein. Action research as a proactive research method for construction engineering and management. *Journal of Construction Engineering and Management*, 136(1):87–98, 2010.

[15] Navid Azimy. Study to assess the security knowledge of stack overflow community members. Bachelor's thesis, Leibniz Universität Hannover, Software Engineering Group, 2020.

[16] Brenda S Baker. On finding duplication and near-duplication in large software systems. In *Reverse Engineering, 1995., Proceedings of 2nd Working Conference on*, pages 86–95. IEEE, 1995.

[17] James E. Barlett, Joe W. Kotrlik, and Chadwick C. Higgins. Organizational Research: Determining Appropriate Sample Size in Survey Research. *Information Technology, Learning, and Performance Journal*, 19, 01 2001.

[18] Sean Barnum and Gary McGraw. Knowledge for software security. *IEEE Security & Privacy*, 3(2):74–78, 2005.

[19] Richard L Baskerville. Distinguishing action research from participative case studies. *Journal of systems and information technology*, 1(1):25–45, 1997.

[20] Alara Basul. The growing importance of cyber security for organisations. https://www.uktech.news/featured/the-growing-importance-of-cyber-security-for-organisations-20191113, 2019.

[21] Ira D Baxter, Andrew Yahin, Leonardo Moura, Marcelo Sant'Anna, and Lorraine Bier. Clone detection using abstract syntax trees. In *Software Maintenance, 1998. Proceedings., International Conference on*, pages 368–377. IEEE, 1998.

[22] Amiangshu Bosu and Jeffrey C Carver. Peer code review to prevent security vulnerabilities: An empirical evaluation. In *2013 IEEE Seventh International Conference on Software Security and Reliability Companion*, pages 229–230. IEEE, 2013.

[23] Wasja Brunotte. Security code clone detection developed as eclipse plugin. Master's thesis, Leibniz Universität Hannover, Software Engineering Group, 2018.

[24] G Campbell and Patroklos P Papapetrou. *SonarQube in action*. Manning Publications Co., 2013.

[25] Brant A Cheikes, Brant A Cheikes, Karen Ann Kent, and David Waltermire. *Common platform enumeration: Naming specification version 2.3*. US Department of Commerce, National Institute of Standards and Technology, 2011.

[26] Mengsu Chen, Felix Fischer, Na Meng, Xiaoyin Wang, and Jens Grossklags. How reliable is the crowdsourced knowledge of security implementation? In *2019 IEEE/ACM 41st International Conference on Software Engineering (ICSE)*, pages 536–547. IEEE, 2019.

[27] Axel Claassen. Optimierung von precision und recall der vulnerability clone detection. Master's thesis, Leibniz Universität Hannover, Software Engineering Group, 2020.

[28] William G. Cochran and Andrés S. Bouclier. *Sampling Techniques*. A Wiley publication in applied statistics. Wiley, 1977.

[29] Mitre Corporation. Common weakness enumeration. https://cwe.mitre.org, 1999.

[30] Mitre Corporation. The growing importance of cyber security for organisations. https://cve.mitre.org/, 1999.

[31] Gordana Dodig Crnkovic. Constructive research and info-computational knowledge generation. In *Model-Based Reasoning in Science and Technology*, pages 359–380. Springer, 2010.

[32] Mark Cuphey and Dennis Groves. Open Web Application Security Project (OWASP). https://owasp.org/, 2001.

[33] Randy B Davenport and Ernesto A Bustamante. Effects of false-alarm vs. miss-prone automation and likelihood alarm technology on trust, reliance, and compliance in a miss-prone task. In *Proceedings of the Human Factors and Ergonomics Society Annual Meeting*, volume 54, pages 1513–1517. SAGE Publications Sage CA: Los Angeles, CA, 2010.

[34] de la Mora, Fernando López and Sarah Nadi. Which library should i use? a metric-based comparison of software libraries, 2018.

[35] Société Vaudoise des Sciences Naturelles. *Bulletin de la Société vaudoise des sciences naturelles*, volume 7. F. Rouge, 1864.

[36] Premkumar T. Devanbu and Stuart Stubblebine. Software engineering for security. In Anthony Finkelstein, editor, *Proceedings of the Conference on The Future of Software Engineering*, pages 227–239, New York, NY, 2000. ACM.

[37] Giorgio Maria Di Nunzio and Federica Vezzani. A linguistic failure analysis of classification of medical publications: A study on stemming vs lemmatization. In *CLiC-it*, 2018.

[38] John Diamant. Resilient security architecture: A complementary approach to reducing vulnerabilities. *IEEE Security & Privacy*, 9(4):80–84, 2011.

[39] Cicero Dos Santos and Maira Gatti. Deep convolutional neural networks for sentiment analysis of short texts. In *Proceedings of COLING 2014, the 25th International Conference on Computational Linguistics: Technical Papers*, pages 69–78, 2014.

[40] Paulo Sergio Medeiros dos Santos and Guilherme Horta Travassos. Action research use in software engineering: An initial survey. In *2009 3rd International Symposium on Empirical Software Engineering and Measurement*, pages 414–417. IEEE, 2009.

[41] Daniel Drescher. *Blockchain basics*, volume 276. Springer, 2017.

[42] Gradle Enterprise. What is gradle? `https://docs.gradle.org/current/userguide/what_is_gradle.html`, 2020.

[43] Stack Exchange. The world's largest programming community is growing. https://stackexchange.com/about, 2020.

[44] Robert Feldt and Ana Magazinius. Validity threats in empirical software engineering research-an initial survey. In *Seke*, pages 374–379, 2010.

[45] Kelly Finnerty, Helen Motha, Jayesh Shah, Yasmin White, Mark Button, and Victoria Wang. Cyber security breaches survey 2018: Statistical release. 2018.

[46] Felix Fischer, Konstantin Böttinger, Huang Xiao, Christian Stransky, Yasemin Acar, Michael Backes, and Sascha Fahl. Stack overflow considered harmful? the impact of copy&paste on android application security. In *2017 IEEE Symposium on Security and Privacy (SP)*, pages 121–136. IEEE, 2017.

[47] Felix Fischer, Huang Xiao, Ching-Yu Kao, Yannick Stachelscheid, Benjamin Johnson, Danial Razar, Paul Fawkesley, Nat Buckley, Konstantin Böttinger, Paul Muntean, et al. Stack overflow considered helpful! deep learning security nudges towards stronger cryptography. In *28th {USENIX} Security Symposium ({USENIX} Security 19)*, pages 339–356, 2019.

[48] Dirk Fox. Open web application security project. *Datenschutz und Datensicherheit - DuD*, 30(10):636, 2006.

[49] Andreas Fuchs and Roland Rieke. Identification of security requirements in systems of systems by functional security analysis. In *Architecting dependable systems VII*, pages 74–96. Springer, 2010.

[50] Alfonso Fuggetta. Software process: a roadmap. In *Proceedings of the Conference on the Future of Software Engineering*, pages 25–34, 2000.

[51] Stefan Gärtner. *Heuristische und wissensbasierte Sicherheitsprüfung von Softwareentwicklungsartefakten basierend auf natürlichsprachlichen Informationen*. Logos Verlag Berlin GmbH, 2016.

[52] Dennis Giffhorn and Christian Hammer. Precise analysis of java programs using joana. In James R. Cordy, editor, *Eighth IEEE International Working Conference on Source Code Analysis and Manipulation, 2008*, pages 267–268, Piscataway, NJ, 2008. IEEE.

[53] GitHub. Most starred javascript repositories. `https://github.com/search?l=JavaScript&q=stars%3A%3E40000&type=Repositories`, 2019.

[54] GitHub. Trending github repositories. https://github.com/trending, 2019.

[55] Github. Github security lab codeql. https://securitylab.github.com/tools/codeql, 2020.

[56] GitHut. A small place to discover languages in github. https://madnight.github.io/githut/, 2019.

[57] Nils Göde and Rainer Koschke. Incremental clone detection. In *2009 13th european conference on software maintenance and reengineering*, pages 219–228. IEEE, 2009.

[58] Li Gong, Gary Ellison, and Mary Dageforde. *Inside Java 2 platform security: architecture, API design, and implementation*. Addison-Wesley Professional, 2003.

[59] James Gosling, Bill Joy, Guy Steele, Bracha Gilad, Alex Buckley, Daniel Smith, and Gavin Bierman. The java language specification. https://docs.oracle.com/javase/specs/, 2020.

[60] Dave Gruber. Modern application development security. https://www.synopsys.com/software-integrity/resources/analyst-reports/modern-application-development.html?cmp=pr-sig, 2020.

[61] Lieve Hamers et al. Similarity measures in scientometric research: The jaccard index versus salton's cosine formula. *Information Processing and Management*, 25(3):315–18, 1989.

[62] Atsuo Hazeyama. Survey on body of knowledge regarding software security. In *2012 13th ACIS International Conference on Software Engineering, Artificial Intelligence, Networking and Parallel/Distributed Computing*, pages 536–541. IEEE, 2012.

[63] Jaap-Henk Hoepman and Bart Jacobs. Increased security through open source. *Communications of the ACM*, 50(1):79–83, 2007.

[64] David Hovemeyer and William Pugh. Finding bugs is easy. *ACM SIGPLAN Notices*, 39(12):92–106, 2004.

[65] J. Howard and S. Ruder. Universal Language Model Fine-tuning for Text Classification. *ArXiv e-prints*, January 2018.

[66] Michael Howard and Steve Lipner. *The security development lifecycle*, volume 8. Microsoft Press Redmond, 2006.

[67] Chaoran Huang, Lina Yao, Xianzhi Wang, Boualem Benatallah, and Quan Z Sheng. Expert as a service: Software expert recommendation via knowledge domain embeddings in stack overflow. In *2017 IEEE International Conference on Web Services (ICWS)*, pages 317–324. IEEE, 2017.

[68] imagine your future (isg). Conducting a successful security risk assessment. https://www.isg-one.de/third-party-management/articles/conducting-a-successful-security-risk-assessment, 2020.

[69] Stack Exchange Inc. Stack Exchange. `https://stackexchange.com/sites?view=list#traffic`, 2009.

[70] ECMA International. Ecmascript 2020 language specification. https://www.ecma-international.org/publications/standards/Ecma-262.htm, 2020.

[71] Sergey Ioffe. Improved consistent sampling, weighted minhash and l1 sketching. In *2010 IEEE International Conference on Data Mining*, pages 246–255. IEEE, 2010.

[72] Jiyong Jang, Abeer Agrawal, and David Brumley. Redebug: finding unpatched code clones in entire os distributions. In *Security and Privacy (SP), 2012 IEEE Symposium on*, pages 48–62. IEEE, 2012.

[73] Kanta Jiwnani and Marvin Zelkowitz. Maintaining software with a security perspective. In *International Conference on Software Maintenance, 2002. Proceedings.*, pages 194–203. IEEE, 2002.

[74] HyunChul Joh and Yashwant K Malaiya. Defining and assessing quantitative security risk measures using vulnerability lifecycle and cvss metrics. In *The 2011 international conference on security and management (sam)*, pages 10–16, 2011.

[75] Jan Ole Johanssen, Fabien Patrick Viertel, Bernd Bruegge, and Kurt Schneider. Tacit knowledge in software evolution. In *Managed Software Evolution*, pages 77–105. Springer, Cham, 2019.

[76] Russell L Jones and Abhinav Rastogi. Secure coding: building security into the software development life cycle. *Inf. Secur. J. A Glob. Perspect.*, 13(5):29–39, 2004.

[77] Jacques Julliand, Pierre-Alain Masson, and Regis Tissot. Generating security tests in addition to functional tests. In *Proceedings of the 3rd international workshop on Automation of software test*, pages 41–44, 2008.

[78] Jan Jürjens. *Secure systems development with UML*. Springer Science & Business Media, 2005.

[79] Jan Jürjens, Kurt Schneider, Jens Bürger, Fabien Patrick Viertel, Daniel Strüber, Michael Goedicke, Ralf Reussner, Robert Heinrich, Emre Taşpolatoğlu, Marco Konersmann, et al. Maintaining security in software evolution. In *Managed Software Evolution*, pages 207–253. Springer, Cham, 2019.

[80] Jan Jürjens, Kurt Schneider, and Dortmund Hannover. The secreq approach: From security requirements to secure design while managing software evolution. In *Software Engineering*, pages 89–90, 2014.

[81] Toshihiro Kamiya, Shinji Kusumoto, and Katsuro Inoue. Ccfinder: a multilinguistic token-based code clone detection system for large scale source code. *IEEE Transactions on Software Engineering*, 28(7):654–670, 2002.

[82] Jacob Kastrenakes. Sec issues 35 million usd fine over yahoo failing to disclose data breach. https://bit.ly/2qYxS3I, 2018.

[83] A. Kedia and M. Rasu. *Hands-On Pythin Natural Language Processing: Explore tools and techniques to analyze and process text with a view to building real-world NLP applications*. Packt Publishing, 2020.

[84] Muhammad Umair Ahmed Khan and Mohammad Zulkernine. Quantifying security in secure software development phases. In *2008 32nd Annual IEEE International Computer Software and Applications Conference*, pages 955–960. IEEE, 2008.

[85] Christopher M King, Curtis Dalton, and Stephen H Foreword By-Beck. *Security Architecture: Design, Deployment, and Operations*. McGraw-Hill Professional, 2001.

[86] Vandana Korde and C Namrata Mahender. Text classification and classifiers: A survey. *International Journal of Artificial Intelligence & Applications*, 3(2):85, 2012.

[87] Rainer Koschke. Survey of research on software clones. In *Dagstuhl Seminar Proceedings*. Schloss Dagstuhl-Leibniz-Zentrum für Informatik, 2007.

[88] Ilpo Koskinen, John Zimmerman, Thomas Binder, Johan Redstrom, and Stephan Wensveen. *Design research through practice: From the lab, field, and showroom*. Elsevier, 2011.

[89] Jens Krinke. Identifying similar code with program dependence graphs. In *Reverse Engineering, 2001. Proceedings. Eighth Working Conference on*, pages 301–309. IEEE, 2001.

[90] Gary Kumfert and Tom Epperly. Software in the doe: The hidden overhead of"the build". Technical report, Lawrence Livermore National Lab., CA (US), 2002.

[91] Richard Kunert. The surprisingly good performance of dumb classification algorithms. https://rikunert.com/dumb_classifier_performance, 2019.

[92] Dominik Kupczyk. Anwendung ausgewählter verfahren aus dem machine learning und dem natural language processing für die identifikation von sicherheitsrelevantem code aus stack overflow. Bachelor's thesis, Leibniz Universität Hannover, Software Engineering Group, 2020.

[93] Paul Lensing, Dirk Meister, and André Brinkmann. hashfs: Applying hashing to optimize file systems for small file reads. In *2010 International Workshop on Storage Network Architecture and Parallel I/Os*, pages 33–42. IEEE, 2010.

[94] Hongzhe Li, Hyuckmin Kwon, Jonghoon Kwon, and Heejo Lee. Clorifi: software vulnerability discovery using code clone verification. *Concurrency and Computation: Practice and Experience*, 28(6):1900–1917, 2016.

[95] Zhen Li, Deqing Zou, Shouhuai Xu, Hai Jin, Hanchao Qi, and Jie Hu. Vulpecker: an automated vulnerability detection system based on code similarity analysis. In *Proceedings of the 32nd Annual Conference on Computer Security Applications*, pages 201–213. ACM, 2016.

[96] Zhen Li, Deqing Zou, Shouhuai Xu, Xinyu Ou, Hai Jin, Sujuan Wang, Zhijun Deng, and Yuyi Zhong. Vuldeepecker: A deep learning-based system for vulnerability detection. 2018.

[97] Bennett P Lientz and E Burton Swanson. *Software maintenance management*. Addison-Wesley Longman Publishing Co., Inc., 1980.

[98] Steve Lipner. Security development lifecycle. *Datenschutz und Datensicherheit-DuD*, 34(3):135–137, 2010.

[99] Ling Liu and M Tamer Özsu. *Encyclopedia of database systems*, volume 6. Springer New York, NY, USA:, 2009.

[100] V Benjamin Livshits and Monica S Lam. Finding security vulnerabilities in java applications with static analysis. In *USENIX Security Symposium*, volume 14, pages 18–18, 2005.

[101] Jeremy Long, Steve Springett, Will Stranathan, and Dale Visser. How does the dependency-check work? https://jeremylong.github.io/DependencyCheck/general/internals.html, 2020.

[102] Jeremy Long, Steve Springett, Will Stranathan, and Dale Visser. Owasp dependency-check. https://owasp.org/www-project-dependency-check/, 2020.

[103] Panagiotis Louridas. Static code analysis. *IEEE Software*, 23(4):58–61, 2006.

[104] Node Package Manager. About npm. https://docs.npmjs.com/about-npm/, 2020.

[105] Node Package Manager. lodash v4.17.20 npm package. https://www.npmjs.com/package/lodash, 2020.

[106] Christopher D. Manning, Prabhakar Raghavan, and Hinrich Schütze. *Introduction to information retrieval*. Cambridge Univ. Press, Cambridge, reprinted. edition, 2009.

[107] Maven. Central maven repository. https://repo1.maven.org/maven2/, 2020.

[108] Maven. Pom reference. https://maven.apache.org/pom.html, 2020.

[109] Jean Mayrand, Claude Leblanc, and Ettore Merlo. Experiment on the automatic detection of function clones in a software system using metrics. In *icsm*, volume 96, page 244, 1996.

[110] Gary McGraw. Software security. *IEEE Security & Privacy*, 2(2):80–83, 2004.

[111] Peter Mell, Karen Scarfone, and Sasha Romanosky. A complete guide to the common vulnerability scoring system version 2.0. https://www.first.org/cvss/v2/guide, 2021.

[112] Microsoft. GitHub. https://github.com/, 2008.

[113] Microsoft. GitHub Security Advisories. https://docs.github.com/en/github/managing-security-vulnerabilities/creating-a-security-advisory, 2008.

[114] T. Mikolov, K. Chen, G. Corrado, and J. Dean. Efficient Estimation of Word Representations in Vector Space. *ArXiv e-prints*, January 2013.

[115] T. Mikolov, I. Sutskever, K. Chen, G. Corrado, and J. Dean. Distributed Representations of Words and Phrases and their Compositionality. *ArXiv e-prints*, 2013.

[116] MITRE. About cpe. http://cpe.mitre.org/about/, 2021.

[117] Mvnrepository. Top indexed repositories. https://mvnrepository.com/repos, 2020.

[118] Col Needham. Internet movie database (imdb). https://www.imdb.com/, 1990.

[119] Huu Kim Nguyen. Enhancement of a vulnerability checker for software libraries with similarity metrics based on file-hashes. Bachelor's thesis, Leibniz Universität Hannover, Software Engineering Group, 2020.

[120] NIST. National vulnerability database - data feeds. https://nvd.nist.gov/vuln/data-feeds, 2020.

[121] Ikujiro Nonaka and Hirotaka Takeuchi. *The knowledge-creating company: How Japanese companies create the dynamics of innovation*. Oxford university press, 1995.

[122] NPM. all-the-package-names. https://www.npmjs.com/package/all-the-package-names, 2020.

[123] Node Package Manager (NPM). Auditing package dependencies for security vulnerabilities. https://docs.npmjs.com/auditing-package-dependencies-for-security-vulnerabilities, 2020.

[124] NVD. National vulnerability database statistics. `https://nvd.nist.gov/vuln/search/statistics?adv_search=false&form_type=basic&results_type=statistics&search_type=all`, 2020.

[125] NVD. National vulnerability database vulnerablity definition. https://nvd.nist.gov/vuln, 2020.

[126] NVD. National vulnerability database cpe. https://nvd.nist.gov/products/cpe, 2021.

[127] NVD. National vulnerability database cvss. https://nvd.nist.gov/vuln-metrics/cvss, 2021.

[128] NVD. National vulnerability database total vulnerabilities. https://nvd.nist.gov/general/nvd-dashboard, 2021.

[129] National Institute of Standards and Technology (NIST). National vulnerability database (nvd). https://nvd.nist.gov/, 2012.

[130] National Institute of Standards and Technology. Weighted cosine similarity. https://www.itl.nist.gov/div898/software/dataplot/refman2/auxillar/weigcorr.htm, 2020.

[131] Erlend Oftedal. Retire.js. https://retirejs.github.io/retire.js/, 2020.

[132] Oracle. Oracle jar file specification. https://docs.oracle.com/javase/8/docs/technotes/guides/jar/jar.h 2017.

[133] Open Web Application Security Project (OWASP). OWASP Top 10 - 2017 The Ten Most Critical Web Application Security Risks. 2017. 2018-09-28.

[134] John Platt. Sequential minimal optimization: A fast algorithm for training support vector machines. 1998.

[135] Luca Ponzanelli, Alberto Bacchelli, and Michele Lanza. Seahawk: Stack overflow in the ide. In *2013 35th International Conference on Software Engineering (ICSE)*, pages 1295–1298. IEEE, 2013.

[136] Marting F Porter. An algorithm for suffix stripping. In *Electronic library and information systems*, volume 14, pages 130–137, 1980.

[137] Tom Preston-Werner. Semantic versioning 2.0.0. http://semver.org/, 2017.

[138] Steven Raemaekers, Arie van Deursen, and Joost Visser. Semantic versioning and impact of breaking changes in the maven repository. *Journal of Systems and Software*, 129:140–158, 2017.

[139] Chaiyong Ragkhitwetsagul, Jens Krinke, Matheus Paixao, Giuseppe Bianco, and Rocco Oliveto. Toxic code snippets on stack overflow. *IEEE Transactions on Software Engineering*, 2019.

[140] Sebastian Raschka. Naive Bayes and Text Classification I - Introduction and Theory. *ArXiv e-prints*, October 2014.

[141] Ralf Reussner, Michael Goedicke, Wilhelm Hasselbring, Birgit Vogel-Heuser, Jan Keim, and Lukas Märtin. *Managed Software Evolution*. Springer Nature, 2019.

[142] Peter C Rigby and Martin P Robillard. Discovering essential code elements in informal documentation. In *2013 35th International Conference on Software Engineering (ICSE)*, pages 832–841. IEEE, 2013.

[143] Peter C. Rigby and Martin P. Robillard. Discovering essential code elements in informal documentation. In *Proceedings of the 2013 International Conference on Software Engineering*, ICSE '13, pages 832–841, Piscataway, NJ, USA, 2013. IEEE Press.

[144] H. Sajnani, V. Saini, J. Svajlenko, C. K. Roy, and C. V. Lopes. SourcererCC: Scaling Code Clone Detection to Big-Code. In *2016 IEEE/ACM 38th International Conference on Software Engineering (ICSE)*, pages 1157–1168, May 2016.

[145] G Salton and M McGill. Introduction to modern information retrieval, 1983.

[146] Jonathan Sandals. Top 7 programming languages of 2020. https://www.codingdojo.com/blog/top-7-programming-languages, 2020.

[147] Riccardo Scandariato, James Walden, and Wouter Joosen. Static analysis versus penetration testing: A controlled experiment. In *Software Reliability Engineering (ISSRE), 2013 IEEE 24th International Symposium on*, pages 451–460. IEEE, 2013.

[148] Kurt Schneider, Kai Stapel, and Eric Knauss. Beyond documents: visualizing informal communication. In *2008 Requirements Engineering Visualization*, pages 31–40. IEEE, 2008.

[149] Ken Schwaber and Mike Beedle. *Agile software development with Scrum*, volume 1. Prentice Hall Upper Saddle River, 2002.

[150] A. Sheneamer and J. Kalita. A Survey of Software Clone Detection Techniques. *International Journal of Computer Applications*, 137(10):1–21, 2016.

[151] Catarina Silva and Bernardete Ribeiro. *Inductive Inference for Large Scale Text Classification: Kernel Approaches and Techniques*, volume 255. 01 2010.

[152] SonarQube. Sonarqube. https://docs.sonarqube.org/latest/extend/adding-coding-rules/, 2020.

[153] Jimmy Spencer. Why is cyber security important in 2019? https://securityfirstcorp.com/why-is-cyber-security-important/, 2019.

[154] Dick Stenmark. Information vs. knowledge: The role of intranets in knowledge management. In *Proceedings of the 35th Annual Hawaii International Conference on System Sciences*, pages 928–937. IEEE, 2002.

[155] Christian Sternitzke and Isumo Bergmann. Similarity measures for document mapping: A comparative study on the level of an individual scientist. *Scientometrics*, 78(1):113–130, 2009.

[156] Christopher Strachey. Fundamental concepts in programming languages. *Higher-order and symbolic computation*, 13(1-2):11–49, 2000.

[157] Daniel Svozil, Vladimír Kvasnicka, and Jirí Pospichal. Intro to multi-layer feed-forward neural networks. *Chemometrics and Intelligent Laboratory Systems*, 39(1):43 – 62, 1997.

[158] Liran Tal and Simon Maple. About npm. https://snyk.io/blog/npm-passes-the-1-millionth-package-milestone-what-can-we-learn/, 2019.

[159] R. Telang and S. Wattal. An empirical analysis of the impact of software vulnerability announcements on firm stock price. *IEEE Transactions on Software Engineering*, 33(8):544–557, 2007.

[160] TIOBE. Programming community index. https://tiobe.com/tiobe-index/, 2019.

[161] P. M. Todd. Heuristics for decision and choice. In *International Encyclopedia of the Social & Behavioral Sciences*, pages 6676–6679. Elsevier, 2001.

[162] Christoph Treude and Martin P Robillard. Augmenting api documentation with insights from stack overflow. In *2016 IEEE/ACM 38th International Conference on Software Engineering (ICSE)*, pages 392–403. IEEE, 2016.

[163] Amos Tversky and Daniel Kahneman. Judgment under uncertainty: Heuristics and biases. *science*, 185(4157):1124–1131, 1974.

[164] US-Cert. United states computer emergency readiness team. https://goo.gl/ZCuCc8, 2003.

[165] Rob Van der Spek and Andre Spijkervet. *Knowledge management: dealing intelligently with knowledge.* Knowledge Management Network, 1997.

[166] Vladimir Vapnik. *The nature of statistical learning theory.* Springer science & business media, 2013.

[167] Cyntia Vargas, Jens Bürger, Fabien Viertel, Birgit Vogel-Heuser, and Jan Jürjens. System evolution through semi-automatic elicitation of security requirements: A position paper. *IFAC-PapersOnLine*, 51(10):64–69, 2018.

[168] Tim Vidas and J Wilson. Cyber forensics the basics. *CERTconf2006*, 2006.

[169] Fabien Patrick Viertel, Wasja Brunotte, Yannik Evers, and Kurt Schneider. Community knowledge about security: Identification and classification of user contributions. In *The 15th International Conference on Risks and Security of Internet and Systems*, 2020.

[170] Fabien Patrick Viertel, Wasja Brunotte, Daniel Strüber, and Kurt Schneider. Detecting security vulnerabilities using clone detection and community knowledge. In *Proceedings of the 31st International Conference on Software Engineering and Knowledge Engineering*, SEKE '31, pages 245–252, 2019.

[171] Fabien Patrick Viertel, Oliver Karras, and Kurt Schneider. Vulnerability recognition by execution trace difierentiation. In *2017 ACM/IEEE International Symposium on Software Performance (SSP)*, Karlsruhe, 2017.

[172] Fabien Patrick Viertel, Fabian Kortum, Leif Wagner, and Kurt Schneider. Are third-party libraries secure? a software library checker for java. In *International Conference on Risks and Security of Internet and Systems*, pages 18–34. Springer, 2018.

[173] Leif Erik Wagner. Konzept und entwicklung eines schwachstellenprüfers für java-bibliotheken. Master's thesis, Leibniz Universität Hannover, Software Engineering Group, 2017.

[174] Mozilla MDN Webdocs. Javascript guide. https://developer.mozilla.org/en-US/docs/Web/JavaScript/Guide/Functions, 2020.

[175] Claes Wohlin, Per Runeson, Martin Höst, Magnus C Ohlsson, Björn Regnell, and Anders Wesslén. *Experimentation in software engineering*. Springer Science & Business Media, 2012.

[176] Edmund Wong, Jinqiu Yang, and Lin Tan. Autocomment: Mining question and answer sites for automatic comment generation. In *Proceedings of the 28th International Conference on Automated Software Engineering (ASE'13)*, pages 562–567, 2013.

[177] Xin-Li Yang, David Lo, Xin Xia, Zhi-Yuan Wan, and Jian-Ling Sun. What security questions do developers ask? a large-scale study of stack overflow posts. volume 31, pages 910–924. Springer, 2016.

[178] Kun Yu, Shlomo Berkovsky, Ronnie Taib, Dan Conway, Jianlong Zhou, and Fang Chen. User trust dynamics: An investigation driven by differences in system performance. In *Proceedings of the 22nd International Conference on Intelligent User Interfaces*, pages 307–317, 2017.

[179] Kun Yu, Shlomo Berkovsky, Ronnie Taib, Dan Conway, Jianlong Zhou, and Fang Chen. User trust dynamics: An investigation driven by differences in system performance. In *Proceedings of the 22nd international conference on intelligent user interfaces*, pages 307–317, 2017.

[180] Misha Zitser, Richard Lippmann, and Tim Leek. Testing static analysis tools using exploitable buffer overflows from open source code. In *ACM SIGSOFT Software Engineering Notes*, volume 29, pages 97–106. ACM, 2004.

List of Figures

List of Tables

Curriculum Vitae

Personal Details

Name: Fabien Patrick Viertel
Date of Birth: 07.04.1990
City of Birth: Salzgitter, Germany

Education

- 06/2016 - Today PhD Student: Computer Science
Leibniz Universität Hannover
Preliminary Title of Dissertation: „Heuristic and Knowledge-Based Security Checks of Source Code Artifacts Using Community Knowledge" Focus: IT-Security

- 10/2012 - 01/2015 Master of Science: Computer Science (2,3)
Technische Universität Braunschweig
Title of Master's Thesis: „Maschinelles Lernen für die Testfallauswahl beim Black-Box-Testen" Focus: Vehicle Computer Science and Datamining

- 09/2009 - 07/2012 Bachelor of Science: Technical Computer Science (1,7)
Hochschule Ostfalia
Title of Bachelor's Thesis: „Erweiterung eines Mitarbeiterinformationssystems um Gestensteuerung auf Touchscreens"

- 09/2011 - 12/2011 Semester abroad in the USA, Wisconsin, Kenosha University of Wisconsin-Parkside
Focus: Softwareengineering and Application Development

- 08/2007 - 06/2008 Advanced Technical Certificate (2,5)
Fachoberschule Technik am Fredenberg, Salzgitter

Professional Experience

- 06/2016 - Today Research Associate, Leibniz Universität Hannover, Hannover
  - Security at Run-Time
  - Security at Design-Time
  - Community Knowledge about Security

- 01/2015 - 05/2016 Test Engineer, IAV GmbH, Gifhorn
  - Hedging Strategy §29 StVZO: Concept Planning for Implementation in ODIS-E&S, Analysis of the Production Processes of the Volkswagen AG
  - Planning, Implementation and Preparation of Reports of the Diagnostic Test of Vehicle Control Units

- 02/2012 - 07/2012 Project Work, Volkswagen AG, Salzgitter
  - Concept Planning and Implementation of an Employee Information System for the Engine Assembly Lines

- 10/2008 - 09/2009 Voluntary Social Year as a First Aider, Johanniter e.V., Salzgitter

Publications

- Fabien Patrick Viertel, Oliver Karras, and Kurt Schneider: Vulnerability Recognition by Execution Trace Differentiation.
  IN: 2017 ACM/IEEE International Symposium on Software Performance (SSP), 2017. [171]

- Fabien Patrick Viertel, Fabian Kortum, Leif Wagner, and Kurt Schneider: Are third-party libraries secure? a software library checker for java.
  IN: 13th International Conference on Risks and Security of Internet and Systems (CRISIS), Springer, Cham, 2018. [172]

- Fabien Patrick Viertel, Wasja Brunotte, Daniel Strüber, and Kurt Schneider: Detecting Security Vulnerabilities using Clone Detection and Community Knowledge.
  IN: International Conference on Software Engineering and Knowledge Engineering (SEKE2019), pages 245-324, 2019. [170]

- Cyntia Montserrat Vargas Martinez, Jens Bürger, Fabien Viertel, Birgit Vogel- Heuser, and Jan Jürjens: System evolution through semi-automatic elicitation of security requirements: A Position Paper.
  IN: IFAC, volume 51, pages 64-91, Elsevier, 2018. [167]

- Jan Jürjens, Kurt Schneider, Jens Bürger, Fabien Patrick Viertel, Daniel Strüber, Michael Goedicke, Ralf Reussner, Robert Heinrich, Emre Taspolatoglu, Marco Konersmann, Alexander Fay, Winfried Lamersdorf, Jan Ladiges, Christopher Haubeck: Maintaining Security in Software Evolution.
  In: Managed Software Evolution, pages 207-253, Springer, 2019.

Editors: Ralf Reussner, Michael Goedicke, Wilhelm Hasselbring, Birgit Vogel- Heuser, Jan Keim, and Lukas Märtin. [79]

- Jan Ole Johanssen, Fabien Patrick Viertel, Bernd Bruegge and Kurt Schneider: Tacit Knowledge in Software Evolution.
  In: Managed Software Evolution, pages 77-105, Springer, 2019.
  Editors: Ralf Reussner, Michael Goedicke, Wilhelm Hasselbring, Birgit Vogel- Heuser, Jan Keim, and Lukas Märtin. [75]

- Fabien Patrick Viertel, Wasja Brunotte, Yannik Evers, and Kurt Schneider: Community knowledge about security: Identification and classification of user contributions.
  IN: 15th International Conference on Risks and Security of Internet and Systems (CRISIS), 2020. [169]

Awards

- Best Paper Award Third Place at SEKE 2019 for "Detecting Security Vulnerabilities using Clone Detection and Community Knowledge" [170]